Judicial Objectivity

Dia-Logos

Schriften zu Philosophie und Sozialwissenschaften
Studies in Philosophy and Social Sciences

Edited by Tadeusz Buksiński / Piotr W. Juchacz

Vol. 28

PETER LANG

Lidia Rodak

Judicial Objectivity

Limits, Merits and Beyond

PETER LANG

Bibliographic Information published by the Deutsche Nationalbibliothek
The Deutsche Nationalbibliothek lists this publication in the Deutsche Nationalbibliografie; detailed bibliographic data is available in the internet at http://dnb.d-nb.de.

Library of Congress Cataloging-in-Publication Data
A CIP catalog record for this book has been applied for at the Library of Congress.

This publication was financially supported by the University of Silesia in Katowice.

UNIVERSITY OF SILESIA
IN KATOWICE

ISSN 1619-005X
ISBN 978-3-631-65214-5 (Print)
ISBN 978-3-653-04679-3 (E-PDF)
ISBN 978-3-631-71122-4 (EPUB)
ISBN 978-3-631-71123-1 (MOBI)
DOI 10.3726/978-3-653-04679-3

Peter Lang – Berlin · Berlin · Bruxelles · New York · Oxford · Warszawa · Wien

This publication has been peer reviewed.

www.peterlang.com

Table of Contents

Introductory Remarks

> 'It is not necessary to regard everything as truth but it is enough to perceive it as necessity before law.'[1]

The topic of objectivity is one of the most controversial in the jurisprudential literature, as the numerous publications on this issue show, with defenders and critics of both the concept of objectivity in general and of legal objectivity, in particular. By looking at these debates, one can think that everything has been said on this topic and, consequently, conclude with Ronald Dworkin that there is no need to talk about objectivity anymore.[2]

Objectivity is often entangled in the interpretative paradigm and often, deliberately or not, serves as an epistemological perspective. Therefore, most often objectivity becomes the subject of attacks from the perspective of anti-realist or so-called critical positions today. At the same time, however, realistic and naturalistic school of thoughts consider it a fundamental category.

For this reason, this book starts with discussing the arguments presented by opposite views on objectivity from both the perspective of philosophy and philosophy of law. This is to prepare the ground for the discourse analysis of jurisprudence of the courts, in order to understand the apparent ambiguity and inconsistencies in the ways *objectivity* is used in the law courts.

The overall aim of this book is to identify the usages of *objectivity* that appear in practical legal discourse, and critically examine them to verify the hypothesis that a special legal meaning of objectivity is created bottom-up by the practical discourse itself. In addition, the results of this research allow to shed new light on objectivity in its relationship with intersubjectivity and subjectivity, in particular with the subjects of law in the legal discourse.

The inspiration for this book came from observing the different ways in which the term 'objectivity' is used in court rulings, as this begged the question of what

---

1 Franz Kafka, *The Trial*, trans. John Williams (Hertfordshire: Wordsworth Edition, 2008) 141.

2 Ronald Dworkin, 'My Reply to Stanley Fish (and Walter Benn Michaels): Please Don't Talk About Objectivity Anymore,' in W.J.T. Mitchell, ed., *The Politics of Interpretation* (Chicago and London: University of Chicago Press, 1983).

objectivity actually means in the legal world and what its function is. Why is it so popular in the discourse of judges? What is behind it?

The discourse analysis proposed in this book shows how highly controversial this term is in the process of applying the law. *Objectivity* is used in many different contexts, which generates different meanings in use, very often contradictory and, sometimes, even against our common intuition of how to use this term. By observing the large number of cases where this term is used simply for its argumentative reasons, one might find it tempting to join the camp of radical critics of legal objectivity and try to identify the power relations hidden behind it. However, the theoretical considerations point out the many types of objectivity which can be ranked according to their force, such as minimal modest and strong objectivity. In addition, they highlight the capacity of objectivity to guarantee certainty, transparency, common acceptance, universalism, equity before law and, in a certain sense, democracy. At the very basic level of legal assumption, objectivity provides the values that constitute law like legitimacy, justification, and its power of authority.

This is the framework for the analysis proposed in this book, where tension appears between practical confusion and what seems a devaluation of the term objectivity on the one hand, and the theoretical necessity to think of law as objective, on the other. By carrying out a critical discourse analysis I reconstruct what could be the reasons for using objectivity in a given context and look at what is behind a given usage. By analysing a variety of meanings used in different legal contexts, I also examine whether there is any special meaning that could be constituted by the legal context and characteristic only for it.

This is the most important aim of carrying our discourse analysis, as mentioned above: to verify whether the practical legal discourse generates its own bottom-up legal objectivity, what it can actually mean, and what can be the results for subjects of law.

However, it is also relevant to understand whether the practical usage of objectivity in the legal discourse is only a chaotic battle of opposite epistemological perspectives applied consciously or not by judges, or there is something more: that the discourse of law, thanks to its performative power generates the conditions for the emergence of certain type of objectivity, which is arbitrary and power-related. The great argumentative power of objectivity indeed may profit from ontological assessments of realism and may open up opportunities to create inequality and exclusion in the legal discourse. This is especially dangerous from the perspective of an authoritative legal body, which creates a legal reality using language.

i. Methodology and Theoretical Perspective

I have carried out research on both a theoretical and a practical level. On the theoretical level, I take mainly an analytical approach. In particular, I begin by describing the main approaches and concepts which are necessary to understand the complexity of objectivity. This is set against the philosophical debate about objectivity from realistic to antirealist and postmodern concepts. The realists' and antirealists' debate about objectivity, together with different approaches to legal objectivity – strong, modest or minimal – are crucial to analyse the practical legal discourse.

The theoretical perspective provides the tools for carrying out the discourse analysis. In particular, I adopt the methods of Critical Discourse Analysis (CDA). First of all, the theoretical perspective provides the framework for the discourse analysis, especially to investigate discursive practices, their intertextual relations (for example between doctrinal and judicial discourse), the institutional practices or the involvement of human aspects, which are fundamental to analyse *objectivity*. For example, to find out whether it is justified to make claims about different types of object and to understand the difference between the objectivity of facts, evaluations, and legal decisions. Secondly, the theoretical analysis points out the relevance of the inter-subjective dimension of objectivity in the legal discourse. Such a perspective, as I argue, is almost invisible at the level of practical analysis.

In my analysis, I only take an epistemological perspective, as this is the most relevant for the legal discourse, and essentially the only one present in judges' considerations. In addition, I do not adopt a comparative approach: if I use some examples from different legal systems to show differences in the perception of objectivity, it is only for illustrative purposes.

The main tool to carry out the discourse analysis, which is the core of my analysis of the practical dimension of objectivity, is the method of CDA by Norman Fairclough,[3] who proposed a 'three-dimensional model' for the qualitative analysis. The main aim of the application of CDA is to create the list of the usages of objectivity in the legal contexts and analyse them to understand if legal objectivity is generated by the discourse itself, what this means, and what are its consequences for the participants to thc discourse.

As the aim of CDA is to find out what are the meanings of objectivity that are used in legal practice, the theoretical foundations of the adapting of 'three-dimensional model' of Norman Fairclough in the form of classifications of the

---

3 Norman Fairclough, *Language and power. Second Edition* (Harlow: Pearson Education, 2001).

meanings of objectivity are the following. The analysis does not start from the semantic level but from the practice of usages, as suggested by the concepts of 'open texture' formulated by Hart and Waismann.[4] Such an approach allows to identify the examples of the practical usages of objectivity and create a list.

However, starting from the semantic pre-organized layer of meanings one can only find meanings which have been already nailed down. To circumvent this problem, one can follow the approach of Langacker, who suggests that instead of perceiving expressions as containers of meanings, one should focus on the symbolic correspondence between the phonological and the semantic structure, which corresponds to the 'term vs. concept' opposition.[5]

Following this approach, by analysing a usage, it is possible to detect non-standard senses of a given word or expression. This allows to describe the whole *family of meanings* of objectivity, using Wittgenstein's terminology.

In this book I mainly analyse Polish law,[6] in particular by analysing courts' ruling in *Lex*, the Polish System of Legal Information. The large quantity of verdicts using the term *objectivity* is a ready source of data for analysis and a proof of how willing judges are to use the term *objectivity*.

ii. The Structure of the Book

The structure of the book is the following: Chapters 1 and 2 introduce the theoretical discussion on objectivity. The central part of the book is the discourse analysis which is presented in Chapter 3. Chapters 4 and 5 focus on two specific problems found in the practical discourse analysis: general clauses and legal facts. In Chapter 6, I draw the conclusions of the discourse analysis. In particular, I describe the ceremonial function of legal objectivity, present some reflections on the relationship between objectivity and subjectivity and, finally, I analyse the key question of why intersubjectivity can fit the law.

Chapter 1 describes the philosophical debate on objectivity. Far from being an exhaustive survey, this chapter proposes a single typology that embraces all the meanings found during my research. This is based on whether objectivity

---

4 Herbert L. A. Hart, *The Concept of Law* (Oxford: Clarendon Press, 1961), Friedrich Weismann, 'Verifiability,' *Proceedings of the Aristotelian Society*, Supplementary Volume 19 (1945): 119–150.

5 Ronald W. Langacker, *Foundations of Cognitive Grammar: Descriptive Application. Volume 2* (Stanford: Stanford University Press, 1987).

6 Some other examples are included but not in a systematic way because this would be too broad a perspective as I have no ambitions to examine all legal systems.

is regarded as being determined by subject, object or it is intersubjectivity-determined. In this way, I tried to take into account the possible ambiguity of 'objectivity,' as it is very easy to get lost in the vast maze of propositions on the meanings and concepts of objectivity. To quote R. Rorty, 'the long and very rich tradition of defending and attacking objectivity makes the attempt of overcoming this problem an unsolvable battle.'[7]

The background of philosophical debate between realists and antirealists about objectivity guides this research. All the concepts analysed, are divided into three groups depending on whether they are determined by the object/the subject or whether they are determined by intersubjectivity. In particular, they are classified with regard to persons, type of statements, knowledge, elements of empirical reality, and values. The subject-determined camp presents the opinion that objectivity is dependent on the author and the context, but to different extents. This leads to the graduated schema, introducing objectivity in its strong, modest and minimal versions, depending on the degree of the subjects' involvement. This classification allows for the analysis of both the relations between those notions and with other concepts related with objectivity, such as truth and universality.

The conclusion of this chapter that guides the theoretical considerations and the analysis of the practical cases of the chapters that follow, is that the realists' approach, which identifies objectivity with truth is the most problematic. The connection with truth is the most common and, in my opinion, the most misleading implication. Objectivity embodies truth only in radical strong approaches that conceptualize objectivity in a way more based on the naive worship of a certain vision of law than on any other form of argument. That is why it is difficult to support strong approaches to objectivity, especially in the domain of law. The empirical research will just confirm this: the courts' use of objectivity in the sense of truth is one of the largest groups of meanings, and the most controversial.

Chapter 2 deals with different conceptions of objectivity in the domain of law. The analysis goes under the banner of questions such as: is objectivity fit for law?; is this concept characteristic for law?; has law its own concept that could be called 'legal objectivity;' and, finally, do we need objectivity for law? The presentation introduces the critical camp and the defenders of legal objectivity. The first represents the opinion that objectivity is a hypocritical notion and should

7 See Richard Rorty, *Objectivity, Relativism, and Truth: Philosophical Papers* Vol. I (Cambridge University Press: Cambridge, 1991) 6.

be completely rejected. The critics claim that it does not fulfil its prescribed role and that it is too easy to smuggle in inequity and injustice under the banner of objectivity. The defenders either argue that law could not be thinkable without the idea of objectivity or directly identify law with objectivity.

My analyses firstly distinguish between objectivity 'of law' and objectivity 'in law.' After an overview of this typology, I will then focus on three approaches to objectivity in law: the metaphysical, epistemological and semantic levels.

Metaphysical objectivity of law could be considered in terms of mind independency, determined correctness, and uniform applicability with regard to legal norms (M. Kramer's proposition). Another approach could be analysed from the perspective of the possible objective status of legal facts (J. Coleman's proposition). These two approaches could be settled in the context of the realism vs. antirealism debate and the graduated typology introduced in the first chapter. It is possible to qualify Coleman's approach in the middle, as representing the modest version of objectivity. Kramer would be counted in the antirealist camp, representing the idea of minimal objectivity, mainly because of his conventionalist approach to law, which is based on an internal legal narrative.

Epistemological objectivity of law is considered as the method that allows discovery of the right answer in the process of legal application. Procedural or methodological objectivity is very often characterized as impartiality or identified with some commonly accepted standards. Being entirely independent and reaching an 'objective point of view from nowhere' is practically impossible. That is why some authors postulate the necessity of making positional judgments, where the standpoint of judging is revealed. In this way, judgments taken from the same, or what appears to be the same, position can be called 'positionally objective.' Such an approach enables a way to reach epistemological objectivity in its minimal version.

The semantic approach centres around the debate on which extent legal interpretation is determined. In this sense, the degree of determination of the sense can be conceived as directly related to objectivity. The semantic approach is developed further in Chapter 5. This chapter leads to the conclusion that it is not possible to think about law without objectivity but highlights the major theoretical problems connected with this concept.

The conclusions of this chapter are that 'objectivity of law' is necessary on the level of assumption, while 'objectivity in law' is the practical perspective necessarily linked with subjects' action and through this necessarily subjective, to a certain extent. The epistemological approach reveals the impossibility of taking a 'view from nowhere' and gives justification for the external observer. The semantic level, on the other hand, reveals the problem with interpretation, which is very often called objective, but in practical terms this is just a myth. The comparison of these two perspectives reveals what conditions are needed to justify claims about objective meanings.

Chapter 3 presents the critical discourse analysis on the rulings of the Polish courts. The main aim of the chapter is to present the classification of the usages of objectivity from the analysis of the most common contexts of occurrence of the term 'objectivity' according to the scheme of object- subject- and intersubjective-determined usages.

The most interesting finding is the group of usages that includes meanings specific to the law, such as 'objective evaluation,' 'objective legal facts,' 'objectivity of legal norms,' 'legal decisions,' and 'objectivity based on legal order.' In other words, objectivity that is given by the authority of law: objective meaning of legal rules, objectivity of linguistic interpretation, objectivity formulated by legal doctrine and repeated jurisprudence of the court or objective judgmental practice, and objectivity used for persuasive aims to make arguments stronger and more convincing.

The most fruitful conclusion from this part of my research was to discover that objectivity could be used to mean nothing more than stated by the authority of law. This can be seen in all the fragments of courts' justifications when the court says that a decision is 'objective' because the court, or another legal body, prescribes it to be so. In other words, the justification for objectivity is upheld by the authoritative power of the legal bodies. It was also possible to note the positive context in which objectivity is always settled. What judges perceive as right, correct, proper, rightful, legitimate, equitable, or reasonable, and what they finally agreed to accept, have all been called 'objective.' The question still remains open as to whether decisions, evaluations, and legal facts can become objective by the power of naming them as such or whether certain legal decisions, opinions, and evaluations are called 'objective' because they have an intrinsic objective quality. The theoretical analyses from the first two chapters would suggest that many cases of this usage of objectivity are not justified, that is, unless objectivity can be justified by the self-created, authoritative power of law. In trying to answer the question 'how much objectivity must be in objectivity?' the main theoretical arguments centre around the justification for the minimal conception of objectivity.

Two special legal senses of objectivity, which appear from the empirical research, deserve special attention – objective judgments/evaluations and objectivity of legal facts. These are dealt with in the next two chapters. I chose these conceptions because they represent two important questions regarding objectivity in law: taking decisions regarding legal facts, and taking interpretative decisions concerning general clauses.

Chapter 4 analyses the problem of objectivity in the context of judicial discretion. The main aim is to examine the subjective character of the evaluation process, which is directly linked with exercising discretion, and the claims about objectivity in the application of general clauses. By examining these two points, my aim is to find the explanation for objectivity that is specific for law. Looking closer at the way both the notions of 'objectivity' and 'general clauses' are applied, it appears that they are in themselves the source of many doubts. The theoretical and philosophical literature is also full of different approaches, conceptions and definitions, which make the problems even more complicated. My main aim was to understand what objectivity of general clauses means, both on the theoretical level and on the level of application. Firstly, I explain the concept of general clauses, then introduce chosen examples from the court rulings to show that the process of application, even if named 'objective' and based on objective standards, is hardly justified. I introduce the general clause of 'reasonable person' as an example that is applied in many different legal systems as an objective measure to demonstrate the different understandings when used for the objective interpretation of contracts. The findings are that objectivity is defined according to the interpretative style: one is linked with the text, one linked with the intention of the authors, and another uses the interpretation from a third-person perspective, yet all of them are called objective.

A possible explanation of the objective character of general clauses may come from the public character of legal discourse in that the judge's decision is not taken in his own name but in the name of the court. The transformation from 'judge' to 'court,' seems to entail a shift from a subjective to an objective perspective. In addition, the public character of law demands commonly shared objective standards. Another explanation could be the necessity to eliminate all that is arbitrary and subjective in all cases where judges must exercise their discretion. This questions what we can conceive as the minimal content of objectivity. The fact that a decision is not arbitrary does not mean it is objective.

Another lesson given by this chapter is that it is necessary to accept subjective elements as part of the process of taking legal decisions. Therefore, to understand a decision introduced as objective, it is necessary to reveal all the elements that go into making the final decision. This could help to avoid creating the impression of lawyers as Egyptian priests who have mysterious, not commonly accessible knowledge.

Chapter 5 is an attempt to answer the question about the objectivity of legal facts. What exactly does it mean that legal facts are objective? And, if so, in what sense? Research about objectivity of legal facts requires long elucidation. The ambiguity of the notion of objectivity also applies to legal facts. At the first look, both are associated with the dominant picture created by the doctrine of realism with its strong presuppositions hidden behind them. Firstly, I introduce the conceptions of legal facts and institutional legal facts, and then I examine them in the context of legal practice. The next step is to analyse legal facts from the point of view of the interpretative semantic theory. To explain how legal facts could be understood as objective, I have utilized the conception of institutional narrative legal order.

On the ontological level, descriptive and evaluative facts have a different status because the former refer to the empirical world whereas the latter are based on values. That is why the status evaluative facts is determined by an assumed theory of values. In this work, I consider what 'objectivity' of legal facts means, because this expression is very often used in judges' justifications of their rulings. Firstly, I introduce some legal facts that are called 'objective' by Polish courts. It seems to be trivial and obvious that at least some legal facts are objective. But, if we have a closer look, it is striking that even evaluative facts, like 'acting in good faith,' are described as 'objective.' However, in the more detailed analyses it became obvious that there is no difference between descriptive and evaluative facts from the point of view of determining their meanings. It means that all legal facts, if they are objective, are objective to the same extent. I argue for minimal objectivity at the semantic level, that is, meaning is set by common acceptance and social practice. However, even this condition is not always fulfilled in the law's domain, as I will illustrate with some examples of difficult cases from the Polish courts.

First and foremost, it is necessary to indicate some differences in interpretative semantic theories. The main differences focus on general assumptions. I rely on the critical semantic theories saying that meaning is set by a shared test of common acceptance, but at the same time I follow Wittgenstein's distinction between 'understanding' and 'interpretation.' This helps me to defend the objectivity of meaning and the objectivity of legal facts in the minimal version.

I argue that legal facts are objective to a minimal sense on the semantic level and that there are no differences between various types of facts on the semantic level. In my argumentation, I follow the antirealist approaches based on Kripke's interpretations of Wittgenstein and the justification theory of meaning. But there still remain doubts about the possible objective status of legal facts after their interpretation, or application. This is another very controversial activity from the point of view of objectivity.

The theory of coherence sheds new light on providing an explanation for the objectivity of legal facts in the process of their application. In order to make sense in law, the category of correspondence is replaced by the category of coherence.[8] The category of correspondence is used to guarantee the objectivity of facts, even in a very strong sense. When the theory of coherence is applied, the status of legal facts changes their character from the point of view of their objectivity. To quote MacCormick, who claims that it is not the case that we cannot get the truth about the past, but only rarely can we be absolutely certain what the truth of the given matter is. Narrative coherence does not operate by calling itself objective. Actually, it never can be fully objective, because it always requires some subjective judgments.[9] Taking into account all the above arguments, it is hard to support the objectivity of institutional facts, even in the minimal sense.

Lawyers and judges seem to speak about the law in terms that presuppose strongly objective standards. This is why this is a point of controversy and, for me personally, the main reason for writing this book.

Chapter 6 contains the concluding remarks. The chapter initially provides some critical remarks on the role of objectivity in practical legal discourse, pointing out its great argumentative role, by which objectivity plays the role of masking power relations of the public authority over the rights of the individual, resulting on violence rather than on dialogue and recognition.

By providing the analysis of the judicial style of argumentation when using objectivity, it was possible to single out some figures of speech which have a ceremonial, not semantic character, as they serve to differentiate the judge from the so-called ordinary people. For example, a figure from which judges profit by using objectivity is like the following: 'It is not me who decides here,' 'The matter is therefore clear and obvious,' 'It is the truth,' 'It is objective because that is what the law says,' 'It is objective because we all think that.' The judge utilizes such figures of speech to impose the validity and authority of his judgment. This situation illustrates the paradox of the situation of adjudication of the judge, who must first introduce himself as non-individual to establish the validity of his decision, and then needs objectivity to assign authority to himself.

The subsequent part of the chapter analyses the relationship between subjectivity and objectivity, pointing out that subjectivity is typically identified with what is emotional and irrational and is only characterized as an individual

8 Monica Den Boer, 'Two in one Trolley: Reflection on the Relation Between MacCormick's Institutional and Narrative Theory of Law,' *International Journal of Semiotics of Law* IV/12 (1991), 263.

9 Neil MacCormick, *Rhetoric and the Rule of Law: a Theory of Legal Reasoning.* (Oxford: Oxford University Press, 2005) 227–228.

perception contrasted with a rational objective assessment of legal standards. In this context, 'subjective' as individual does not deserve consideration, unless it is institutionally recognized as one of the legal categories. An important, though not surprising, observation is that the 'subjective' is often completely eliminated from the discourse, as an argument not deserving recognition due to its insignificant character.

This indicates that this imperialist – objectivist way of thinking, by ignoring individual and historical experience as unnecessary complexities, eliminates conflicting points of view due to the lack of developed tools to deal with the tension between objectivity and subjectivity. These remarks bring to the conclusions on the role of intersubjectivity as a possible way out of the many difficulties described in the book. In fact, the law, due to its deliberative character, creates more relevant conditions for intersubjectivity. Furthermore, as intersubjectivity is a precondition for communication, it would guarantee the inclusion of subjectivity, by providing the most important aspects of transparency and awareness of what we agree and what we disagree on. Since the minimal condition for intersubjectivity is communication, it is a more democratic solution compared to objectivity.

Chapter I The Conceptions of Objectivity

The discussion developed in this chapter begins with the necessary assertion that objectivity is an ambiguous term. To use it correctly it is obligatory to specify exactly what one has in mind. But what can one have in mind?

This chapter introduces the many different and often contradictory meanings of objectivity. What I am trying to do here is to make a single typology that embraces all the meanings that I have found during this research. My initial attempt to find a way to approach objectivity through dictionaries and philosophical encyclopaedias revealed many different concepts, which at first sight create a very confusing picture. It is very easy to get lost in the overviews offered by different authors. One of them even identifies twelve different meanings of objectivity.[10] But what eventually becomes clear is that all the different meanings and approaches mirror the complex relation between object and subject. Objectivity can be approached from an object-subject or a subject-object perspective. This touches upon metaphysical and epistemological foundations, including the basic question of what is first, ontology or epistemology? Standing behind this debate are philosophical systems providing justifications for certain views and explanations on what could be objective and under which conditions. All these debates are in a certain sense the prolongation of the debate on realism versus antirealism (which I will explore later in this chapter). In other words, this debate could be formulated as a question about what determines the relation between object and subject. Is it object dependent or subject dependent relation? Or, perhaps, it is somewhere in the middle, combining elements from opposite sides? The key I offer to deal with the conceptions of objectivity is to make a typology according to two main criteria, namely, from the object point of view and from the subject's point of view.

Subjectivity is commonly treated as the opposite of objectivity. This debate starts with a general characterization based on juxtaposing the following notions: on the one hand, objectivity is connected to the object and with regard to the object, whilst subjectivity is connected to the subject and with regard to the subject.[11]

---

10 See Józef Herbut, ed., *Leksykon Filozofii Klasycznej* [*Lexicon of Classical Philosoph*] (Lublin: Towarzystwo Naukowe KUL, 1997) 404–406. verbo: Stanisław Judycki.

11 See Roman Ingarden, 'Rozważania dotyczące zagadnienia obiektywności,' ['Considerations on the issue of objectivity'] in *U podstaw teorii poznania* [*At the Foundations of the Theory of Knowledge]* (Warszawa: PWN, 1971) 451.

The sense of this pair of notions is commonly treated as obvious but if we have a closer look at them, it is possible to see that they are not so clear as they seem. This juxtaposition reveals two main problems with defining these notions: their interdependence and the consequent ambiguity of both notions.

When dealing with their ambiguity, one may explain the problems with these notions could through the many meanings of both objectivity and subjectivity. Not only is objectivity ambiguous but subjectivity also has many different meanings. I am not going to go deep into the ambiguity of subjectivity, but it is helpful to briefly introduce some approaches. There are a few versions of subjectivism, which started with the Greek philosopher Protagoras of Abdera. His claim was that man is a measure of statements, which leads to the conclusion that knowledge is related to the knower. Subjective idealism, represented in the radical version by George Berkeley, says, the mind is the most basic reality and that is why the physical world exists only as an appearance to or as an expression of mind[12]. At the other extreme, we have all the postmodern positions that refer to subjectivity as being in accordance with other subjects.[13] The postmodern subjects' statements approach is closest to the intersubjective position.

Regarding the interdependence of these two notions, there would be no problem with objectivity if there was no intervention by the subject, but the object clearly has to be accessible by the subject. As Brian Fay observes:

> objectivism and subjectivism (relativism) need each other: without its opposite, neither position would get off the ground (...) they are opposite sides of the same coin (...) the only difference between them being that objectivists believe access to the world is attainable, at least in theory, while relativists deny that it is even theoretically possible.[14]

This perspective gives the background for an explanation of the phenomenon of gradation of objectivity, which can be described as strong, modest, and minimal.[15] I will explain the phenomenon that objectivity comes in degrees at the end of the chapter.

---

12 See Edward Craig, ed., *Concise Encyclopedia of Philosophy*, Vol. 8. (London: Routlege 1998) 378–379.

13 See e.g. Jacques Derrida, *Of grammatology*, trans. G. Spivak (London: The Johns Hopkins University Press, 1976).

14 See Brian Fay, *Contemporary Philosophy of Social Science. A Multicultural Approach* (Blackwell Publishing 1996) 220.

15 See Connie S. Rosati, 'Some puzzles about objectivity of law,' Law and Philosophy Vol. 23, No. 3 (May, 2004): 273–323.

Let us note that in order to avoid possible misunderstandings about the structure of this chapter, I have grouped all the meanings of objectivity found in my research into two main camps. The first one I will call object dependent (2.1.), that is, determined by object. The second is subject dependent (2.2.), which means that it is determined by the subject. To help clarify my approach to objectivity, I have made a short overview of all the meanings of objectivity I found in the philosophical field. But before doing this, it is important to explain the background of all the meanings in the light of the realism/antirealism debate (1).

At the end of this chapter, I will approach the phenomena of gradation of objectivity (4), described as strong, modest, and minimal.[16] Then I will explain the relation of objectivity with truth (5) and universality (6) and state why I have found the most misleading claims concerning objectivity within these two notions. Finally, I will present my conclusions (7).

1.1. The Realism Versus Antirealism Debate

The widely held connection between objectivity and realism offers a certain vision of reality and has its roots in the traditional realist approach.[17] But just as philosophical views of realism have changed over time and differ between different schools of philosophy, so have our interpretations of the meaning of objectivity.[18] One could be said to follow the other. It is now even possible to talk about objectivity within an antirealist approach, which has very little in common with the realist approach. Given the many types of realism and the way objectivity is used in wide ranging contexts, it is perhaps not surprising that there is no single definition of the term objectivity. While at first this may seem confusing, the great diversity of meanings offers us different ways to understand objectivity and, when viewed together, they can be seen as a gradation. This is reflected in the literature, where there are three main approaches to objectivity described as strong, modest, and minimal.[19]

Let us look closer at the doctrine of realism. The first assumption identified with realism is that ontological and epistemological objects exist independently

16 See Rosati, 'Some puzzles about objectivity of law.'

17 See Antoni Podsiad, ed., *Słownik terminów i pojęć filozoficznych*, [*Dictionary of philosophical terms*] (Warszawa: PAX, 2000) 574.

18 See Jan Woleński, *Epistemologia*, [*Epistemology*] (Warszawa: WN PWN, 2005) 465.

19 See Rosati, 'Some puzzles about objectivity of law.'

from human minds.[20] This is the starting point. Although there are many types of realism, they all have a common core that can be characterized in the following way: 'realism with regard to T-objects, means that these objects exist, or that one considers them as existing.'[21] The opposite position, namely antirealism, claims that nothing exists outside the mind or that we have no access to mind-independent objects. This is the main difference between these two approaches. Even though both realism and antirealism have holistic, global and local versions, this assumption remains valid for all of them.

Epistemological realism indicates that our perception is the focus on objects that exist independently of our act of recognition. Ontological realism says that objects exist independently of our perception, mainly in the sphere of existing structures and features. The ontological approach is not free from epistemological elements, mainly because existing independently is related to our acts of perception. The world is transcendent on acts of consciousness in two meanings:

(1) The world exists outside the consciousness.
(2) The world really exists in an absolute way; it exists independently of anybody's consciousness.

It is very hard to make a defence of either realism and antirealism in their holistic or absolute versions as the conclusion would be either everything exists or nothing exists[22]. Summing up, it is possible to characterize holistic realism as follows:

- Objects described in certain domains exist.
- The existence of these objects is independent of human minds, i.e. they are not artifacts of our minds, languages or notions.
- Sentences belonging to certain domains are not reducible to different types of sentences; otherwise it would be possible to claim that they refer to something other than what they actually refer to.
- Sentences belonging to certain domains have conditions that enable them to be verified as true or false. These sentences are direct descriptions of aspects of the world and facts make them true or false. 'Snow is white' is true if and only if snow is white.

---

20 See Mieczysław Szymczak, ed., *Słownik języka polskiego,* [*Polish Dictionary*] (Warszawa, 1994) 114.

21 See Woleński, *Epistemologia*, 234.

22 See Woleński, *Epistemologia*, 466–470.

- We are able to reach the truth in certain domains and it justifies why we accept formulated statements.[23]

Many authors reject one of these five premises. Sceptics either reject the first premise or deny that it can be proved. Conceptualists and idealists reject the second premise, reductionism rejects the third one, instrumentalists and projectivists the fourth one, and constructive empiricists the fifth one. And, of course, there are many possibilities for making very different combinations of the above arguments.[24] These possibilities and combinations of choices demonstrate the degrees of objectivity. Rejecting all five premises leads to the rejection of strong realism in the direction of antirealism. The more premises that are rejected, the weaker the conception of objectivity that is approached. This process of getting weaker shows a controversial picture of objectivity working both in the realistic and antirealist doctrine under the same name. As one may be convinced now, the content can be radically different and still classified as objective.

1.2. The Typology of Objectivity with Regard to the Object

To the first camp, the object-determined camp, belong all that meanings that could be explained in relation to the different kind of objects to which objectivity refers. To grasp the particular and subtle differences in meaning I would like to characterize the objects that are described as objective (i.e. what objectivity refers to) as follows:

1.2.1. persons recognized as objective,
1.2.2. certain types of statements,
1.2.3. knowledge,
1.2.4. elements of empirical reality.[25]

---

23 See Simon Blackburn, *Oksfordzki słownik filozoficzny*, [*Oxford Dictionary of Philosophy*] trans. Cezary Cieśliński, Paweł Dziliński, Michał Szczubiałka, Jan Woleński (Warszawa: Książka i Wiedza, 2004) 338–339.

24 For example, Kant has joined empirical realism with transcendental idealism, he accepts objective reality but considers it as structured by mind.

25 See Jan-Reinard Sieckmann, 'Legal System and Practical Reason. On the Structure of a Normative Theory of Law,' *Ratio Juris* Vol. 5 Is. 3 (1992).

1.2.1. Persons Recognized as Objective

Persons recognized as objective are commonly understood as impartial. It means that for the participating subject the process of cognition is impartial, free of bias and personal opinion. Objectivity with regard to persons is characterized as a lack of tendency[26] and the limiting of influences of individual preferences in situations of choice. Of course, these influences are impossible to eliminate in full, which is why it is necessary to use external criteria for making decisions. Personal influences are limited just to choosing these criteria, which must be subsequently used. This way of acting protects against personal bias in every case where objectivity is demanded.

The epistemological approach is identified with a method that can give the guarantee of verification, whether a statement is true or false. From a realist position, qualifying statements are verified by the correspondence theory of truth, with analytical or *a posteriori* verifications. Antirealist approaches move the central point to the area of common acceptance: the pragmatic test of applicability, the strong convincing argument, etc.

1.2.2. Objectivity of Different Types of Statements

The most general characterization says that semantic objectivity is a property of the statements.[27] I will try to explain this with regard to both the realistic and antirealist approaches. Generally speaking, semantic realism defines the meaning of statements on the basis of the classical correspondence theory of truth. It says that the statements correspond to the actual state of affairs. In contrast, the antirealist perspective defines the meaning of statements on the basis of the justification theory of truth, based on the assertability of the conditions of the statement. This is the most basic and the most significant difference.

For the realistic approach it is necessary to know which conditions have to be fulfilled to make the sentence true in order to understand the meaning. In the antirealist approach, to understand the meaning of the sentence, it is necessary to know which conditions justify a certain statement. The justification theory

26 See Klemens Szaniawski, *O nauce, rozumowaniu i wartościach. Pisma Wybrane*, [*About Science, Reasoning and Values. Selected works*] (Warszawa: PWN, 1994) 8–17.

27 See Brian Leiter, 'Law and Objectivity' in *The Oxford Handbook of Jurisprudence and Philosophy of Law*, ed. Jules Coleman, Scott Shapiro (Oxford: Oxford University Press, 2002) 975.

of meaning, at least in its deepest forms, rejects the theory of bivalence (i.e. that statements have to be necessarily true or false).[28]

So, as mentioned above, semantic objectivity is verified according to the semantic structure of a certain type of statement. It means that, different types of statements would be treated differently depending on whether they are descriptive, normative, moral or evaluative. According to the correspondence theory of truth, only descriptive statements could be classified as semantically objective. All other kinds of statements, like normative, ethical[29] (especially according to the emotivism doctrine[30]), performative, and evaluative statements are excluded from the group of truth statements. This is because they do not refer to anything really existing independently of consciousness.

Let us first consider normative judgments. They do not refer to empirical facts because they postulate a certain state of affairs that should happen but has not happened yet. That is why their verification is not possible. The second more controversial example is moral judgments that refer to certain types of moral systems. A moral system has its own hierarchy of values and that is why it dictates what is morally good or bad in an objective sense. Moral judgments may also be treated as objective[31] under the conditions of strong ontological assessments with regard to existence of the system's values.[32] Performative statements are not objective because they constitute or instantiate the objects to which they refer.[33] They are not truth evaluated because they are uttered in the performance of illocutionary acts.[34] Their aim is not to state something. Finally, we have evaluative

28 See Tadeusz Szubka, *Antyrealizm semantyczny. Studium analityczne*, [*Semantic Antirealism. Analitical Study*] (Lublin: Redakcja Wydawnictw KUL, 2001) 62–91.

29 See more, Paul K. Moser, Thomas L. Carson, ed., *Moral Relativism* (Oxford: Oxford University Press, 2001) 335.

30 See more, Jasse J. Prinz, *The Emotional Construction of Morals* (Oxford: Oxford University Press, 2007) 334.

31 See J. L. Mackie, 'The Subjectivity of Values,' in *Moral Relativism*, ed. Paul K. Moser, Thomas L. Carson (Oxford: Oxford University Press, 2001) 265–268.

32 The assessment of Max Scheler's theory of values is that values are objective, eternal, given a priori and are sensible phenomena. See also Roman Ingarden, *Spór o istnienie świata*, [*Controversy over the Existence of the World*] (Warszawa 1987).

33 See more, John R. Searle, *Speech acts: An essay in the Philosophy of Language* (Cambridge: Cambridge University Press 1969) 185.

34 Although for example J. Searle claims that 'the successful performance of the speech act is sufficient to bring about the fit between words and world, and to make the propostional content true.' In 'How Performatives Work,' *Linguistics and Philosophy* Vol. 12 No. 5 (1989).

judgments, which are also not objective. The core of evaluative judgments relies on expressing subjects' personal approval or disapproval on certain types of objects or phenomena.[35] In law, evaluative judgments are the most controversial group. According to the semantic analyses, they are subjective, but in practice there many examples where expressions such as 'objective evaluation' are used in the legal discourse.

That is why it is important to distinguish between logical sentences and other types of statements when it comes objective validation. Logical sentences are objective because it is possible to give them a true or false value. With other types of statements, it is necessary to look for other measures that could make them valid in order for them to be called objective. Where it is impossible to guarantee validity in a logical way, the strongest possible criteria are used. Examples include non-contradiction, cohesion, coherence, rational justification, acceptance of universal auditorium,[36] or, according to the social constructivist and minimal objectivism theories, qualifying as objective from the results of social dialogue. Fulfillment of the above conditions allows us to distinguish the next type of objectivity, namely 'discursive' or 'methodological.'

'Methodological objectivity' defines certain types of statements as objective depending on whether or not they are true or false according to the correspondence theory of truth. It is important to point out that a different theory of discourse justifies the objective validity of certain statements in different ways. It depends on the specific features and character of the discourse, which in turn define the specific conditions. In law, the main stress is put on legal argumentation; because of the normative character and interpretive nature of law, *mutatis mutandis*, it is not possible to justify statements by truth conditions.

1.2.3. Objectivity with Respect to Knowledge

Objectivity is used in a different sense for mathematics and logic, and for the humanities and social sciences. Objectivity in mathematics is regarded as universal, timeless, outside intentional relations and is fully intersubjective. Conversely, *a posteriori* judgments are subjective and, in light of this, humanities and social sciences are not objective. As the hermeneutic movements stress, it is necessary to use the procedure of understanding and, through this, go into a

---

35 Maria Ossowska, *Moral Norms. A Tentative systematization* (North – Holland – Amsterdam – New York – Oxford: PWN Warszawa 1980) 259.

36 See Chaïm Perelman, *L'Empire rhétorique* (Paris: Vrin, 1977); Chaïm Perelman, *Imperium Retoryki* (Warszawa: PWN, 2002) 42.

hermeneutic circle.[37] Application of hermeneutic methods excludes any conception of objectivity.

Some authors stress that objectivity as a condition for sciences could be also understood as impartiality, lack of preconceptions, intersubjective verification, the requirement being that we can work with a method that allows us to check whether certain statements are true or false.[38]

One way to consider objectivity connected with objective knowledge is to identify it with knowledge that is true by its object. The most spectacular example of the proposition of objective knowledge is an idea of Karl Popper. According to him, objective knowledge 'consists of the logical content of our theories, conjectures, and guesses.[39] According to Popper's approach, physical objects are in the first world, our conscious experience is the second world, and the logical content of books, libraries, computer memories, and suchlike are in the third world. The third world, according to Popper, is the example of pure objectivity, which could be thinkable without any reference to subjectivity, at least in some sense. The content of this world is a human product, but after the moment of creation, the existence is completely independent of the subjective perspective.

Popper's third world includes legal norms because they have a real existence but they are not part of the material world. 'They exist as elements of intersubjective meaning available to human understanding through interpretation.'[40] So legal norms could be treated as objective without or before interpretation and provide a way of accessing what is objective. However, the process of interpretation changes the status of legal norms. The act of accessing the legal norms, the process of interpretation, removes their objective status. One could say that the third world is the world of language, so if legal facts are interpretative facts, they will finally lose their objective character. What I would like to present in further consideration is that legal facts (treated as part of legal norms) are institutional facts, and through this they are interpretative facts. The first possibility suggests that if they are objective in pre-interpretative state, after the act of interpretation, they will lose it. A second possibility follows Wittgenstein's dichotomy

37 There is a movement postulate not to separate law from the humanities. See More, Gregory Leyh, *Legal Hermeneutics. History, Theory and Practice* (Berkeley, Los Angeles, Oxford: University of California Press, 1992) 325.

38 See Szaniawski, *O nauce, rozumowaniu i wartościach*, 8–18.

39 See Karl R. Popper, *Objective Knowledge. An Evolutionary approach* (Oxford: Oxford University Press, 1979) 73.

40 See Ota Weinberger, in *An Institutional Theory of Law*, Neil MacCormick and Ota Weinberger (Dordrecht: D. Reidel & Co, 1986) 165.

on understanding and interpretation. If one accesses legal norms in the act of understanding it is possible for them to hold their objective character. At the moment I only foreshadow this question and will come back to it at the end of this book.

1.2.4. Elements of Empirical Reality: Objectivity of the External World and the Ontology of Brute and Institutional Facts

This meaning of objectivity gains its sense with regard to elements of the external world. In this case objectivity is a feature of reality because its existence does not depend on the subject. The meaning of objectivity in this sense is important because it distinguishes between what really exists and what is only an illusion. One could differentiate between elements of the external world that are entirely independent from human beings, for example stones or rocks, and those that would not have been existed without human actions, such as chairs and cars. However, the latter are still regarded as objective because, once created, they can continue to exist without further human intervention.

The most important division from the point of view of this work is the distinction between brute and institutional facts. Brute facts exist in the world independently of any rules, values or conventions. They could be subject to regulation by rules, for example regulative rules. In contrast, institutional facts have a presupposition in the body of rules that create them. Examples of brute facts are empirical facts that construct our physical reality like chairs and stones. In opposition, there are institutional facts that belong to an objective, social reality and are constructed as a subjective ontological group of convictions. They are ontologically subjective in the sense that people create them and give them functions to perform. Institutional facts are characterized as collective and socially accepted. They are also constitutive rules; they constitute some action and at the same time regulate them. When institutional facts are working in a social reality, they become elements of an objective social reality, mainly because they have common acceptance, are generally agreed upon, and have collective intentionality.[41]

John Searle, one of the authors who conceptualizes institutional facts, defends realism, namely the theory according to which the real world exists independently of our ideas and representations, whatever human beings are thinking or seeing. Institutional facts include such things as money or legal institutions. In contrast to the objective external world, everything that is internal or psychological for

---

41 See J. Searle, *The Construction of Social Reality* (London, New York: The Free Press) 1995.

human beings, everything connected with emotions, experiences, feelings, and imagination, is subjective. This third group, Searle calls mental facts.

As one can see, it is possible to distinguish three types of facts: brute, institutional and mental. The first two could be counted in the object dependent camp, while mental facts are subject dependent. However, there are a lot of problems with institutional facts with regard to legal facts because of their interpretative character in the domain of law. I will devote a separate chapter to deal with this issue.

1.3. The Explanation of Objectivity with Regard to the Subject's Determination

One encyclopaedia of philosophy says that objectivity has no definite meaning and that the notion of objectivity depends on the author and the context.[42] Probably this is the most radical definition to be found, mainly because it denies the most common intuitions of objectivity and suggests that the notion of objectivity could be filled in by the subject who is dealing with it. When such an operation is possible to do, it means that objectivity is an empty notion. According to the above comments, it seems that all attempts at grasping one cross-disciplinary, universal, absolute and firm meaning of objectivity are impossible. The thesis that objectivity is an empty notion contradicts its claims to universality and general validity

1.3.1. Overcoming the Subjective Perspective[43]

As human beings, we necessarily make our determinations from a subjective perspective. We always stand at a certain viewpoint and each of us has her or his own individual perspective. Nobody can be free of it; it is not possible to look from nowhere, which could be recognized as the guarantee of being objective. Always we are looking as 'somebody,' as somebody who is the sum of experiences that are not possible to cancel, or suspend. We cannot go into the structures of experience and consciousness of others. It is a kind of impassable border, something that is not always possible to describe in an intersubjective way. To go beyond subjectivity would mean to be the other than a human being. At the same time, we cannot lose our subjective perspective because we are always in a certain place and we cannot escape from this. That is why one could say that

---

42 See Herbut, *Leksykon Filozofii Klasycznej*, 404–406. verbo: S. Judycki,

43 See Herbut, *Leksykon Filozofii Klasycznej*, 404.

it is not possible to be fully objective. An objective perspective demands what Thomas Nagel called a 'view from nowhere' or Hilary Putnam's 'God's-eye view.' As Nagel tries to demonstrate: 'it's not possible to explain objectivity in relation to a reality that exists entirely independently of our human perspective. It's necessary to look for other ways to explain it – one of which is to explain objectivity with regard to subjectivity.'[44] However as Nagel stresses, the relation between objectivity and subjectivity is not absolute in character. Statements or thoughts are more objective if they are less dependent on individual subjects and their standpoints. So, the more subjects who can reach a similar understanding, the less dependent the thoughts and statements become on individual opinions and feelings, and the more objective in character they become.[45]

1.3.2. Rejecting the Influences of Individual Elements

The assumption is that individual emotional or volitional influences, habits and tastes, or even common elements rooted in traditions and culture, are not the conditions for making judgments. Here, judgments can only be objective if they are formulated solely with regard to the object. If we analyse the relations between the first and second understandings mentioned above, we could say that the lack (of existence) of the former is not disturbing in the sense of having an influence on the second one. It is possible to have judgments that will be independent of emotional or volitional influences and, in this sense, objective, but it is impossible to be free of being the subject.[46] In this approach, independent criteria are always used when objective judgments are required and these are designed to prevent emotional and volitional influence on the judging process. The decisions of court judges should be objective in this sense.

1.3.3. Esse Obiectivum

The third meaning of objectivity accepts the possibility of the essence of the subject's consciousness. This is the scholastic notion known as *esse objectivum* or, in more modern terms, the psychological fact of knowing. It expresses all essence present in the subject's mind. However, only part of this essence could be objective in the sense that it regards objects existing independently from the human mind. But be aware that everything could be thinkable by a human mind,

44 See Thomas Nagel, *The View from Nowhere* (New York, Oxford: Oxford University Press, 1986) 14.

45 Thomas Nagel, *The View from Nowhere*, 17.

46 See Herbut, *Leksykon Filozofii Klasycznej*, 404.

even such objects as a rectangular circle, the essence of negative judgments,[47] and mythical creatures like unicorns.

Esse obiectivum characterizes the peculiar being of cognitive objects insofar as they exist in the human intellect. This may be regarded as qualification of the more general expression *esse intelligible*. Duns Scotus used *esse objectivium* interchangeable with *esse cognitum*, *esse representatum*.[48]

1.3.4. Forms of Expressing the Essence

The next meaning could be thought of with regard to the forms in which the essence is expressed. For example, Kantian's forms of perceptions like time and space are categories that are obligatory for all human beings. According to this understanding, all *a posteriori* judgments are objective because they are organized in an intersubjective way; they are forms of categories that are common for all subjects. These kinds of judgments do not reach the thing in itself (object existing independently of the human mind) because of impossibility knowing it at all, and so they are not objective in the sense of a realistic theory of perception.[49]

1.3.5. The Dichotomy Given to the Subject

The fifth understanding is based on the following dichotomy: what is given to the subject as external and what is internal for the subject. The former is what is given to the subject in the sense of perception or the grasping of sensory phenomena, the latter is what could be called psychological essence. But everything that is external for the subject could be also thinkable. In opposition to such an understanding of objectivity, one could say everything that is psychological is subjective.[50]

1.4. The Explanation of Objectivity with Regard to Intersubjectivity

Intersubjectivity is one of the basic categories in the humanities. Similarly to objectivity, intersubjectivity is marked with polysemy and conceptual vagueness. As a result, we face many kinds of intersubjectivity and its many approaches,

---

47 See Herbut, *Leksykon Filozofii Klasycznej*, 404.

48 Leen Spruit, *Species intelligibilis. From Perception to knowledge. Classical roots and Medieval Discussions* (Leiden: E. J. Brill, 1994) 279–280.

49 See Herbut, *Leksykon Filozofii Klasycznej*, 404.

50 See Herbut, *Leksykon Filozofii Klasycznej*, 404.

depending on the contexts they occur in, or different approaches proposed by philosophy, psychology, sociology or anthropology. Each of these fields invokes their own definition of intersubjectivity, stressing its different aspects. Social psychologists, for example, exemplify even six different kinds of intersubjectivity.[51]

There are different stances related to the very origin of the term as well. On the one hand, modernity is indicated as the launching of intersubjectivity, emphasizing that it has its roots in Cartesianism, but as well as in the tradition of German idealism and British empiricism.[52] On the other hand, there are also such authors, as e.g. M. Siemek, who points out that the roots of intersubjectivity may be found in the debate of post-Socratic Greeks. The ancient philosophers, as emphasized by M. Siemek, entered into intersubjective dialogue in *dia-logos* constituted by them, where a thought was created in the social space of communication. Dialoguing is based, however, on polis, or political democracy, which is a context here. Intersubjective dialogue, which occurs between its participants, arises in Socratic dialectics. What is common for the dialogue participants, is not only 'found' by them, but also commonly 'created.'[53]

As for the philosophical perspective, we might say that intersubjectivity occurs in three main approaches: communicative-ontic,[54] epistemological in the discussion on the issue of the acceptability of scientific tasks and the ontological approach.[55] The first context, which is the most distributed, is related to the field of communication among subjects, different forms of interhuman contacts and relations, being the element of communicative space. Intersubjectivity in the second approach is described from the epistemological perspective as a category, which fulfils a basic role in accessing genuine facto, formulating true authentic utterances, as well as judging/constituting the objectivity of objects. The ontological context concerns the fact what this communication is preceded by.[56] As S. Judycki indicates, the ontological context is primary in relation to the

51 Alex Gillespie and Flora Cornish, 'Intersubjectivity: Towards a Dialogical Analysis,' *Journal for the Theory of Social Behaviour*, 40 (2010) 19–46.

52 Paweł Dybel, 'The problem with intersubjectivity,' in *Intersubjectivity*, ed. Piotr Makowski (Kraków: Universitas, 2012) 17–28.

53 Marek J. Siemek, *Freedom, mind, intersubjectivity* (Warszawa: Oficyna Naukowa, 2002), 27–56.

54 Dybel, 'The problem with intersubjectivity,' 17–28.

55 Stanisław Judycki,'The mystery of interhuman communication,' in Intersubjectivity, ed. Piotr Makowski (Kraków: Universitas, 2012) 94–96.

56 Dybel, 'The problem with intersubjectivity,,' 17–28.

communicative context (tonic) and refers to the issue of the existence of other subjects considered with reference to idealism.

The communicative intersubjectivity, as it is emphasized in the literature, also referred to as relative or tonic, comprises many Assumption, e.g. that intersubjectivity occurs among people, subjects, who are simultaneously incorporated in the common communicative space, where the subjects exceed their distinctiveness and individuality.[57] With regard to this, what requires explanation is a status of communicating subjects functioning in given space, where their mutual existence and perceptions are conditioned.

Accordingly, what would require justification in the first place would be the existence of other minds, which become equally questionable as the existence of the world[58]. In this respect, however, the ontological context remains out of direct scope of this chapter and subsequent considerations are focused on the communicative and epistemological aspects.

1.4.1. Intersubjectivity and Communicative Context

True to its Latin etymology, with *inter-* meaning 'between, among' and *subiectivus* meaning 'subjective,' intersubjectivity refers to the field of what is inter-subjective. However, the concept often points simply to the public sphere, as intersubjectivity in the social dimension presented above by M. Siemek.

In colloquial terms, intersubjectivity is understood as a viewpoint, which exceeds the subjective perspective, of what belongs to the sphere of interhuman space, and what is not the erroneous reference, as emphasized in the literature,[59]

57 Dybel, 'The problem with intersubjectivity,' 17.

58 Stanisław Judycki in *Powszechna Encyklopedia Filozofii* Vol. 4 (Lublin: Polskie Towarzystwo Tomasza z Akwinu, 2003) 893–894: If this, what we unquestionably are given, is only 'my' own mind (Descartes), and then the existence of other minds (as cognitively assisted by their bodies) is at least as doubtful as the existence of the physical world. Therefore, there is a necessity to prove the existence of other minds, so that the idealism was not solipsistic whether in the metaphysical or epistemological sense. See Berkeley, Fichte, Husserl). Simultaneously, Husserl's considerations on the issue of intersubjectivity, which according to him are based on the experience of other subjects, who are analogized (foreign body and subsequently foreign psyche), emphasized the issue of the words accessible via intersubjective experience, the so-called 'simple life experiencing' (Lebenswelt) and the scientific world whose objectivity is formed as a result of intersubjective methods and idealized constructive procedures. The issue was used by A. Schütz and in phenomenological sociology.

59 Dybel, 'The problem with intersubjectivity,' 21.

although it is questionable and doubtful. Although it seems that the definition of intersubjectivity in a negatively way as being solely subjectivity is very vague, it may be the first step to define the scope/boundaries/criteria of this notion.

The first clarification, which seems to be useful, is the distinction between subjectivity and monosubjectivity. Non-communicability is the antonym to intersubjectivity, and 'monosubjectivity,' 'privacy,' 'solipsism' are considered the opposite notions,[60] or such approaches, which are strictly associated with non-transferability of individual experiences. Such a situation would denote the impossibility to communicate individual states of a given entity to other subjects, by not allowing the access in the form possible to be considered by others.

Therefore, intersubjectivity in the communicative context will occur only when subjective contents will be a matter of consideration by other subject. The basic conditions for intersubjectivity to occur will be the expressions of contents in the language comprehensible to others, but other forms of communication may occur, such as the emphatic communication.

The problem of communication among subjects in the above approach was problematized, however, both in philosophy and in other fields of knowledge dealing with intersubjectivity. We may pose a question here of this kind: how do we know that others understand us and to what extent they do so and how we may justify it.

The initial assumption in intersubjective communication is that we have direct access to our self, and the states of other people are co-assisted by body and language and with this sense we have direct access to them. That is why there remains a problem to be considered. How can we justify our belief that other people have minds similar to ours to analogically deduce about the states of other people based on individual experience.[61] These issues have been described for the last 50 years as the so-called problem of *other minds*.[62] Philosophy and psychology have been extensively searching for the answer to the question about the possibility to communicate in the face of occurring doubts. We have a debate, then, oscillating around the problem of confidence and scepticism as well as the questioning of the chances of agreement, or recurring solipsistic argument. The

---

60 Judycki in *Powszechna Encyklopedia Filozofii*, 893–894.

61 Stanisław Judycki, 'Tajemnica komunikacji pomiędzy osobami' [The mystery of interhuman communication], in *Intersubjektywność* [*Intersubjectivity*], ed. Piotr Makowski (Kraków: Universitas, 2012) 94–96.

62 See more, A. Hyslop, 'Other Minds' in *The Stanford Encyclopedia of Philosophy* (Fall Edition), ed. Edward N. Zalta, Accessed June 13, 2016, plato.stanford.edu/archives/fall2010/entries/other-minds/>. Section 1.

problems below will be discussed via the considerations on the nature of language and the possibilities of the so-called private language by L. Wittgenstein, the intersubjective anchoring in the context called 'thought communities' and on the research on the emphatic communication.

1.4.1.1. Wittgenstein's Argument

The argument presented by L. Wittgenstein (the so-called private language argument), in Philosophical Investigations (§ 243–315)[63] aims at indicating that the notion of the language which may be understood by one person and whose subjective reference of expressions would be private experience of this entity is impossible. The use of language must rely on the current rules applying to a given language. Therefore, only other language users may verify the appropriateness of its use and they become the instance controlling its use. That is why the use of the rules of a given language requires reference to a group of interlocutors-subjects in a given language, because it guarantees the appropriateness of its use. If an individual person constructed the so-called private language, then only its author would verify the appropriateness of its use and they would not be certain whether it was used appropriately.[64] It would be, as Wittgenstein states, a set of sounds incomprehensible for the remaining subjects.

Wittgenstein's argumentation, as emphasized by Judycki, would point out to the impossibility of the existence of truly private (solipsistic) language. But we could advance and see, as demonstrated by Wittgenstein's argument about the impossibility of the existence of private language, the justification of the thesis on the intersubjective communicability occurring at the language level. If language is co-dependent on 'the community of its users constituting its appropriateness, then expressing individual contents in it in an appropriate way is simultaneously the entry into private space, opening to the considered or deliberated possibility

63 See Ludwig Wittgenstein, *Philosophical investigations*, trans. Gertrude E.M. Anscombe (Oxford: Blackwell, 1958). 'Can we think of a language in which someone at one's own expense would record or utter one's internal experiences – feelings, moods, etc.? – Or cannot we do it in our own language? – I do not mean this. The expressions of such language would refer to something only a speaker knows about; to his/her direct, private experiences. The other person would not be able to understand this language' (§ 243). 'How should I refer to a language describing my internal experiences, which only I am able to understand? How do I mark these experiences with words?' (§ 256). 'Instead "private language" could denote sounds which cannot be understood by anyone else, I, however, "seem to understand them"' (§ 269).

64 Judycki in *Powszechna Encyklopedia Filozofii.*

by others and making it intersubjective. Language is since a form of communication with others assisted by rules of a given community. In this respect, as emphasized by Wittgenstein, privacy is an exaggerated concept.[65] There are no, e.g. private feelings because as one tries to express them, they become assisted by what is common. Wittgenstein, by emphasizing the role of community in shaping language, pays attention, however, to the fact that the concept of privacy is simultaneously constructed by this community.

The thesis about the very opportunity to express a message in a language understandable for other subjects would make them communicable, hence possible to be considered by other subjects in public discourse, is supported in Wittgenstein's argumentation only if this message is appropriately expressed in a given language.

Any impossibility of private language by L. Wittgenstein may be regarded as a strong argument against solipsism within the justification of the possibility to communicate at the language level, the subsequent specification of the issue of intersubjectivity was noted in recent literature. It took the form of a debate between two stances: cognitive individualism and cognitive universalism. The arguments from two opposites poles clashed here. On the one hand, the arguments emphasizing the importance of difference at the individual level, which disturb or forbid communication, on the other hand, the arguments emphasizing what is common for the entities, what binds them and what enables agreement.

1.4.1.2. 'Thought Communities'

The stance, which is a kind of compromise between the position of cognitive universalism, denoting commonality and universality of our thinking and individual cognitivism, emphasizing radical individualization, deserves a particular attention. It was formulated by E. Zerubavel, who focusing on the problems in communication resulting from differentiation at the individual level places them in the context of what is common among entities, of what binds them and what is a common horizon of communication. Zerubavel's intersubjective approach assumes that we are neither individual nor universal thinkers, but we belong to different 'thought communities.'

'Thought communities' are defined as communities of differing beliefs. They include churches, professions, scientific beliefs, generations, nations, and

65 Ludwig Wittgenstein, *Philosophical investigations…*

political movements.[66] Each of 'thought communities' shares a certain kind of experiences, which shape the beliefs of their members, but they differ from other 'thought communities.' This what affects the entity most strongly and individually is usually a group it belongs to, but not the species human beings are. E. Zerubavel constrained the scope of the influence of external context on the entities by placing them in a specific ethno-context.

These experiences, which are gained by us as the entities in our 'thought communities' are not entirely subjective or individual, but in other words they profoundly exceed this subjectivity.[67] The beliefs at the individual level are genuinely the same beliefs, which function at the community level, because they are profoundly affected by social environment. Thanks to that they may be divided by other entities from a given community and subsequently as entities we meet in common intersubjective space.

E. Zerubavel's stance clarifies the distinction at the individual level due to belonging to common contexts, which consists of various thought communities. Simultaneously, he clarifies the unification indicating the influence of community on forming individual beliefs. This approach is intersubjective in this matter and additionally supports Wittgenstein's thesis about the community privacy character.

1.4.1.3. Intersubjectivity as Agreement/Disagreement

The conducted analyses indicate that the basic condition of intersubjectivity is expressing the contents in a language comprehensible for others, while the comprehension may be determined by context with 'thought communities.' The opportunity to make contact occurs thanks to it and the opportunity for intersubjective agreement in a form of relation commences.

Intersubjectivity in the above approach is therefore comprehended mainly as a relationship among people, and more precisely as 'a variety of possible relations between people's perspectives.'[68]

The analyses related to the discussion on intersubjectivity, conducted so far, mostly focus on the aspect of agreement when they formulate the conditions vital for its occurrence. However, as it has been emphasized in literature, agreement,

---

66 Eviatar Zerubavel, *Social Mindscapes: An Invitation to Cognitive Sociology* (Cambridge, Massachusetts: Harvard University Press, 1997).

67 Zerubavel, *Social Mindscapes.*

68 Alex Gillespie and Flora Cornish, 'Intersubjectivity: Towards a Dialogical Analysis,' *Journal for the Theory of Social Behaviour* 40 (2010) 19.

in a sense of consent, or sharing the definite individual states by other entities, is not a central element of intersubjectivity. The more precise definition of intersubjectivity is emphasized. It focuses on lack of consent and agreement among entities, simultaneously being a result of deliberative activity.

The classic approach emphasizes that intersubjectivity refers to an agreement in the sense of having a shared definition of an object.[69] Such definition is the closest to the approach, in which intersubjectivity is certain common sense. If people share common sense, then they share a definition of the situation.[70] However, as other authors problematized this traditional definition of intersubjectivity understood as 'a state of overlap of individual understandings' because it 'overemphasizes agreement and de-emphasizes disagreement among the participants in joint activity.'[71]

Several different types of relations, which may occur in intersubjective communication, have been distinguished in the research conducted by social psychologists on the intersubjective communication among subjects. During the research it was established that we may enumerate at least three relations as far as relative intersubjective communication is concerned: agreement/disagreement, understanding/misunderstanding and realization of Understanding/misunderstanding. What becomes equally important is the mutual awareness of agreement or disagreement and even the realization of such understanding or misunderstanding.[72]

The additional aspect of being aware of the occurring agreement or disagreement as well as understanding/misunderstanding, added here, which seems to be the key to intersubjective communication, may simultaneously be the argument in favour of freeing from solipsism via awareness. Simultaneously, the character of intersubjectivity reinforces by the discussion of its deliberative character, which must lead to consent, and solely to awareness of occurring differences and similarities.

---

69 Junko Mori and Makoto Hayashi, 'The Achievement of Intersubjectivity through Embodied Completions: A Study of Interactions between First and Second Language Speakers,' *Applied Linguistics* Vol. 27 Issue 2 (2006) 195–219.

70 Clive Seale, *Researching Society and Culture* (London, Thousand Oaks, New Delhi: Sage Publications, 2004).

71 Eugene Matusov, 'Intersubjectivity without agreement,' *Mind, Culture and Activity*, Vol. 3 Issue 1 (1993).

72 Ronald David Laing, Herbert Phillipson, A. Russell Lee. *Interpersonal Perception: A Theory and Method of Research* (London: Tavistock Publications, 1966).

1.4.1.4. *The Emphatic Communication*

As it has been mentioned above, intersubjective communication is assisted mainly by body and language. Language has been discussed on the occasion of Wittgenstein's argument, however this paragraph will comprise other aspect of communication related to the transfer observable in body and via emotions. The integral co-activity of body during thinking is indicated in the latest neuroscientific research, called embodied theories.

Individual experiences may be communicated via different ways and may, for example, take the form of emphatic communication, where subjective individual states are shared by other individuals. Thomas Scheff defines intersubjectivity as 'the sharing of subjective states by two or more individuals.'[73] In accordance with this approach, one of the ways of experiencing other human being is via division of their subjective states, which may occur thanks to empathy.

The current renaissance of research on empathy run mainly by neuroscience indicates that empathy, as a state of co-experiencing with others, is not only the most significant way of communicating with others, but also understanding others and learning. In accordance with classic, but revalidated views, empathy played an important role at the early stages of child development and as we tended to think we gradually refrain from emotional communication when socialization occurs. As it is observed by the latest neuroscientific research, emotional communication is a basic and dominant form of interhuman communication and interaction with environment during lifetime.

Empathy, as sharing the same mental state by different people, is also defined as the intersubjective form of communication. However, both comprehension of empathy and the very emotions as well as their role changed in connection with the research conducted by neuroscience.[74]

---

73 Thomas Scheff, et al. *Goffman Unbound!: A New Paradigm for Social Science (The Sociological Imagination)* (CO: Paradigm Publishers, 2006).

74 In the light of the latest neuroscientifc research, to which I refer to in this chapter, it does not correspond to the traditional distinction into cognitive and affective empathy, because empathy seems to be an active state, an embodied simulation. See e.g. W. Załuski: 'Literature discusses mainly three types of empathy, complete empathy, truncated empathy, and contaminated empathy. Our attention will focus on complete empathy as the most basic form. Truncated empathy and contaminated empathy are blended forms. Truncated empathy occurs when one of 3 elements included in complete empathy becomes deficient. Complete empathy is defined as the combination of three elements: cognitive empathy (the capacity for a comprehensive and ethically proper understanding of other people's emotions), affective empathy (the tendency to

First of all, neuroscience redefines emotions and their role in human life as the main drives for action. Antonio Damasio's in the 'Descartes's error'[75] claimed that 'the reasoning system evolved as an extension of an automatic emotional system with emotions playing diverse role in the reasoning process.'

It denotes that emotions play a central role in cognition, communication and communication with others. Attention, perception and memory are directed by emotions. They also influence reasoning and decisions.[76]

Two accounts to emotions in the process of processing information are known mainly in psychology and cognitivism. They are as follows: modal and amodal.

Amodal account, which symbolic mind theories are based on,[77] assumes that mind encodes information in an analogue way in different conceptual systems (sight, hearing, smell, etc.). Subsequently, information is processed into abstract notional form, functionally and structurally separated from primary sources in which it was stored. As a result, amodal symbols (notions) occur, which take part in high level cognitive processes such as categorising, deducing and language. Most generally speaking, the amoral account assumes that digesting emotional information is done in exactly the same manner as each different kind of information.

On the other hand, embodied cognition theory assumes modal account.[78] According to it, high cognitive processes (thought, language) involve partial

---

emotionally respond to other people's emotions in an adequate way: sorrow to sorrow, and joy to joy), and a tendency to undertake an ethically proper action (e.g., to relieve the sufferer's pain) as a result of the emotional response to other people's emotions.' Wojciech Załuski, 'O trzech rodzajach empatii: pełnej, częściowej I skażonej' ['On Three Types of Empathy: the Complete, the Truncated, and the Contaminated'], *Logos i Ethos*, Vol. 46 Issue 2 (2017) 51.

75 Antonio Damasio, *Descartes's error* (Random House, 2008).

76 Damasio, *Descartes's error;* Piotr Winkielman, Brian Knutson, Martin Paulus and Jennifer L. Trujillo, 'Affective influence on judgments and decisions: Moving towards core mechanisms,' *Review of General Psychology* Vol. 11 Issue 2 (2007) 179.

77 Jerry A. Fodor, *The Language of Thought* (Cambridge, MA: Harvard University Press, 1975); Allen Newell, 'Physical symbol systems,' *Cognitive science* Vol. 4 Issue 2 (1980) 135–183.

78 Lawrence W. Barsalou, 'Perceptual Symbol System,' *Bahavioral and Brain Science* Vol. 22 Issue 4 (1999) 576–660; Andy Clark, *Being There: Putting Brain Body, and World Together Again* (Cambridge MA: MIT Press, 1997); Jessy J. Prinz, *Furnishing the Mind Concepts and their perceptual basis* (Cambridge MA: MIT press, 2002); Margaret Willson, 'Six views on Embodied Cognition,' *Psychonomic Bulletin and Review*, Vol. 9 Issue 4 (2003) 625–636.

reactivations of states in modality-specific, sensomotor systems and partially 'reliving' experience in its sensory. These theories assume that high cognitive processes are based on partial reactivations of sensorimotor states. According to these theories, human knowledge requires, in a sense, a recurrent 'experience' of a given event via sensual processes, which took part in the primary perception of this stimulus. It also means, that there is no redescription into abstract symbols. Sensorimotor/affective states are captured and stored in modality specific association areas and then partially reactivated.[79] In accordance with embodied theory during the experience of some emotional stimulus, the record in association areas takes place, thanks to which during the recurrence to this state (recovery of the experience in consciousness), e.g. while thinking about it, the area is reactivated. Therefore, this phenomenon is called embodied simulation, because a part of experience is regenerated or even recreated in such manner as if the individual was re-affected a given experience but in real time.[80]

What is worth emphasizing here is that simulation is regarded as an active process, not a passive one.

This dynamic aspect of embodiment, or body reactivations during a cognitive process demonstrates that body is strongly connected with a cognitive process (hence a name – embodied theory).

According to some researchers the reconstruction of the emotional state is conducted via the activation of mirror neurons or the entire system of mirror neurons. As the latest research indicates, mirror neurons are responsible for human abilities within sparing emotions, or empathy.[81] As Rizzolatti states 'Mirror neurons allow us to grasp the minds of others not through conceptual reasoning but through direct simulation. By feeling, not by thinking.'[82]

In accordance with the research conducted in this field, seeing an action causes firing/stimulating the same areas of the brain as doing a given action. It is sufficient, then, to observe someone affected by pain so that the part of the

79 Piotr Winkielman, Paula M. Niedenthal, Ucieleśniony, emocjonalny umysł społeczny (Embodied emotional social mind) In: Psychologia poznania społecznego (Psychology of social cognition), Wydawnictwo Naukowe PWN, 2009.

80 Vittorio Gallese, 'The roots of empathy: the shared manifold hypothesis and the neural basis of intersubjectivity,' *Psychopathology* Vol. 36 Issue 4 (2003) 171–180.

81 Marco Iacoboni, 'Grasping the Intentions of Others with One's Own Mirror Neuron System,' PLoS Biol Vol. 3 Issue 3 (2005).

82 Sandra Blakeslee, 'Cells That Read Minds,' *New York Times. Science* (January 10, 2006), accessed 13 June 13 2016, http://www.nytimes.com/2006/01/10/science/cells-that-read-minds.html?_r=0

brain connected with feeling pain would react actively. If we observe a scene of violence we experience terror, because mirror neurons activate this emotion in us. However, understanding a given activity of other person is possible because our brain refers to a certain template created on the basis of prior experience.

The possibility of sparing emotions is then directly related to the functioning of mirror neurons. The system of mirror neurons is responsible for stimulating an activity, however, as for the reflected emotions, a new name 'shared circuits' was introduced, because somehow the entire family of neurons functions here[83], situated in the part of the brain called insula.[84]

Moreover, it is confirmed that the research demonstrating that empathy is based on embodied simulation. In particular, we may refer to the research on the suffering of other people.[85] However, what is emphasized as particularly significant in the conducted research on embodied theories is that empathy is determined by psychological context, quality of relation with the observed person and belonging to a group. Empathy is not automatic then,[86] but individually variable and it requires mental consent to be involved in the relations and enter empathy.

In the research on the difference in reactions to emotional and non-emotional notions, in a similar way the reaction to emotional notions is characterized by the fact that it activates a specific modality – internal representation of a corporal state, which is basically related to motivation. It also organizes information in accordance with the rules of subjective value, but not external-objective one. During cognitive processing they create priorities for internal purposes, but not external-objective ones.[87]

---

83 There is no entire consent as for the fact whether neurons are located in the area of the brain called Broadmann's area (Vittorio Gallese, C. Keysers and G. Rizzolatti, 'A unifying view of the basis of social cognition,' *Trends in Cognitive Sciences* 8 (2004) 396–402; or whether they constitute a system or simply whether they fulfil reflection functions being in different areas of the brain. It was proved that the people with the so-called high empathy have very active mirror neurons. Regardless of the controversies related to reflecting neurons, it is certain which functions they cause.

84 Christian Keysers, *The emphatic brain* (Kindle Edition, 2011) 98.

85 Neuron mapping technique, subjects tested via MRI. See William D. Hutchison, et al., 'Pain related neurons in the human cingulate cortex,' *Nature Neuroscience* 2 (1999) 403–405.

86 Piotr Winkielman, Paula M. Niedenthal, and Lindsay Oberman, 'The embodied emotional mind,' *Embodied grounding: Social, cognitive, affective, and neuroscientific approaches* (2008) 26.

87 Winkielman, Niedenthal, Oberman. 'The embodied emotional mind,' 263–288.

To conclude, embodied theory demonstrates that emotions are involved not only in emotional terms but even in the act of processing information and in abstract terms.

Under the examination is the ability to connect simulation with more abstract knowledge depending on the current goal people can represent, no matter whether a given concept is more modal or amodal. People can engage different amount of perceptual simulation to more symbolic forms of knowledge representing and processing of abstract information (social, legal concepts, e.g. contract, expropriation or e.g. logical notions such as eminent domain).[88]

However, what needs to be emphasized is that these two extreme and different types of information: emotional and the most abstract are processed in a different way. We react more subjectively to emotional notions and also our body is more strongly activated and more abstract notions, such as legal concepts, are characterized by a kind of processing information resembling the amodal mode, with a low commitment of body and emotions.

The significance of the discussed research on empathy is constrained mainly to questioning of division of reactions to contents due to their cognitive subject in two modes: modal and amodal. It seems that a factor determining empathy is mainly a degree of commitment of a given person. This factor is determined by their subjective motivation and psychological context.

Apparently, we cannot underestimate the stimulation of experiencing states by other people via assisting them in our prior experiences, which enhances the easiness of empathy. We cannot forget either about a sphere of conditioning and genetic determination, which causes that thanks to the inheritance from our ancestors, we react to their experiences, which we have not experienced ourselves (e.g. research on fear against snakes conducted among city dwellers).

Eventually here the argument from solipsism recurs, however constrained mainly to dependence on the degree of individual motivation and consent to enter a relationship. The otherness of experiences may be, but does not have to negatively affect our possibility to be engaged in the other person and share their subjective state.

88 Lawrence W. Barsalou, 'Abstraction in perceptual symbol systems,' *Philosophical Transactions of the Royal Society of London: Biological Sciences*, 358 (2003) 1177–1187.

1.4.2. Epistemological Intersubjectivity as a Condition for Knowledge Creation

The analysis of intersubjectivity in a communicative context points to a great deal of controversies related to the very act of communication. However, what may be evidently stated is the fact that intersubjective communication occurs when other people have access to individual subjective states of entity and may interpret them. However, what remains controversial as well is the aspect of awareness of agreement/non-agreement by the entities immersed in a communicative contact. Despite many previously discussed arguments indicating the possibility for intra-subjective communication, a rather not entirely solved problem of solipsism is recurrent. It is observable in uncertainty related to the fact whether experiences of entities in communication are identical for both parties. Even in case of emphatic contact a situation in which the retrieval of a similar experience initiates a different set of emotions. There is no 100 % certainty whether two subjects experience precisely the same. In this regard even the arguments from thought communities and impossibility of Wittgenstein's private language reporting on community assistance in individual experiences does not solve the problem, because it does not guarantee entire accomplishment of simultaneity conditions and conscious experiencing a communicative process for both parties.

We may certainly assume that a communicative context of intersubjectivity may be treated as some kind of a preliminary stage or a basis being a foundation to transfer to the subsequent stages of intersubjectivity. While accomplishing a communicative intersubjectivity between subjects, a stage of content verification between subjects is likely to occur. The analysis via methods playing a role of verification procedures is the establishment of what we know and may lead to building knowledge.

Knowledge analysed and verified by repetitive procedures is in fact itself called intersubjective, thus intersubjectivity may also constitute property of knowledge, judgments or utterance, which is available to others, but it may be verifiable by others in accordance with established methods or tests. In this context we may state that intersubjectivity is a method of verifiability or testability, which is mandatory in a specific discourse and may decide about property of knowledge, or scientific character of a given discourse.

Intersubjectivity fulfils a double function, as a category of mutual intersubjective agreement, but also as a category of verifiability of our statements, judgments, knowledge or eventually the qualification of the scientific character of discourse. The requirement of intersubjectivity is approved in general methodology of sciences as a criterion overlapping scientific explanations, which both these requirements should meet. Firstly, scientific statements should be intersubjectively communicational or should be expressed in a language comprehensible for others and, secondly, they should meet the requirement of controllability, or be verified by other researchers by means of tests, so that their result of control could be compared.

The control procedures verifying knowledge concern the fact how we collectively verify the created knowledge and what character it has in relation to it.

Firstly, it is import ant that the very method of verifiability could be available for many subjects, if possible, specializing in a given field. Thus, the methods of intersubjective verification may be placed both narrowly and widely.

If the methods of verification are placed narrowly, namely solely sensually, then the views of introspective psychology are not allowed for intersubjective research and scientific accordingly. On the other hand, the wide approach of verification methods includes introspection into the methods of intersubjective verifiability and allows for research and as an aftermath introspective psychology is regarded as science.[89]

According to Judycki, the results of a narrow approach may be the thesis that no phenomenon is intersubjective: either two researchers observe it one after the other, and then it undergoes a change or they see it simultaneously, but then each, from a diverse spatial location, sees something different. As a result of it, the regulation of intersubjectivity was treated regulatively: we should approve of in science only the things which may be easily verifiable by others.[90]

1.4.3. Proximity of Objectivity and Intersubjectivity

The communicative and verifiable context of intersubjectivity, described above, is important as well for the conducted elaborations on objectivity. The discussion on the issues of verifiability and reasonableness of scientific sentences, transforms, however, in the subsequent stage into the discussion on the issue of methods verifying the objectivity of knowledge and its authenticity. Hence, the discussion/theme on the verifiability of products of science or knowledge is already the issue of objectivity. However, the literature comprises stances of different views, therefore the discussion on the relation of objectivity and subjectivity requires an elaboration on two more issues, which will be described below.

---

89 Judycki, 'The mystery of interhuman communication,' 94–96.

90 Judycki in *Powszechna Encyklopedia Filozofii.*

Considering the relation of objectivity to intersubjectivity, we may commerce with the analysis of the argumentation presented by S. Judycki. He identifies objectivity with truth, which creates knowledge and intersubjectivity with condition to gain this knowledge. As a result, the problem with the relation of objectivity and intersubjectivity is presented as a relation of knowledge to the conditions of regarding something as knowledge.

Discussing the relation of intersubjectivity to objectivity, S. Judycki compares their scopes by skating that objectivity is a wider notion with relation to intersubjectivity, because there may be non-communicable truth. He states that intersubjectivity does not belong to essential components of the notion of knowledge.

> Something is knowledge not because it is intersubjective, but because (except for other conditions) it is true. Intersubjective communicability and verifiability are conditions of approving of something as knowledge, but the very conditions do not exclude that monosubjective (solipsistic) knowledge may exist in significant sense.[91]

Objectivity is, according to Judycki, a notion wider in scope than intersubjectivity because objective (true) knowledge, which is monosubjective, may exist. However, the argument Judycki makes about the possibility of the existence of monosubjective knowledge, confronted with L. Wittgenstein's argument concerning the issue of the impossibility of the existence of a private language (the so-called private language argument), sheds new light on the relations of objectivity and intersubjectivity, particularly in the context of the proximity of these two notions.

As it was mentioned earlier, constructing a private language requires the use of rules. The verification whether these rules are appropriately used may be conducted solely by other users of a language, but not by someone who creates the rules of a language. The person who constructs the rules will never be able to verify whether they use them appropriately, because only the language community verifies the appropriateness of the use of rules (otherwise they are not the rules of a language). In this sense intersubjectivity is incorporated in the very use of a language, which has a public nature.

Something is expressible; therefore it is expressed in a language. As a result monosubjective objectivity (truth), which is meant by S. Judycki, remains exclusively solipsistic truth, because it is not only non-expressible, but also unknowable. If something cannot be expressed in a language, which is based on the meanings shared by users, then in general, based on the assumption of linguistic

91 Judycki in *Powszechna Encyklopedia Filozofii.*

philosophy, there is no access to this kind of 'truth' or reality. Language is here, in a sense, a form enabling cognition.[92]

Thus, intersubjectivity is somehow incorporated in truth, which may be only expressed through language, or intersubjective medium. As a result, Wittgenstein's argumentation presenting the impossibility of a private language is simultaneously an argument against a solipsistic language, which is not able to express 'truth' and is an argument against solipsistic knowledge.

The argument from Wittgenstein's private language (the so-called private language argument), indicating that there must be a community, which controls the rules used by it, approximates objectivity and intersubjectivity to each other and enhances the position of intersubjectivity as a form of objectivity. Just like a private language is not possible, monosubjective knowledge is not possible either. As a result, we may observe not only the approximation of objectivity to intersubjectivity to each other, but also the conditioning of objectivity with intersubjectivity.[93]

1.4.4. Separation of Objectivity and Truth

The elaborations on the approximation of objectivity and intersubjectivity reveal one more possibility, however, namely the separation of objectivity from truth and the justification for other forms of objectivity, which are not identified with truth.

Placing intersubjectivity in objectivity causes that we may pertain to a wider scope of relation than only the relation: objectivity – truth.

We may then think about at least three types of relations of objectivity and intersubjectivity, where intersubjectivity may be:

(1) a way of expressing (objective) state of affairs, where intersubjectivity is applied at the communicative level,
(2) a way to confirm (objective) state of affairs when the results of intersubjective tests are unanimously confirmed; intersubjectivity is applied at the epistemological level,
(3) a way to agree how (objective) state of affairs looks like; the applied communicative intersubjectivity, with awareness that the version of this what is assumed as (objective) state of affairs is verified, because we

92 Certainly, an open question is other forms of extralinguistic cognition, which I leave out of the frames of discussion in a monograph, such as irrationalism or mysticism.
93 I wish to thank prof. Zirko-Sadowski for the idea, which was presented in the review of the original version of a PhD dissertation.

> accept it by consent or by a democratic vote. What is the most significant in the agreement generated by communicating subjects is the fact what the subjects agree on and how conscious they are of the relations among each other.

The proximity of objectivity and intersubjectivity causes that the case (1) and (2) may overlap. As a result, the separation of objectivity from truth occurs in practically two possible cases, which is assisted by different types of intersubjectivity.

1.4.5. Conclusions

The lesson from this chapter is that the notion of objectivity should be used very carefully and in a precise way. The main aim of this first chapter is to shed a new light on 'objectivity' as an ambiguous concept, which will then be considered in more detail in further chapters. The misleading content of the notion appearing under the banner of 'objectivity' hides different content, from the claims to truth on the one hand to universality on the other. After all the considerations I have highlighted it will be easier to recognize and realize why this notion is still in use. Even authors themselves are often not conscious of the meaning of the notion they are using. What is more, even on the level of analytical consideration, it is possible to see that objectivity could have non-justified claims which are still identified with very powerful concepts such as truth and universality. That is why, when one shifts to the level of practical discourse and tries to interpret objectivity, it is easy to still think of it in its original philosophical meaning, even though it has been interpreted differently in different discourses.

Grasping its richness of meanings only seems possible to me through describing the way the notion of objectivity is perceived in certain types of languages and in certain types of discourses. Engagement in Herbert Hart's 'open texture'[94] approaches become more appropriate in this context. Through the descriptions of usage and the explanations of authors' assumptions and analyses of the contexts it should be possible to grasp the steps in the process of the changing meaning of objectivity. That is why I carried out the empirical analyses of legal language and examined the rulings of the Polish courts to get to know the meanings of objectivity at the level of legal practice. The findings of this empirical research in are set out in Chapter 3.

---

94 See more, Herbert Hart, *The Concept of Law* (Oxford: Oxford University Press, 1994) 124–154; verbo: S. Judycki.

1.5. The Characterization of Objectivity Due to Its Different Extent/Gradation

A common core of all these understandings of objectivity is the principle of decreasing relation of objectivity with regard to the subject, *mutatis mutandis*, and increasing of the autonomy of objectivity. If you understand objectivity as connected with the object and subjectivity as related to the subject, it is necessary to explain all those usages of objectivity which are related to the increasing role of the subject's activity and still named as objective.

In the jurisprudential literature, it is possible to find examples of strong, modest and minimal objectivity. If we divide these distinctions into two groups according to the activity of subject, the first group will be entirely connected with the object, namely the strong version of objectivity, and the second connected with an increasing role of the subject, namely the modest and minimal version of objectivity.

Strong objectivity as completely independent from a subject is characterized as pure objective entity. Strong objectivity is the representation of the theory of realism, which rejects the subject's dependence with regard to existence and perception. For example, a stone which exists completely independently from the subject or any of their activity, no matter whether the subject perceives it or not.

The other two approaches of objectivity are connected with the activity of the subject, which is necessary and not possible to eliminate. The modest version of objectivity is characterized with regard to the subject, determined by the ideal epistemological conditions (as I will explain later). These conditions have to be fulfilled to make it possible to think about objectivity as in some way independent of the subject. In this sense, for example, the activity of measuring could be objective. Effects of measuring would be the same for everybody who is doing it under the same conditions. One can observe that within the same group of notions it is possible to find different extensions of the subject's indeterminacy. This is possible because the minimalization of the subject's intervention is not always possible to the same degree and there are situations when objectivity is desirable. The example of measuring is one of the strongest, but there are there a lot of situations in which it is impossible to eliminate in subject's determination to any large extent. All these cases could be situated between the minimal version of objectivity and the strongest modest version. The minimal version of objectivity is based on the acceptance of the majority in a certain group. Take fashion as an example. What is fashionable in a certain society or group is accepted by the majority of that group.[95] Both modest and minimal versions of objectivity

95 See Rosati, 'Some puzzles about objectivity of law,' 275.

could be characterized as an attempt to minimalize subjective elements, but with the reservation that subjective elements are not excluded entirely. It is important to point out that on the semantic, epistemological and ontological levels, there are these three kinds of objectivity.

After this short analysis and presentation of some of the understandings and approaches to objectivity, one question needs to be answered or at least put forward. What is objectivity? Is it the relation of the object, or the features of the object, to the features of the subject? Or just common experience and common judgment? There is no definitive answer to this question. The realistic ontological perspective tells us that objectivity is a feature of the object; the epistemological perspective tells us that it is the style of perception, where the subject is just like an instrument.

Generally speaking, in a realistic approach, one can say that is the immanent feature of object to be connected with the general assumption about the possibility of an independently existing reality and a pure style of perception. In an antirealist approach the gravity point has moved to the subject, so the subject's judgments are objective where judgments are accepted by a majority or based on external criteria.

1.6. Objectivity and Truth/Correctness/Validity

One of the central issues of objectivity is its relation with truth, correctness, and validity. One of the strongest common intuitions regards objectivity as linking these notions. But what kinds of relations exist between these notions and objectivity, and do the commonly implied relations have a justified character? The most controversial relation is that between objectivity and truth. Let me explain why.

Some philosophical traditions, like Platonism and realism, used to identify objectivity with truth.[96] The very long philosophical tradition of using 'objectivity' in this way has linked its claims to truth. One could easily say that everything that is true is at the same time objective, but it does not work the other way around. I mean what is objective would not necessarily be the truth.

I would like to introduce Kant's explanation about the difference and separation between these two notions and then comment on the position of truth in law. On the basis of this separation, I will try to support the hypothesis that the objectivity has started to play the role that used to be identified or linked with

96 Every time I write about truth I mean the classical Aristotelian theory of truth.

truth. We have started to notice difficulties connected with the notion of truth in the domain of law, but the same kind of problems are characteristic of the conceptions of objectivity. Some authors claim that law without truth is possible.[97] But law without objectivity is a very controversial and radical approach. Some authors also postulate to dismiss objectivity because of its potentially destructive function. I do not believe that law without objectivity is possible, but the first step in that consideration is to make the notion of objectivity more precise. The crucial point in this consideration is in revealing that objectivity comes in degrees. What does this actually mean?

One can claim that there are different degrees of objectivity, namely strong, modest and minimal. The strong form of objectivity proposes to identify objectivity with truth. Such a position is characteristic for realism and it is highly controversial and strongly criticized, especially in the domain of law. What follows from such a strong approach is the criticism of the concept of objectivity in law and the claim that it is better to reject it entirely from the legal discourse.[98] Such claims refer to the strong form of objectivity because even when applied in its minimal meaning it is always open for abuse and can potentially cause destructive effects by virtue of the powerful character of objectivity. That is why the impact of objectivity in the legal domain could be perceived as disturbing. The picture of legal reality in strong objective terms is hardly possible and one can suspect smuggling political and ideological ideas under the banner of natural law. This radical approach introduces problems connected with the application of objectivity, which surely deserve to be taken into account. I will try to defend the thesis that it is not possible to think about law without objectivity, but first it is necessarily to separate objectivity from truth. In doing so, I would like to follow the separation thesis proposed by Kant. Before doing so, I would like to briefly mention that, at the level of law's application, in court rulings, the phenomenon of embodying objectivity with truth is very common. I found nearly 350 Polish court justifications that used objectivity in the sense of meaning 'truth.' I will develop and examine court practices in Chapter 3, which deals with how the Polish courts understand objectivity in their rulings.

97 See more, Dennis Patterson, *Law and Truth* (Oxford, New York: Oxford University Press, 1996) 189; Anna Pintore, *Law without truth*, ed. Bernard Jackson (Deborah Charles Publications, 2000) 273.

98 Catharine A. MacKinnon, *Toward Feminist Theory of the State* (New York: Harvard University Press, 1989) 308.

1.6.1. Objectivity as not Equal to Truth

Kant, in his Critique of Pure Reason,[99] distinguishes objectivity from truth. He tries to explain it by making the distinction between conviction and persuasion. Conviction is identified with truth and it depends 'upon the agreement of the judgment with the object.[100]' As far as we cannot reject subjective influences and subjective conditions in the process of verifying the agreement between the object and the judgment about it, we are not sure about the truth. This is the main reason why establishing truth is so difficult. The best we can do is to establish the possibility of objectivity. How it is possible? The judgment of each subject must be in agreement with the judgments of others. This is the way of providing objectivity, which Kant understands as intersubjectivity. That is why persuasion plays an important role in the process of formulating judgments. A certain judgment is considered by others and then could be potentially accepted or shared by others. it is important to stress the reasons for this kind of acceptance. It is an acceptance made by reasonable agents or, in other words, what makes them share a certain judgment is a reasoned and independently formulated judgment.

This is how it works in the sphere of the theoretical reason. But it seems that, in the sphere of the practical reason, understanding of objectivity is exactly the same, despite it dealing with different kind of realm, namely moral judgments, or norms. The difference in perspective between theoretical and practical reason is not caused by the different metaphysical status of the judgment's object, but because of its autonomy in morality. Kant said, 'Moral judgments or norms are objective if they are rationally inescapable and if they meet the tests supplied by practical reason itself, namely universality and necessity'[101]. One could draw the conclusion that objectivity here is also identified with universal intersubjective validity.

For Kant objectivity based on intersubjective validity is substantiated by morally free agents and he puts the accent on the independence of such a judgment. This is not an acceptance based on other motives but a deep, independent, individually formulated judgment made by rational, free and equal agents. Minimal objectivity, as mentioned above, is also based on common agreement

99 Immanuel Kant, *Critique of Pure Reason*, trans. Norman Kemp Smith (London: St. Martins Press, 1965) 517; Immanuel Kant, *Krytyka czystego rozumu* [*Critique of Pure Reason*], trans. Roman Ingarden (Kęty, 2001) 634.

100 Kant, *Critique of Pure Reason*, 58; Kant, *Krytyka czystego rozumu*, 67.

101 Kant, *Critique of Pure Reason*, 257. See also interpretation of John Rawls, 'Kantian Constructivism in Moral Theory,' *Journal of Philosophy*, No. 77 (1980) 559–572.

and the sharing of judgments, and also refers to the intersubjective character of judgments, but it is important to stress the main differences. The motives of the same judgments do not have to be the result of reasonable and independent research. They can be just emotional motives, an effect of following a certain authoritative judgment, etc. It does not matter whether they are independent or not. The accent lies on sharing the same judgments, like following the fashion trends, for example. Obviously, this kind of objective judgment does not have any metaphysical justification.

Summing up, Kant's objectivity of legal or moral judgments is transcendental with regard to a subject who formulates it, because it has been grounded in metaphysics. This is not a matter of conviction but persuasion, as has been shown above. That is why one does not tell the truth when making 'an objective judgment.' The latter has transcendental justification.

This is the most significant difference between Kant's approach to objectivity, which is based on the separation from truth, and that formulated by contemporary authors in their minimal conception of objectivity, which also rejects the truth, is the latter not only rejects truth but the whole metaphysics. This is why sharing judgments have no transcendental justification, and why they have no external, independent criteria to be based on. Such conceptualized objectivity does not fulfill the basic conditions to be called objectivity.

1.6.2. Objectivity Versus Correctness and Validity

A very common assumption is to identify objectivity with correctness or validity in objective judgments. But what criteria allow us to formulate correct or valid judgments? A possible way of thinking about objective judgments in this sense is, I presume, the formal way. I mean that there are certain criteria that have to be applied which constrain or even eliminate subjective, individual, arbitrarily made decisions in the process of judging. Judgments based on the proper application of such external criteria could be recognized as valid or correct. Validity could be provided by the acceptance of other participants but it is important to stress how the conditions of such acceptance are derived and how it is possible to get acceptance. There are different sources that deliver very different reasons to create their convictions about the objectivity of judgments. Judgments could be rooted in metaphysics or dismiss metaphysics entirely. Judgments could be based on certain external criteria, fixed from outside, or could be based on criteria fixed by the same subject who at the same time is formulating the judgments. A valid judgment could also be an effect of a shared opinion or agreement of judgments. To make sure a certain judgment is objective, it needs validity and to obtain its validity one needs acceptance. How is acceptance achieved? Again, the sources can be very different; it could be in the process of discovering but it could also be created. As Aristotle said 'mathematics does not need any justification.' The same applies to validity; it should be self-justifying.

1.7. Universality

The next concept strongly connected with objectivity is universality. A closer look at this relation reveals big flaws in this concept, especially with regard to objectivity and law. I claim that universality is necessary at the level of assumption of law, as a necessary assumption for the hierarchical built pyramidal system, which applies the same values to all subjects of law. As well as law's normative necessity, it must also be thought as universal with regard to all subjects who are subjected to the law. I will present research advocating a different approach, which goes beyond the level of normative assumption but focuses on the practical dimension of legal discourse. In Chapter 3, where I present my analyses of empirical data from the rulings of the Polish courts, I will show how misleading it is using objectivity in the sense of universality, or universality itself, in the practical legal discourse. For now, I would just like to briefly characterize the concept of universality.

Generally, universality could be characterized as grasping some phenomenon which omits the individual features of subjects, or which transcends individual elements. For Kant such a method takes place when based on rationality and intersubjectivity, as previously mentioned (5.1.), when intersubjective validity is based on the activity of morally free agents who follow a universal moral law. The accent is then put on the independence of such judgments. This kind of perception of transcendence, which is valid for one particular realm and one particular context, is possible to hold on to, but problems occur if there are many equal and different discourses. Legal theory shows why such a method in not compatible in the realm of law. First of all, it is possible to see how many types of discourses are taking place in law, representing different types on rationality, and mirroring a different hierarchy of values. Following Habermas' idea, one could say that we are living in a post-secular society, meaning that people are no longer all living in the same circle of norms and values. It was the former function of religion to unite state and citizens. In the post-secular society we are living in, there is no common validity of norms or values, no criteria that can be accepted by everyone, and no agreement about values. That is why the idea of universality in law is now difficult to hold on to.

The next aspect of universality in law is a holistic horizon on which one could impose a certain vision. This is the possible aim of every worldview, which is also present in law. But, as postmodern philosophies show, we have no claims to be universal. The postmodern approach has consciousness of being fragmented and does not even ascribe such a feature as reason, calling it 'discursive reason.' Postmodernists stress that the time of meta-narration is over. They have no commonly valid function anymore. We see that generalized views are often over-simplified and we no longer consider things in simple terms. We learn how to recognize multiplicity and reject all support for the power of myth. Here, it is very useful to recall two paradigms of law: one based on a pyramidical structure and one pictured as a group or archipelago.[102] In the pyramidical system, it is possible to use at least some concept of universality that will be common on every stage. The pyramid is based on common values for all citizens. The group or archipelago picture allows a pluralism of perspectives and accepts rather than rejects differences.

Despite the many controversies, universalism is still widely practiced in legal discourse, but it is possible to observe that what is called universal or objective is just *a priori* and subjectively imposed. The level of observation is also very important: distance makes it possible to reach a justification for making or recognizing universal claims. As I have mentioned before, distance is helpful in justifying universal and objective claims.

In this book I will defend that the value of universality and objectivity is just a myth deeply rooted in many cultures. So, what do we need universality and objectivity for?

I see other reasons, like the need to organize our lives, to take some control over our existence, or to feel some sense in being. The second one is the need of certainty, the need for believing in sense, or to avoid agreeing that the world could be accidental, in what appears a situation of impermanence.[103] Another important aspect that draws attention to the presence of myth is epistemology, which I have presented in my overview of the meanings of objectivity. T. Nagel, in his idea of a 'view from nowhere,' expresses that only God's perspective could offer an objective view, which could be guaranteed as a coherent and truthful vision of reality. So, what is next? The end of philosophy? Or a painful

102 François Ost and Michel van de Kerchove, *De la pyramide au réseau? Pour une théorie dialectique du droit* (Bruxelles: Publications des FUSL, 2002) 608.

103 See Leszek Kołakowski, *Obecność mitu*, [*The Presence of Myth*] (Warszawa: Prószyński i S-ka, 1972) 18.

conscious agreement on multiple rights of individual perspectives; in other words, 'anything goes'? Of course, this question is too radical to be accepted, because it presupposes another holistic vision of reality. One could say that it is hubris or just absurd thinking about the categories of universality or holisticism.

Chapter II Objectivity in Law Versus Objectivity of Law

As we saw from the previous chapter, the concept of objectivity can be approached on different levels and from different points of view. In this chapter, I would like to discuss some of the problems concerning the objectivity of law versus objectivity in law. My first step is to try to answer the following questions as a useful way to introduce two different approaches regarding the objectivity of law and the ways it is used within law (1.).

For any given domain, can claims within it be objective? Is objectivity a proper notion to be used to law; is it fit for law? Is objectivity a kind of a specific term, characteristic for a certain domain? Or should it be the same for all the disciplines, a cross-disciplinary notion?

Then I would like to stress the difference between the objectivity of law (2.) and objectivity in law (3.). After a short overview, I will then focus on three approaches to objectivity in law: metaphysical (3.1.), epistemological (3.2.), and semantic (3.3.). Consideration of this chapter will lead us to further analyses of two particular problems regarding objectivity in law: the objectivity of legal facts (Chapter 5) and the objectivity of general clauses (Chapter 4).

2.1. Is Objectivity Fit for Law?

Is objectivity fit for law?[104] Is it the proper notion that allows us to deal with legal problems? Or, as critics of this concept claim, should we reject the notion of objectivity all together?

In the jurisprudential literature, there are several different camps regarding the role of objectivity in law. The first takes its inspiration from the naturalistic approach and is based on the critical question of whether conceptions of objectivity fit all domains. According to the followers of naturalistic conceptions 'objectivity in any domain must be understood on the model of the natural sciences, whose objects of study are objective in the sense of being 'mind-independent.'[105] This

104 See more, Gerald Postema, 'Objectivity fit for Law,' in *Objectivity in Law and Morals*, ed. Brian Leiter (Cambridge: Cambridge University Press, 2000) 99–143.

105 See Sigrún Svavarsdóttir, 'Does Meta-ethics Rest on a Mistake?' I am citing that after: Brian Leiter, *Objectivity, Morality and Adjudication* (The University of Texas School of Law, Public Law and Legal Theory Working Paper, No 004, March 2000) 2.

generally means that only natural sciences could employ the concept of objectivity with legitimacy. According to such a perspective, law perceived as a social science cannot belong to the framework where objectivity in a strong sense could be applied.

There is also the idea that objectivity may be applied to all domains, proposed by naturalistic view as the cross domain, cross-disciplinary test. The naturalistic view is grounded on scientific epistemology, based on a causal explanation test.[106] Such a position is full of controversy[107] and it may be considered necessary to change the conception of objectivity as understood by the naturalistic camp. Once it has been accepted that it is not possible to reach objectivity in a strong sense, social sciences can start to apply the conception of objectivity in its modest or minimal versions. Argumentation in favour of objectivity is presented within the framework of changed notions where objectivity is no longer in full opposition to subjectivity.[108] Objectivism and subjectivism have started to be perceived as if one is part of the other. Objectivity is impossible to imagine without subjectivity, but not the other way around. There is no access to objectivity other than from a subjective perspective and because of subjective perspective. Particular authors differ in their positions on how large an extension is acceptable in order to talk about objectivity. One could say, that in that sense, these notions are strongly correlated.

Regarding these analyses of the law's objectivity, one can introduce a group of defenders[109] and a critical group. The critical

---

106 See more, Postema, 'Objectivity fit for Law,' 67, 134.

107 See more, Postema, 'Objectivity fit for Law,' 135.

108 Dennis Patterson, 'Objectivity and Normativity,' *William & Mary Law Review*, Vol. 43 (2001–2002) 326.

109 Ronald Dworkin, *Law's Empire* (Cambridge: Harvard University Press, 1986); Ronald Dworkin, 'Objectivity and Truth: You'd Better Believe It,' *Philosophy and public affairs* 25 (1996) 87–139. Kent Greenawalt, *Law and Objectivity* (New York, Oxford University Press, 1992); Michael Moore, 'Moral Reality Revisited,' *Michigan Law Review* 90 (1992) 2424; Michael Moore, 'A Natural Law Theory and Interpretation,' *Southern California law Review* 58 (1985) 279; Jules Coleman and Brian Leiter, 'Determinacy, Objectivity, and Authority,' *University of Pennsylvania Law Review* 142 (1993) 549, reprinted in Andrei Marmor, ed., *Law and Interpretation: Essays in Legal Philosophy* (Oxford: Oxford University Press, 1995); Nicos Stavropoulos, *Objectivity in Law* (Oxford: Oxford Clarendon Press, 1996); Hilary Putnam, 'Are Moral and Legal Values Made or Discovered?,' and 'Reply to Brian Leiter,' *Legal Theory* 1 (1995) 5–19 and 69–80; Jules Coleman, 'Truth and Objectivity in Law,' *Legal Theory* 1 (1995) 33–68; Brian Leiter, 'Objectivity and the Problems of Jurisprudence,' *Texas Law Review* 72 (1993) 187; Brian Leiter, 'The Middle Way,' *Legal Theory* 1 (1995) 21–31; Brian Leiter,

group[110] consists mainly of followers or writers who identify themselves with the Critical Legal Study movement, Feminist Jurisprudence[111], and Critical Race Theory.[112]

Followers of Feminist Jurisprudence call for a complete rejection of objectivity, describing it as a 'hypocritical notion.' They mainly highlight the internal incoherence of objectivity. As they explain, there is a clash between rules and norms, which are perceived as objective, and the practice, which makes objective rules and norms fail when they are judged by implicit standards.[113] The only remedy for this tension between explicit and implicit standards is to reject the notion of objectivity, as the feminist movement claims.

The theme of rejecting objectivity also is prevalent in followers of Critical Race Theory (CRT). Basically, they share the same objections as the Feminist

---

'Legal Indeterminacy,' *Legal Theory* 1 (1995) 482–492; Brian Leiter, 'Rethinking Legal Realism: Towards a Naturalized Jurisprudence,' *Texas Law Review* 76 (1997) 267; Brian Leiter, 'Objectivity, Morality, and Adjudication,' in *Objectivity in Law and Morals*, ed. Brian Leiter (New York: Cambridge University Press, 2001) 66–98; David O. Brink, 'Legal Theory, Legal Interpretation, and Judicial Review,' *Philosophy and Public Affairs* 17 (1988) 105–148; David O. Brink, 'Legal Interpretation, Objectivity, and Morality,' in *Objectivity in Law and Morals*, ed. Brain Leiter (Cambridge: Cambridge University Press, 2000) 12–65; and Heidi Li Feldman, 'Objectivity in Legal Judgment.' *Michigan Law Review* 92 (1994) 1187; Andrei Marmor, *Positive Law and Objective Values* (Oxford, New York: Oxford Clarendon Press, 2001); Patterson, 'Objectivity and Normativity,' 325–363. Joseph Raz, 'Notes on Values and Objectivity,' in *Objectivity in Law and Morals*, ed. Brain Leiter (Cambridge: Cambridge University Press, 2000) 193–233. Postema, 'Objectivity fit for Law,' 99–143. Rosati, 'Some puzzles about objectivity of law.' Matthew H. Kramer, *Objectivity and the Rule of Law* (Cambridge: Cambridge University Press 2007); George Pavlakos, *Our Knowledge of Law. Objectivity and Practice in Legal Theory* (Oxford and Portland, Oregon: Hart Publishing, 2007).

110 The critical group is also very varied. See more, for example, Joseph Singer, 'The Player and the Cards: Nihilism and legal Theory,' *Yale Law Journal* 94 (1984) 1. Duncan Kennedy, 'Form and Substance in Private Law Adjudication,' *Harvard Law Review* 89 (1976) 1685. Richard Delgado, 'The Inward Turn in Outsider Jurisprudence,' *William and Mary Law Review* 34 (1993) 741.

111 Ann C. Scales, 'The Emergence of Feminist Jurisprudence: An Essay,' *Yale Law Journal* 95 (1986) 1373.

112 See Derrick Bell and Preta Bansal, 'The Republican Revival and Racial Politics,' *Yale Law Journal* 97 (1988) 1609, 1611; John O. Calmore, 'Critical race Theory, Archie Shepp, and Fire Music: Securing an Authentic Intellectual Life in a Multicultural World,' *University of South California Law Review* (1992) 65, 107.

113 MacKinnon, *Toward a Feminist Theory of the State*, 54.

Movement to the use of objectivity in law. This American movement is sceptical about concepts such as justice, truth and reason, since they reveal their complicity with power.[114] They attempt to expose the manner in which these ideas are 'racialized' in American law.[115] The Critical Race Movement typically shift the perspective of consideration from the objective to the subjective level. Using a storytelling model, utilizing subjective accounts of experiences of racism, they seek challenge mainstream cultural assumptions.

The autobiographical approach is used to analyse and criticize social and legal relations. For example, Patricia Williams in her 'The Alchemy of Race and Rights' combines legal analyses with personal narrative in order to criticize legal subjectivity (by deconstructing legal arguments to show that legal principles are not consistently applied). The representatives of Critical Race Theory explore how both literary knowledge in the sense of autography writing once's own story and legal knowledge are produced, to make a postcolonial mimicry of the dominant discourse.[116] Through this, they show that particular experience should be taken into account instead of the standardized experience of the dominant objective narration.

The hostility of traditional legal scholarship to the autobiographical perspective is perceived by CRT as a means to dissociate the law from everyday social and cultural problems, especially racial and gender discrimination.[117] From this perspective, they identify objective discourse with the dominant discourse that is imposed.

Members of Critical Legal Studies movement mainly advance arguments based on the 'indeterminacy critique.' The broad outline of their argumentation says that adjudicative reasoning is not free of political, ideological or other influences external to law, as it should be. Judicial decisions must be impartial, free of arbitrary influences and constrained by the character of their profession.

---

114 Angela P. Harris, 'Foreword: The Jurisprudence of Reconstruction,' *California Law Review* 82 (1994) 741, 743.

115 Derrick Bell, *And We Are Not Saved: The Elusive Quest for Racial Justice* (New York: Basic Books, 1987).

116 Richard Schur, 'Critical Race Theory and The Limits of Autobiographical Reading; Patricia William's *The Alchemy of Race and Rights* Through Postcolonial Theory,' *Biography* Vol. 25, No. 3 (2002).

117 Shoshana Felman, *The Juridical Unconscious, Trials and Traumas in the Twentieth Century* (Cambridge and London: Harvard University Press, 2002).

The core of the problem is that the character of the profession embodies political forces.[118] That is why the circle is closed.

On the other side, there are of course authors who defend objectivity. This camp is also very diverse. Some hold the position that postulates the necessity of objectivity in all domains and, through this, its necessity in law. Others try to prove that every domain has its own individually tailored objectivity and so law has its own brand of objectivity. But this kind of view makes the notion of objectivity empty and contradicts the very basic assessment about a minimum of universality of objectivity. There is also middle a position, which tries to structure objectivity partly as a notion that has certain elements in common in all domains but also with its own specific characteristics in law. G. Postema, who claims both that objectivity is fit for law and that law is a domain that can claim objectivity for itself, represents such a position.

Postema explains it by the law's general claim to legitimacy for itself. Law demands allegiance of all citizens and this provides the law's objectivity. This is the main reason for legal objectivity. What is most interesting about Postema's position is that he reformulates the meaning of objectivity and offers the conception 'objectivity as public acceptance.' He argues that law is such a discipline where 'objectivity can be understood as public acceptance,' mainly because of the public character of justification, which is capable of leading to consensus. And consensus, Postema claims, is a sufficient condition to allow us to speak about objectivity. I will explore this approach in the part of this chapter dealing with the epistemological conception of objectivity. I see it as meaningful to place Postema's approach on the map of authors dealing with the concept of objectivity: its defenders, critics, authors taking a middle position, and adherents of the reformulation of this concept.

Of course, there are wide variations of views within groups and what I have introduced above is a simplification for the purpose of helping to grasp the problems. Generally speaking, what certain groups have in common is their general acceptance or disagreement on objectivity, in particular legal objectivity.

Now I would like to point out two main spheres discussed in jurisprudential literature, namely the objectivity of law and objectivity in law.

---

118 See more: Mark Kelman, *A Guide to Critical Legal Studies* (Cambridge and London: Harvard University Press, 1987); Costas Douzinas and Adam Gearey, *Critical Jurisprudence: The Political Philosophy of Justice* (Oxford and Portland, Oregon: Hart Publishing, 2005); Roberto M. Unger, *The Critical Legal Studies Movement* (Cambridge, London: Harvard University Press, 1983); Duncan Kennedy, *A Critique of Adjudication [fin de siecle]* (Harvard University Press, 1997).

2.2. The Objectivity of Law

The discussion of the objectivity of law centres mainly on the character of law, asking such questions as: Is law objective in itself? How could law be objective? In which way? Under which conditions? Has law an objective core?

One perspective about the nature of law, which I use to open the debate, comes from the School of Natural Law. It focuses on the dilemma of the objective character of law[119] and takes the position that the law is objective. According to this stream of thinking, the law is objective, firstly because it is given by nature, that is independently of people's wills and their influences on it, and secondly because the source of its existence makes law valid to everyone and everywhere. The content of natural law is also objective because it is simply given to people; their task is just to read what has been written for them and they have no influence on the material dimension of law.[120]

Some authors, who don not identify themselves with a natural law position, stress that law can be understood as objective when everybody treats it in the same manner in the same situation, when law is equal for all its subjects[121]. To quote another author 'objectivity of law in first line means that it is a normative order which is the same for everyone, independently of anyone's'[122]. It seems to me that this understanding is connected with the sense of objectivity is based on impartiality and corresponds more closely to the formal understanding of objectivity, whereas the former relates mainly to the material sense of objectivity.

---

119 Czesław Martyniak, *Obiektywna podstawa prawa według Św. Tomasza* [*The Objective Foundation of Law according to Tomas Aquinas*] (Kraków: Towarzystwo Naukowe KUL, 2005) 45.

120 There are many different theories of natural law. One can see the sources from the antiquity to the present moment. See more, Aristotle, *Nicomachean Ethics, book IV of the Eudemian Ethics*, trans. Terence Irwin (Indianapolis: Hackett, 1985); Thomas Aquinas' doctrine in Tony Burns, 'Aquinas's Two Doctrines of Natural Law,' *Political Studies* Vol. 48, Is. 5 (December 2000); Thomas Hobbes and Hugo Grotius in Hedley Bull et al., ed., *Hugo Grotius and International Relations* (Oxford: Oxford University Press, 1990); Samuel von Pufendorf, *The Political Writings of Samuel Pufendorf*, ed. Craig L. Carr (Oxford and New York: Oxford University Press, 1994); John Locke, *Questions Concerning the Law of Nature* (definitive Latin text, with facing accurate English translation in John Locke, *Questions Concerning the Law of Nature*, ed. Robert Horwitz et al. (Ithaca: Cornell University Press, 1990); John Finnis, *Natural Law and Natural Rights* (Oxford: Clarendon Press, 1980).

121 See Leiter, 'Law and Objectivity,' 977–979.

122 Jan-Reinard Sieckmann, 'Legal Reasoning: The Methods of Balancing,' (2010).

What is important to stress is that we have two different conceptions of law (the natural law position and the positivist approach), which both claim that law is objective, but they understand and define objectivity in different ways.

The key question that appears is: 'does the notion of objectivity change its meaning according to the object which is described by it?' In the first case, objectivity is understood in terms of its content from the material perspective and in the latter in terms of formalism. In both cases, the definition of law is different; the former represents the material conception of law and the latter the formal conception of law. Anyway, the question the meaning of objectivity is determined by the object to which the feature of objectivity is refers still remains important, though there seems to be no one easy answer.

This problem could be reformulated into a more general question about the direction of cognition. Then one could ask, does the object determine the subject, or is the object determined by the subject. In other words, is the effect of the process of cognition objective because the object itself is objective or because the subject is able to recognize it in an objective way? Is the feature of objectivity prescribed to the process of cognition or to the object itself? Is the law objective because it has an objective content or because the cognition can be done objectively? Going further, we have to ask whether the questions about objectivity should be epistemological or metaphysical, It seems that these two levels are related to each other and there is no possibility to answer this question without taking a position regarding what comes first, epistemology or ontology?

Now we reach the fundamental problem and the way of solving it depends on the access to a certain philosophical system. It has been a dream of all philosophers to create a philosophical system without any assumptions. As we know this is still just a dream, and that is why we should reveal the basic premises of our thinking each time. In the case of objectivity, revealing preferences about primacy of ontology or epistemology would mean joining one of the philosophical camps we are dealing with, namely realism or antirealism.

With any inquiry into the objectivity of law, the primacy of epistemology or ontology in our perception is at issue. It is the question about the direction and the level of determination of the subject and object.

I will not continue the consideration about the objectivity of law, because it is out of the scope of this book. I just would like to map the problem and draw the attention to the differences between the objectivity of law and objectivity in law. I would also like to stress that both approaches objectivity of law and objectivity in law can be considered on the metaphysical, epistemological and semantic levels. This typology in the issue of convention and depends on definition of law, one assesses[123]. The main field of my consideration will be now the objectivity in law.

2.3. Objectivity in Law

As one Polish theorist says, 'objectivity mainly concerns the decision-making process. With regard to law, there are three main spheres where applying objectivity seems to have a sense and is most often used: with regard to the decisions which are the effects of applying law, with regard to interpretative decisions, and with regard to decisions about fact setting.'[124]

Indeed, there are different approaches to fact setting because there are different types of facts in law. Some authors divide all facts in law into so-called brute facts and institutional facts. Other authors claim that all facts in law are institutional because, even though they are composed of brute facts, they are made institutional by the application of law. When one claims there are brute facts in law, the problem of objectivity in law focuses upon the principle of material truth in criminal law or the formal conception of truth in civil law. In these cases, objectivity means that something is in accordance with what happened in reality.

The latter approach to legal facts makes the situation more complicated because interpretative decisions have to be taken in the process of setting brute facts. This that one does not get to know what legal fact is before the particular concrete decision of the case. Such an approach needs to treat the process of setting legal facts as equally problematic to that of taking interpretative decisions. I will examine this problem in more detail in a separate chapter about the objectivity of legal facts.

Objectivity related to interpretative decisions shows a whole variety of conceptions of possible access to the so-called 'real meaning,' 'true meaning,' or the existence of the ideal objective method, which enables such access. At the

123 It is also important to stress how the definition of law influences of such kind of typology. For American Realists, law is 'law in action,' the effect of applying law. According to such a perspective, my typology would look differently. What I call objectivity in law would be objectivity of law at the same time. What is more, some of them would never call law objective, e.g. Jerome Frank is famously credited with the idea that a judicial decision might be determined by what the judge had for breakfast.

124 Jerzy Wróblewski, *Wartości a decyzja sądowa*, [*Values and Judicial Decision*] (Wrocław – Warszawa – Kraków – Gdańsk: Zakład Narodowy im. Ossolińskich, 1973) 150.

same timee, there are conceptions that also call themselves 'objective,' but in the modest or minimal senses, which accept the subjects' influence on the interpretative process. I will focus upon these problems in a separate chapter.

Objectivity of final judicial decisions[125] is a value directly linked to the activity of the courts, which should fulfil the features of certainty and uniformity. In practice, taking a final decision is nearly always based on choosing between two or more contradictory interests, which are examined to be objective or not. Objectivity in this sense could be approached by the positivist metaphor of the 'right answer.'

Another problem area discussed under this banner is the objectivity of judging, in the sense that judges should be impartial and only follow the law and not their personal opinions or prejudices. Legal decisions have to be objective in the sense that they have to be taken and based on law and in accordance with law alone. Generally, all procedures in law have an aim to protect against personal influences of judges when they apply law. That is why fragments of legal norms that are about 'objective external standards in the process of applying law' are so popular.

In jurisprudence, there are many analyses of objectivity in many contexts. I would like to follow them according to the systematization used in philosophy, namely, from the ontological, epistemological and semantic perspectives. These three approaches create a complex view on the problems of objectivity both of and in law, because it is not possible to understand one perspective separately from the others. These three spheres are of course interdependent and an analysis of relations between them gives a clearer picture of each of them.

This correlation will especially be useful when analysing the objectivity of legal facts, taking in the crucial question of whether the semantic status of facts is determined by its metaphysical status. In other words, do different types of facts have an influence on setting their meaning? Are meanings set or do we discover meanings? Could setting the meaning of statements be called objective? If yes, do legal facts become objective and, if so, in which context? To answer the above questions, I would first like to analyse all three approaches in relation to law: metaphysical objectivity, epistemological and finally semantic objectivity.

I will begin by reviewing the concept of realism and then I will set out and evaluate the stated objectives of the realist perspective. From this, I will go on to present my research advocating the antirealist approach. It is important to take note that all three approaches can be found in strong, modest and minimal forms.

---

125 Wróblewski, *Wartość a decyzja sądowa*, 151.

2.3.1. Metaphysical Objectivity of Law and in Law

Realism or antirealism? Examining the relation between realism and antirealism can illuminate the background to metaphysical considerations. This is the starting point to all further debates, because the joining of these camps provides the justification for further claims. The general line of this typology can be simplified as follows:

(1) The doctrine of realism refers all debates to the status and structure of facts.
(2) The doctrine of antirealism rejects the facts' dependency thesis. They offer a remedy to main line of criticism towards realism through rejecting the dependency on the metaphysical perspective as a necessary condition for starting semantic or epistemological qualifications. Antirealists do not need the history to make further claims. They deny that the world is independent of the human mind or that humans have independent tools that can give them access to the world. So, one can say that antirealism in its radical version entails subjectivism. This is their main argument to justify why there is no need for metaphysical considerations.

To take a realist perspective, one should start at the metaphysical level. The order is important because epistemological and semantic objectivity rely on metaphysical assumptions. It means that the status and structure of facts determines their epistemological and semantic dimensions. The facts' dependency thesis assumes that the direction of determination goes from the ontological status of facts to the subjects' process of cognition or interpretation. It also means that all considerations should be regarded to the ontological level, whatever they deal with.

From the realist perspective, epistemological and semantic objectivity is entirely dependent on the ontological status of facts. This means that if facts in a certain domain are treated as objective from ontological point of view, they could be, but are not necessarily, objective at further levels. It also means that if facts cannot be qualified as objective at an ontological level, it will be impossible to say they are objective at further levels.

This is why if one wants to talk about objectivity in certain domain, objects of the discourse have to be qualified as objective or not. Brute facts could be qualified or be treated as an essence possible to be taken into the framework of realism and so qualify as objective. Some problems have appeared when it is difficult to grasp or constrain facts of certain domain as brute facts. For example, when one has to analyse facts with questionable ontological status, like quantum physics, psychological experience, or legal facts in law. That is why it is necessary at this moment to ask this question with regard to the domain of law.

When analysing law on the ontological level, one needs to be more precise in stating what kind of objects could be qualified as objective. Different authors give different propositions on what the objects of reference are. Some claim that legal norms[126] (3.1.1.) and others that legal facts[127] (3.1.2) are the objects of reference on the ontological level.[128] I have found these two answers the most meaningful because they picture two different approaches to the objectivity of the metaphysical status of law. One could say that they name the same, albeit very complex phenomenon, in a different way. Both these conceptions touch the same phenomenon but put different emphasis on which elements qualify as most important. I will introduce both approaches and show the differences between them.

As I have tried to show at the beginning of this chapter, the typologies documented in jurisprudential literature are very varied and authors very often have their own approach to objectivity and build their own set of notions. Some distinguish objectivity in a weak and strong sense,[129] others claim that objectivity comes in three degrees: minimal, modest and strong.[130] They also give different answers about metaphysical objectivity in law. In this part I will introduce two approaches to metaphysical objectivity. The first, represented by M. Kramer (3.1.1.), identifies the subject of metaphysical status of law with legal norms.[131] The second approach, made by J. Coleman and B. Leiter (3.1.2.), consider the status of legal facts as proper reference point for examination of the metaphysical status of law.

2.3.1.1. M. Kramer's Conception

M. Kramer characterizes objectivity in order to ask the question about the metaphysical status of law. He claims that consideration of objectivity is identified with a question about the nature and existence of things. What makes his position special is the thesis that the existential status of law is considered in referring

126 Kramer, *Objectivity and the Rule of Law*, 56.

127 Jules Coleman and Brian Leiter, 'Determinacy, Objectivity, and Authority, in Law,' in *Law and Interpretation: Essays in Legal Philosophy*, ed. Andrei Marmor (Oxford: Oxford University Press, 1995) 275.

128 It is important to make an assessment about the definition of legal facts and legal norms. There are conceptions that assess that legal facts are part of legal norms. This means that there will be no need to differentiate objects of reference.

129 Kramer, *Objectivity and the Rule of Law*, 45.

130 Rosati, 'Some puzzles about objectivity of law,' 48.

131 Kramer, *Objectivity and the Rule of Law*, 6.

to general legal norms. At the same time, he maintains that both the legal system and legal norms have a conventional character.[132] This set of theses about the conventional nature of law and the objective character of law seem controversial on the ontological level, so it is necessary to have a closer look at them.

Elucidation of the ontological dimension of law's objectivity expresses questions about mind-independence (3.1.1.1.), determinate correctness (3.1.1.2.), and uniform applicability[133] (3.1.1.3.). Within the dimension of law, the mind-independence question could be asked with regards to legal norms. How could they be mind-independent and in what extension? This question deals with the occurrence or continued existence of law, which Kramer maintains is a social convention in an institutionalized form.

2.3.1.1.1. Mind –Independence

Kramer's approach to the metaphysical objectivity of law is mind independent in both its existential and observational dimensions. The weak version of existential mind-independence means that something is not dependent on the mental activity of any particular individual. The strong version[134] says that that something is not dependent on the mental activity of any group, individually or collectively.[135] The weak version of observational mind-independence says that the nature of something is not dependent on what it is taken to be by any particular individual. The strong version says that the nature of something is not dependent on what it is taken to be by the members of any group, individually or collectively.[136] Kramer claims that law is existentially objective in the weak sense because the existence of law is not dependent of the individual will of the subjects, but it is dependent on the will and acceptance of society. This is enough to qualify it only as objective in a weak sense. He also claims that law is observationally objective in the strong sense and, as such, it applies in an all or nothing manner and is not matter of degrees.[137] The implication of this is that it

132 Kramer, *Objectivity and the Rule of Law*, 12.

133 Kramer, *Objectivity and the Rule of Law*, 2.

134 This aspect is not in accordance with most other authors in jurisprudential literature, who identify the strong approach to objectivity with the realistic position. What Kramer calls strong objectivity is identified with the minimal version of objectivity by other authors. What is perceived by the majority of one group is called minimal objectivity by most authors, but Kramer identifies it with the strong version. Most other authors (J. Coleman, B. Leiter, C. Rosati) understand the 'strong position' as being when facts are independent of anybody's mental access or influences on these facts.

135 Kramer, *Objectivity and the Rule of Law*, 6.

136 Kramer, *Objectivity and the Rule of Law*, 6.

137 Kramer, *Objectivity and the Rule of Law*, 100.

possible for a whole community of legal officials to be wrong about an interpretation; they could make a global mistake. This part of Kramer's conception is controversial and other authors, like Andrei Marmor, maintain that law is observationally objective only in a weak sense. Marmor and Kramer share the same convictions about conventional nature of law. The conventional nature of law makes it independent for the individual; the will of the people is what is enough to prescribe objectivity in weak sense. Besides, 'if a given concept is constituted by social conventions, it is impossible for a pertinent community to misidentify its reference (...). There is nothing more we can discover about the content other than that which we already know.'[138]

Another argument that could be taken into account here is the lack of necessity to analyse the existential dimension of law, as on the level of assessment it already has a prescribed conventional character. This leads us to the conclusion that the conventional position is necessarily bound with the minimal approach to objectivity and, however controversial it may seem, it is coherent to argue that this is an antirealist vision of law. The point of this discussion is to demonstrate the main difference between a strong conception of objectivity, which resembles realism, and other weaker conceptions of objectivity, which move closer to the antirealist position. This raises further questions:

(1) When there are no references to facts, how can the theoretical position be named as strongly objective?
(2) Is it possible to accord realism with conventionalism? And, if it is possible, on which conditions could it be possible?
(3) Which position in reference to facts has more force? The modest position (e.g. Coleman) or the weak position, which can be identified with minimalism?

2.3.1.1.2. Determined Correctness

The second metaphysical approach to objectivity of law made by Kramer concerns the question of 'determinate correctness.' He follows a typology that identifies objectivity with determinate correctness and indeterminacy with the negation of legal objectivity. This means that the greater the determination of legal questions, the greater the extent of objectivity. Considered in practical terms, the more leeway left to a legal official in arriving at concrete decisions, the less objective the decision is and *vice versa*.[139] So, objectivity is identified with

138 Marmor, *Positive Law and Objective Values*, 138.
139 Kramer, *Objectivity and the Rule of Law*, 17.

the absence of subjective influences of legal officials when taking decisions. In effect, the more mechanical the decision-making process is, the more objective it becomes. As Kramer claims, indeterminacy exists to some extent in all legal systems, but its extent is exaggerated when it comes to legal practice, especially in its interpretation by the Critical Legal Scholars. That is why the extent of objectivity, according to Kramer, is the matter of degree, situated between the positions of the strong correct answer, as represented by Ronald Dworkin, and the defenders of radical indeterminacy, as represented by the Critical Legal Scholars.

2.3.1.1.3. Uniform Applicability

As Kramer claims, it is also possible to find a third dimension of objective ontological consideration in law connected with uniform applicability, that is the law is applied in the same way to everyone within a jurisdiction.[140] This entails that equality and impartiality are substantial features of the law. Kramer indicates that categorical imperativeness is of prime importance; legal requirements are the same for everyone no matter of inclines or preferences,[141] and everyone is judged with the reference to the same criteria.

It also explains the phenomenon of law providing itself with so-called 'objective standards,' which are applied in all cases where the individual is to be judged. Anglo-American tort law, in its legal construction of a reasonable person, delivers one such example. The standard of negligence is defined by reference to the level of care that would be taken by a reasonable person, which is represented by objective standards to be someone of average intelligence and physical ability. What follows from this is that law distinguishes some groups of subjects to be treated differently (in this case people with above or below average intelligence and physical ability) by excluding them from the general standards and, in so doing, it contradicts uniform applicability. This is visible in all cases where law regards the individual measure of responsibility according to certain abilities or inabilities in order satisfy the standards it demands.

I will explore the topic of objective standards and general clauses in more depth using examples from Polish law in Chapter 4.

2.3.1.2. J. Coleman's and B. Leiter's Conception

Let me offer a differently formulated answer about the metaphysical objectivity of law proposed by Jules Coleman and Brian Leiter. As mentioned before, they

140 Kramer, *Objectivity and the Rule of Law*, 2.
141 Kramer, *Objectivity and the Rule of Law*, 38.

are concerned with the metaphysical consideration of legal objectivity in relation to legal facts. They do not treat legal facts as part of legal norms, as some authors do, but they bind them with legal practice. According to them, the justification of objectivity of the metaphysical dimension of law is that legal practice is objective in a modest sense, and legal practice is dependent on the status of legal facts, which are also objective in a modest sense.

They claim that the question about the metaphysical objectivity of law yields the correct answers to the legal, political and moral questions.[142] When one claims that law is metaphysically objective, it means that its correctness is independent of anyone's beliefs about it.[143] The problem of the metaphysical objectivity of law is now focused on whether the decisions that judges reach are objectively correct or if they are correct just because judges regard them to be correct.[144] They identify this problem as a worry about the metaphysical status of legal facts because they see the legitimacy of authority as referring to objective facts and not depending on objective procedures.[145] Such a view in its extreme version is mostly held by natural lawyers, who claim that law is objective in a strong sense. The second option from this perspective is to follow Ronald Dworkin in his view that almost all cases have one right answer.[146] At the other extreme, there is a position that law is metaphysically objective in a very narrow number of cases.[147] For example, the American Legal Realists claim that metaphysical subjectivity takes place when a judge makes claims about the status of a legal fact based on individual beliefs.[148]

Jules Coleman and Brian Leiter uphold the objective metaphysical status of law but only in the modest sense. What does it mean that legal practice

142 Coleman and Leiter, 'Determinacy, Objectivity, and Authority, in Law,' 244.

143 Coleman and Leiter, 'Determinacy, Objectivity, and Authority, in Law,' 244.

144 Coleman and Leiter, 'Determinacy, Objectivity, and Authority, in Law,' 211.

145 By legal facts they mean, any statements of what law requires on some point. Coleman and Leiter, 'Determinacy, Objectivity, and Authority, in Law,' 244.

146 Leiter, 'Law and Objectivity,' 977.

147 The problem appears when one is referring to objects that have questionable status, like values. This is important because claims about objectivity in ethics implicate claims about objectivity in law. This could be a problem when moral reasoning is necessary in the process of justification, especially in those theories where law has to fulfill moral criteria. Problems are also possible where the sources of law contain moral concepts. In both situations the status of values will decide about the metaphysical objectivity of law.

148 Coleman and Leiter, 'Determinacy, Objectivity, and Authority, in Law,' 245.

is objective in modest sense? In order to give an answer to this question it is necessary to explain what the strong, modest and minimal versions of objectivity mean.

2.3.1.2.1. The Strong Objectivity

Strong objectivity is identified with the realist approach. Following Crispin Wright, facts are claimed to be objective on the metaphysical level by the conjunction of two premises:

(1) The independency of facts can be affirmed by our epistemological access to them.
(2) It is possible to secure knowledge of such facts.[149]

Applying this perspective to legal facts would mean that the existence and the nature of legal facts are independent of what lawyers or judges believe. Such a position raises some objections. Firstly, the possibility of getting access to such facts is questioned. How it is possible? The realist[150] response is that it does not matter if judges have access to legal facts or not. Legitimate authority depends on the correct answer to the legal dispute. They claim that judges have access to the correct answer on legal disputes in the same way as ordinary people have access to facts. The difference is that judges gain this knowledge though the process of adjudication. Treating the process of adjudication as the form of gaining justified beliefs creates a very important question: what kind of epistemology of judging is demanded to fulfil the standards of the realist conception of legal facts?[151] Michael Moore is a realist representing a coherent approach to the justification of beliefs. He claims, the coherence in our beliefs is supposed to track the strongly objective requirements of law.[152] Such an answer may seem unconvincing in defence of strong objectivity because it fails to deal with a ready-made picture of mind-independent facts. The subjects' job is to discover the existence of facts not to create them. Moore's argument about coherence seems more suitable for a softer conception of realism.

149 Crispin Wright, *Realism, Meaning and Truth* (Oxford: Wiley-Blackwell, 1993) 72.
150 Metaphysical realists about legal fact in that strong sense are in jurisprudential literature Michael Moore and David Brink.
151 Coleman and Leiter, 'Determinacy, Objectivity, and Authority, in Law,' 275.
152 Michael Moore, as cited in Coleman, 250.

2.3.1.2.2. The Minimal Objectivity

The minimal version of objectivity says that legal facts are fixed by what the majority of judges take them to be.[153] This position seems to be attractive mainly because of it solves the problems about access to facts. Minimalists simply reject the necessity to consider the metaphysical status of facts. They offer a way of fixing facts not discovering them. That is why the process of cognition is outside their scope of interest.

This version of objectivity seems to be unproblematic and open to adopt everything that would be accepted by the majority of people. But is it really so? Critics' objections to the minimal version of objectivity include the possibility of global or so-called large-scale error, and problems connected with dominant ideology.[154] I see no point in discussing the first problem because it simply does not exist in terms of the minimal approach to objectivity. It seems to be self-evident that if a certain position denies the existence of a reference point outside its own system, there is no need to consider the possibility of large-scale error. Arguments concerning dominant ideology come as both semantic and metaphysical arguments. Semantic arguments, like the one proposed by the Kripkenstein approach, try to establish the indeterminacy of meaning. When human practice establishes meaning, it is nothing different than reflecting the hierarchy of certain society and the interests of the dominant culture. Law then becomes a tool of the enforcer of the dominant ideology and culture behind the mask of objectivity.[155] This line of argumentation reveals a few interesting conclusions. Usage of this argument shows how tricky the ambiguity of the term objectivity can be. First of all, the critic of the minimal version of objectivity is mixing different meanings of the term objectivity. The critic makes the accusation of objectivity as if it were used in the strong sense, where it clearly being stated in the minimal version. As the critic said: 'Law is a tool of the enforcer the dominant ideology and culture behind the mask of objectivity.'[156] But according to the minimalist position, the meaning of objectivity is nothing more the acceptance of majority. It has no implication to truth at all. As this example shows, users of language connect objectivity with truth and universality so strongly in their minds that it very often difficult to appreciate the differences in meaning.

---

153 Coleman and Leiter, 'Determinacy, Objectivity, and Authority, in Law,' 260.
154 Coleman and Leiter, 'Determinacy, Objectivity, and Authority, in Law,' 260.
155 Coleman and Leiter, 'Determinacy, Objectivity, and Authority, in Law,' 260.
156 Coleman and Leiter, 'Determinacy, Objectivity, and Authority, in Law,' 260.

The above argument suggests that the critic's comments were directed towards large narrations, where the domination of one culture or group over the interests of others imposes the truth definition of the 'one right answer,' turning our pluralistic societies into homogenous entities. The only difference is the kind of justification provided by strong and minimal versions of objectivity. In the case of strong objectivity, the critic accuses the stronger minority of imposing the right paradigm of interpretation of reality over the majority. With weak objectivity, the critic accuses the majority, which is also stronger and behind the argument of common acceptance, but there is no implied homogenous vision of an imposed truth that is hidden behind a veil of objectivity.

The second element that deserves to be considered is the relation of objectivity to violence. From the above arguments, it can be seen that objectivity is the kind of notion that can be accused of imposing certain values in violent way. This is the big paradox of the concept of objectivity: it should provide transparency and equity and prevent the domination of the stronger over the weaker, and the domination of one subjective element over another. Objectivity should exclude what is arbitrary, resist the domination of individuals, and prevent the domination of subjectivity. Using an example from political philosophy, this was one of the main arguments against ideologies such as totalitarian systems.

So, what kind of discourse would be free of violence and domination? According to what has been said above, the answer would be one that provides equity for the non-equal. In other words, such a discourse that does not follow objective standards, but provides formal equity. Otherwise it could turn into injustice. This is the tension between justice and equity that objectivity in law creates.

Objectivity also reveals itself like a false concept that is not able to provide the aims that it promises to fulfil. What is more, the application of this notion is necessarily linked with violence even on the unawareness dimension of language.[157]

The metaphysical argument against the minimal version of objectivity sounds even more controversial. From the point of view of legal practice, legal facts are objective in a minimal sense when they are fixed by lawyers or judges and the outcome of the application reflects how they understand them. J. Coleman points out that judges are generally white males and suggests that this is why objective legal facts turn out to be expressed with a bias towards wealthy white

---

157 Andrzej Zybertowicz, *Przemoc i poznanie: studium z nie-klasycznej socjologii wiedzy*, [*Violonce and Cognition. Non-classical Study of Sociology of Knowledge*] (Toruń: Wydawnictwo Uniwerystetu Mikołaja Kopernika, 1995) 58.

men.[158] This is exactly the same argument that feminist movement puts against every conception of objectivity.

This short characterization of the minimal version of objectivity raises some basic doubts. Is the minimal version of objectivity still objectivity? Or is it so weak that it is hard to qualify such position as objective? And finally, what are the minimal standards to qualify a certain phenomenon as 'objective'?

The characterization of minimal objectivity presented above seems very similar to the representation of subjectivity, the one difference being that it finds its justification in common acceptance. Arguments about sharing the same standards seem to be enough to talk about objectivity. This position is closer to the intersubjectivity position but, for me, the core of the argumentation is what kind of standard they share or respect?

Are the standards or criteria external or internal for a certain group that shares the same position? If the standards are internal, this implies that they were set subjectively. The only feature that makes a difference is the common agreement for applying such standards.

But there is still a gap of potentiality between the rejection of ontology, which provided the external justification, and external standards, which can provide criteria from an external system of reference, for example, without any necessary relation to ontology. Another option is to follow Kant's understanding of intersubjectivity, which is justified by the independent decisions taken by rational moral agents (as explained in Chapter 1).

According to such an understanding of the minimal conception of objectivity, everything represented in sufficient quantity would be called objective. Internal justification, by the group itself, seems to be nothing more than transparency. It would at least be more precise to talk about transparency, rather than intersubjectivity or objectivity, in cases where there is no external justification at all.

I see in external justification as both the core of and the minimal requirement for objectivity. Otherwise, there is nothing else but a transparent group project, which represents the sum of a group of subjective individuals.

2.3.1.2.3. The Modest Objectivity

According to the version of modest objectivity, what seems right under 'ideal epistemological conditions' determines what is 'right.'[159] The difference between the minimal and the modest version of objectivity, I would say, is the external

158 Coleman and Leiter, 'Determinacy, Objectivity, and Authority, in Law,' 260.
159 Coleman and Leiter, 'Determinacy, Objectivity, and Authority, in Law,' 56.

kind of justification. According to the modest version of objectivity, a certain group of people can make a mistake. It means that everybody could be wrong about his or her interpretation of the rules of law, but there still exists a certain external pattern for comparison. With the minimal version, it has absolutely no meaning if somebody or group of people are wrong.

As authors on modest objectivity stress, this approach shares some elements of both strong and minimal objectivity, but what makes this position better is that it avoids the criticisms directed at the extremes of the other two.

Firstly, in contrast to the realist vision, legal facts are not transcendent on evidence. They are fixed by judgment under ideal epistemological conditions. This helps to avoid the problems that strong objectivity must face, as the method and the character of access to facts in order to gain knowledge about them is firmly established.

The main argument against minimal objectivity concerns the linguistic level of legal facts. Meaning is set by social practice, which, according to the authors, may generate the possibility of mistakes. They give the example of the meaning of gold. When a new discovery appeared about the chemical content of gold it was necessary to change its definition. In my view this type argumentation misses the point because it uses notions that belong to the opposite philosophical camp. As we have seen, the critics of antirealism use the tools of realism in their arguments. Antirealists do not care about truth or about mistakes. These notions have no consequence because the antirealist does not admit that statements can either be true or false. The antirealist wants to be free of such points of reference and to break this link between meaning and objects. What Jules Coleman names a mistake, the Kripkenstein antirealist position would constitute an advantage.

Modest objectivity is free of such mistakes because of the ideal epistemic conditions prevent them. Modest objectivity could be explained as follows: judges do not take decisions by virtue of their individual beliefs because then it would be subjective; they have to meet certain objective requirements of the law when taking decisions. This means that, on the one hand, legal practice has an objective component in the requirements of the law that judges have to obey, but there is also the question of the indeterminacy of law, which challenges the objective status of law. Combining these two elements is what makes the characterization of law in terms of objectivity so complicated. That is why law is being seen as composition of objective and subjective elements. Coleman and Leiter are trying to combine these two tendencies that exist together in law. These two contradictory tendencies create a specific characteristic of law, which can be used to grasp a specific meaning of objectivity; what Coleman and Leiter call the modest version.

There are several sources of legal indeterminacy represented at different levels of law. One can claim the indeterminacy, inconsistency or even contradictory nature of legal sources in the fundamental way. The source of inconsistency that has been seen in the thesis is that, 'the set of legal reasons are too impoverished or too rich.'[160] What the authors are trying to explain is that that indeterminacy is the effect of the poverty of available or authoritative sources. No matter how rich they are, there will always be cases where it is not possible to apply the law according to actual binding legal standards, leaving gaps in legal systems.[161] There are also general sources of indeterminacy that come from the nature of language and are not specific to law.

According to Coleman and Leiter, meeting these two opposite tendencies in law, which are not possible to eliminate, creates a specific legal type of objectivity in the modest version. From the one side, the indeterminacy of law makes objectivity impossible in the strong sense; from the other side, the standards required by law also makes minimal version of objectivity inappropriate. This points to the need of the middle way as proper for dealing with legal objectivity.

Let me introduce a set of ideal epistemic conditions, which an ideal judge should fulfil:

(1) the judge should be fully informed about all relevant factual information and authoritative legal sources
(2) fully rational
(3) maximally empathetic and imaginative
(4) free of personal bias
(5) conversant with and sensitive to informal culture and social knowledge.[162]

2.3.1.3. Summary

Summing up, the differences between Kramer's and Coleman's approaches to the metaphysical objectivity of law could be characterized according to the line of division between the doctrines of realism and antirealism. I would like to make this characterization to gain the same theoretical of point of reference for both authors. I find it the best way to make a comparison between them and to understand them. The main reason for such a methodology is that there are not only

160 Coleman and Leiter, 'Determinacy, Objectivity, and Authority, in Law,' 218.
161 Coleman and Leiter, 'Determinacy, Objectivity, and Authority, in Law,' 219.
162 Coleman and Leiter, 'Determinacy, Objectivity, and Authority, in Law,' 277.

differences on the level of sets of notions and their typology but also with what they identify as the metaphysical objects of reference for law.

Kramer considers legal norms as ontological objects while Coleman considers legal facts. What is the difference and what is the meaning of such a difference? Kramer understands legal norms as conventions and Coleman understands by legal fact 'any true statement the law requires.'[163] Now it is possible to see the difference between the two approaches; one is conventionalist and the other 'soft realist.'

It means that one can place these two positions on a map showing the history of development of ideas from realism to antirealism. (Note: I will do this according to the map of notions introduced in Chapter 1 rather than the authors' own networks of notion.)

Coleman takes the middle position between strong realism and strong antirealism. But, as he still keeps in mind the point of reference within the body of legal facts, it means that he could qualify as a soft realist. 'Modest objectivity about legal facts treats them as judgment dependent.' This type of thinking is in accordance with philosophical realism, mainly because it holds justification as the ontological point of reference.

In the case of Kramer, I would say that he is a representative of the antirealist camp, mainly because of his references to the conventionalist legal norm. This characteristic matches exactly with the minimal conception of objectivity based on common agreement of majority. But Kramer's proposition has a very specific approach to metaphysical objectivity. Although he maintains that law is objective in the ontological sense, even strongly so in its observational dimension, it is very hard to qualify his position as realist. His consideration of legal norms, which he identifies with conventions, means that they are a different kind of entity to referential facts. The ontological structure appears in three dimensions: determinate correctness, uniform applicability and mind independence. For Kramer, legal norms cannot be wrong. If it was possible for them to be wrong, then they could not be objective in strong sense. 'There is no objective answer to the specific legal question. Every answer is correct (in the sense of not being incorrect) but no answer is determinately correct.'[164] He identifies the question of correct answer with the extent of determinacy by law and in consequence it becomes a question about the predictability and certainty of law. As Kramer claims: 'Philosophers and ordinary people who mull over these

163 Rosati, 'Some puzzles about objectivity of law,' 276.

164 Kramer, *Objectivity and the Rule of Law*, 14.

matters are especially interested in ascertaining whether the legal consequences of people's actions in a particular jurisdiction are determinately settled by the terms of the prevailing legal norms.'[165]

Omitting the incoherent and misleading points, I would not characterize his position as going from ontology to the statements; it is not from a bottom up direction. For Kramer the criteria of correctness are identified with what the law is saying by its legal norms and the internal legal order, and internal legal narrative-constituted by the normative legal order. As Kramer says it is impossible for norms of a legal system not to be address to all the matters covered by particular legal question because the norms are open ended.[166]

After this short summary, it is possible to see two opposite tendencies dealing with the ontological status of law. One which is directed from bottom up and related to metaphysics, albeit in a modest way, and the second one which is created by common agreement of people, directed by the normative dimension of law.

2.3.2. Epistemological Objectivity of Law

The law is treated as epistemologically objective when the method that allows us to discover the right answer in the body of adjudication or the legal reasoning is a right one. This method is a guarantee of impartiality and eliminates any distortion of the effects of the procedure.[167]

The epistemic dimension of law is also called the procedural or methodological dimension. Sometimes it is called justificatory or presented as discourse objectivity.[168] Mainly it is recognized as a lack of partiality in the decision-making procedure for reaching objective decisions. Which decisions could be called objective is determined mainly by the kind of justification employed in reasoning. Realists say that being impartial and following legal procedures in legal reality will lead to the discovery of the 'right answer.' Effects of cognition can be verified and/or justified as objectively valid. It also means that a sentence can be qualified as true or false and so, in consequence, everybody must accept its validity.

165 Kramer, *Objectivity and the Rule of Law*, 14.
166 Kramer, *Objectivity and the Rule of Law*, 56.
167 Leiter, 'Law and Objectivity,' 977.
168 See Sieckmann, 'Legal System and Practical Reason.'

In opposite to a strong realist perspective, a weaker form of epistemic objectivity is correctness. As Leiter stresses, any reasonable agent must accept a certain position as free of mistakes and, in the case of law, free of distorting factors.[169]

There is also antirealist approach saying that what is accepted by majority of auditorium is objective.[170] Decisions are objective if they are an effect of discourse, but what is important is that discourse itself has to fulfil certain conditions. Agents taking part in this discourse have to conduct it in a proper way so that the effect of the procedure can be called objective. This characteristic is reminiscent of Habermas' 'ideal speech situating' picture. Postema, the author who advocates such a position, argues that a judgment can be objective in a specific domain and, at the same time, maintains 'objectivity is fit for law.' Law is such a discipline in which 'objectivity understood as public acceptance' is suitable, mainly because of the public character of justification, which is capable of leading to consensus. And consensus, Postema claims, is a sufficient condition to allow us to speak about objectivity. A legal proposition is objective if is 'maximally supported by the arguments and the balance of reasons available for articulation are assessed by reasonable and competent persons in a fully public deliberative process.'[171] This position, of course, makes no assertions about the metaphysical status of legal facts.

2.3.2.1. Methodological Conception of Legal Objectivity by G. Postema

According to Postema, there are three main components that create the concept of objectivity: the independence of judgments, their validity or correctness, and invariance across judging subjects.[172] These three components are necessary for accepting the definition of objectivity in all the domains where objectivity is demanded. This feature of objectivity means that a certain judgment has to be independent in the sense that it is transcendent on the subjectivity of the judging subject. Of course, being entirely independent is not possible, because it is not possible to reach the 'objective point of having no view.'[173] Arthur Ripstein says 'some influences make us . . . better judges, while others make us worse, but the total absence of influences would leave us as no judges at all.'[174] According to

169 See Coleman and Leiter, 'Determinacy, Objectivity, and Authority, in Law,' 234.
170 See Postema, 'Objectivity fit for Law,' 213.
171 See Postema, 'Objectivity fit for Law,' 117.
172 See Postema, 'Objectivity fit for Law,'108.
173 Postema, 'Objectivity fit for Law,' 102.
174 Arthur Ripstein, 'Questionable Objectivity,' *Nous* 27 (1993) 359.

such a view, the question is which influences are desirable and which are inappropriate. This direction of thinking leads us to consider objectivity as impartiality, which boils down to a definition that objectivity is 'partiality in the right direction.'[175] The limitation of this position has been seen in the answer to the question about 'the right direction.' As always in such cases, it is necessary to apply the process of balancing values.[176] It can give the answer to the question about the right direction, in other words, which values are preferred and for what reasons.

The decision-taking process in the argumentation model is very different from that of the traditional, syllogistic model. Decisions are not taken out form the legal norms, but they are effects of balancing competing principles.[177] According to the argumentation model, decisions are mainly or even entirely reduced to the adequate balancing of the principles and aims of law.[178]

Another author claims that law based mainly on balancing principles within rational discourse is applying 'soft law.'[179] The balancing operation, with arguments 'for' or 'against' the competing interests means that system of law

---

175 Zygmunt Tobor, 'Bezstronność sędziego,' ['Impartiality of a Judge'] *Przegląd sądowy* No. 6 (2005) 3.

176 Robert Alexy, *Teorie der Grundrechte* (Baden-Baden: Suhrkamp Verlag, 1985) 146; see also Tomasz Gizbert-Studnicki, 'Konflikt dóbr i kolizja norm,' ['Conflict of Goods and Collision of Norms'] *Ruch Prawniczy, Ekonomiczny i Socjologiczny* No. 1 (1989) 10; Krzysztof Płeszka, *Uzasadnianie decyzji interpretacyjnych przez ich konsekwencje*, [Justification for Interpretative Decisions by its Consequences] (Kraków: Tow. Aut. i Wydaw. Prac Nauk. Universitas, 1996) 179 ff.; Piotr Tuleja, *Normatywna treść praw jednostki w ustawach konstytucyjnych RP* [Normative Content of Rights of the Individual in Constitutional Acts of the RP] (Warszawa: Wydawnictwo Sejmowe, 1997) 72 ff.; Bartosz Wojciechowski, 'Dyskursywny model sądowego stosowania prawa – wybrane aspekty,' [Discursive model of judicial application of law. The chosen aspects] in *Filozofia prawa wobec globalizmu*, ed. Jerzy Stelmach (Kraków: Wydawnictwo Uniwersytetu Jagiellońskiego, 2003) 161.

177 Ota Weinberger, '*Prima Facie* Ought. A Logical and Methodological Enquiry,' *Ratio Juris* Vol. 12 No. 3 (September 1999) 239: 'Rules stating principles or purposes are always applied as views determining the decision by weighting (but not by subsumption) (...).'

178 Wojciechowski, 'Dyskursywny model,' 153.

179 Marek Zirk-Sadowski, 'Wykładnia i rozumienie prawa w Polsce po akcesji do UE,' [The interpretations and understanding of law in Poland after the accession to EU] (Paper presented on conference in Gniezno), 13; Also: Marek Zirk-Sadowski, 'Instytucjonalny i kulturowy wymiar integracji prawnej,' [Institutional and cultural dimension of legal integration] in *Zmiany społeczne a zmiany w prawie. Aksjologia, konstytucja, integracja*

is rejecting the deductive way of applying law and its so-called subsumption model.[180]

I would like to consider as one of the central problem of the argumentation model, the matter of objectification of criteria, which will be useful for balancing competing standards (principles, values, aims). In this case it is not possible to use such a rule like 'lex posterior . . .,' 'lex superior . . .,' etc, which allow us to make a choice between rules as adequate or appropriate.

In the Polish jurisprudential literature, one of the most famous directives used in cases where there is a conflict of rules is the 'Weight Formula' conceptualized by Robert Alexy also known as the process of balancing or weighting.

'The higher the level of infringement or non-fulfilment of one of the conflicting principles, the more important the implementation of the other principle becomes.'[181] It is important to mention the universal character of this principle, which exists mainly because of its formal nature. This principle does not indicate how to establish the degree of infringement or how to decide on the relative importance of conflicting principles.

The postulate that the realization of certain values (principles) should be done according to the proportionality of their weight poses its own justification in the concept of justice. It is simple realization of what justice demands.[182] By justice, I mean, following Aristotelian definition: 'the distribution of certain goods.'[183]

---

europejska, ed. Leszek Leszczyński (Lublin: Wydawnictwo UMCS, 1999) 41; Tuleja, *Normatywna treść praw jednostki*, 127.

180 Wojciechowski, 'Dyskursywny model,' 166.

181 Alexy, *Teorie der Grundrechte*, 146; Compare, Gizbert-Studnicki, 'Konflikt dóbr,' 10; Płeszka, *Uzasadnianie decyzji interpretacyjnych*, 179 ff.; Tuleja, *Normatywna treść praw jednostki*, 72 ff.; Wojciechowski, 'Dyskursywny model,' 161;

182 See Lothar Hirschberg, *Der Grundsatz der Verhältnismässigkeit* (Göttingen: Schwartz, 1981) 86: '(...) Grundsatz der Verhältnismäβigkeit und Zweckformel, Prinzip des überwiegenden Interesses und Güteraabwägungsprinzip (...) wie auch weitere denkbare allgemeine Formeln sind deshalb nur sprachliche Variationen über ein und dasselbe Thema der Fallgerechtigkeit;' Chaim Perelman, O sprawiedliwości, [Justice at raison] (Warszawa: Wydawnictwo Naukowe PWN, 1959) 130.

183 Aristotle, The Nicomachean Ethics, 'The justice with which we are concerned has two branches: distributive, of honours and the like among citizens by the State, and of private property by contract and agreement; and corrective, the remedying of unfair distribution. There are always two parties, and justice is the mean between the unfairness which favours A and the unfairness which favours B. Distributive justice takes into consideration the merits of the parties; corrective justice is concerned only with restoring a balance which has been disturbed. The distribution is a question not of equality, but of right proportion; and this applies to retribution, which is recognized as

As T. A. Aleinikoff claims balancing is very tempting, mainly because it is consistent with the common understandings of justice, fairness, and reasonableness. Themis, the Greek goddess of justice, is commonly depicted with a blindfold over her eyes holding a pair of scales, weighing 'for' and 'against' to decide which party prevails.[184] Today, we might picture the goddess of justice holding a calculator in her hand, doing very sophisticated analyses. 'Balancing provides a careful, sensitive, thoughtful way to dispense justice, to give each his or her due.'[185]

The function of correction in the hard definition of justice is to take into account the circumstances of all individuals in order to optimalise the final decision in each case. In other words, fairness plays the part of correction in the formulation of justice[186]. Fairness, as Ch. Perelman claims, has a function of supporting justice to implement it in a necessary way.[187]

It is the role of the judge to evaluate each of the principles and to assign values to the identified interests. The judge has a right to make one of the principles more important and to decide which of the principles will be implemented.

The balancing process has to be flexible and relevant to individual circumstances. There are no objective criteria that can provide an absolute solution. To eliminate everything that is arbitrary is possible when there is common agreement in the matter of values within normative system. As Perelman claims, because of the arbitrary and mutually contradictory character of the values in legal system, there is no possibility of perfect justice entirely based on reason.[188] It is very common that arguments for one solution are counterbalanced by arguments for the opposite solution.

'There are very rare cases when arguments supporting one solutions are not balanced by better or worse arguments for different solutions. Only exceptionally

---

one of its aspects, e.g. the retribution for an officer striking a private and for a private striking an officer. Proportional requital is the economic basis of society, arrived at by the existence of a comparatively unfluctuating currency, which provides a criterion.'

184 Thomas Alexander Aleinikoff, 'Constitutional Law in the Age of Balancing,' *The Yale Law Journal* Vol. 96 No 5 (April 1987) 962.

185 Aleinikoff, 'Constitutional Law in the Age of Balancing,' 962.

186 Henryk Piętka, *Słuszność w teorii i praktyce* (Warszawa: Instytut Wydawniczy Kasy Mianowskiego, 1929) 33 ff.; I. Szabó, 'Pojęcie słuszności w różnych systemach prawnych,' *Państwo i Prawo* No. 5 (1971) 673–680.

187 Perelman, *O sprawiedliwości*, [Justice at raison], 64.

188 Perelman, *O sprawiedliwości*, 105, 107.

evaluation of values can be done by arithmetic and measure. Evaluation can change with the subject and stress personal character of decision-making.'[189]

The second feature, namely correctness or validity of the judgment says that the judgment fulfils certain necessary conditions and that is why it is possible for it to be accepted. The third feature, invariance across judging subjects,[190] leads us to the approach objectivity as intersubjectivity. Postema juxtaposes considerations about impartiality with the concept of so-called 'positional objectivity.'[191] The core of this concept lies in the distinction between subjectivity and positional objectivity. A subjective judgment would, according to this theory, be made one person. A positional objective judgment is determined by individual circumstances from a particular position, but it is then confirmed by another subject who is in the same position. A. Sen, the author of this idea, gives 'the moon looks small' as an example of an observational judgment. Such a judgment could be confirmed by another person who observing the moon from the same position[192] This conception seems to me more like multiplied subjectivity. Calling such a judgment objective is unjustified. It is the same as an observational fact, like saying this apple is good or tasty. Such an approach to objectivity as intersubjectivity is equal to the minimal conception of objectivity, mentioned in the first chapter. There are no external reasons for it to cross the border of subjectivity and become objective. There is nothing that makes it transcendental. There is also no possibility for mistake, because in that case everybody will repeat it. And what would this mean if 80 % of the group confirm the same judgment. What does it mean then? It could be only the statistical majority.

The second juxtaposition of types of intersubjectivity is the so-called 'relativized judgment,' which transforms a 'subjective judgment into an objective one.'[193] How is this possible? By defining the position. However such a formulation raises

---

189 Chaim Perelman, *Logika prawnicza. Nowa retoryka*, [Logique juridique] (Warszawa: Wydawnictwo Naukowe PWN, 1984) 36.

190 Postema, 'Objectivity fit for Law,'108.

191 See More, Amartya Sen, 'Positional Objectivity,' *Philosophy and Public Affairs*, Vol. 22 (1993).

192 Amartya Sen, 'Objectivity and Position: Assessment of Health and Well-Being,' in *Health and Social Change in International Perspective. Health and Social Change in International Perspective*, ed. Lincoln Chen, et al. (Boston, Mass.: Harvard School of Public Health, 1994).

193 Greg Currie, 'Interpretation and Objectivity,' *Mind* 102 (1993): 413–28. According to Greg Currie 'the degree of objectivity depends on the degree to which a judgment needs to be relativized before it is capable of gaining closer agreement.'

problems; does something really change from subjective to objective by simply revealing the point of reference and making it visible or public? Such a metamorphosis raises many doubts because it breaks the relation with the point of reference.

The main argument lies in the character of the point of reference, which according this theory makes a judgment objective. We could choose a point of reference that is both subjective and partial, and find everybody who repeated this exercise of relativized judgment would reach the same effect. The question is how this point of reference is chosen, in other words which is right direction.' Answering such questions would always comprise the process of balancing values.[194] How could it be objective? The character of a judgment is not only revitalized to the point of reference or criterion, but it also inherits the character of the system that created it.

2.3.3. Semantic Objectivity of Law

Three types of semantic theory can be distinguished in the literature:

(1) semantic theories that explain what links a word to the object(s) to which it refers, like theories of reference,
(2) criterial semantic theories[195] that claim that the link between a word and its object is an uncontroversial text shared by speakers, like Kripke's rigid designators,
(3) interpretative semantic theories that claim that the link is a theory or interpretation,[196] like Berthelot's conception of modeling facts using theories.

This mapping will help to see why I choose the criterial semantic theories as more suitable for law. I will analyse and explain why the first and the third theory seem to be inadequate for the analysis of legal facts.

The bridge between the objectivity of law and semantic conception can be found in Brink's, who wrote: 'debates about law's objectivity can be seen as debates about the extent to which legal interpretation is determinate.'[197]

---

194 Alexy, *Teorie der Grundrechte*, 100 ff., Robert Alexy, 'On the Structure of Legal Principles,' *Ratio Juris* Vol. 13 No. 3 (September 2000) 297 ff.

195 I follow T. A. O. Edincott typology referring to different types of semantics. Timothy A. O. Endicott, 'Review book of Objectivity in Law by N. Stavropoulos,' *Law Quarterly Review* (1997) 20.

196 See Endicott, 'Review book,' 21.

197 See Brink, 'Legal Interpretation, Objectivity, and Morality,' 13.

Generally speaking, semantic objectivity applies to statements or sentences. If one conceives them as having a referential character, then they refer to facts. The semantic concept of law treats law as a creation of language, so the focus is on the analyses of the structure of statements characteristic for law. When we use words, we rely on accepted principles that provide our criteria for using and giving meaning. Semantic theories assume certain criteria of stating the truth, falsity, validity or acceptance of legal statements. The most important question is what are these criteria? Each semantic theory has different criteria that determine the meaning.

I will start with a brief presentation of semantic conceptions, first the traditional theory of meaning, then the Kripke–Putnam theory of meaning, and then two interpretations of Wittgenstein's view on meaning, the sceptical one by Kripke and the non-sceptical one. In a separate chapter, I will deal with both interpretations of Wittgenstein's conceptions in more detail.

Semantic consideration of the terms of law reflects the debate on the determinacy and indeterminacy of law. Advocates of law's determinacy mainly rely on the realistic assumption and cognitivist approach. The indeterminist camp is mainly connected with the antirealist approach and is influenced by Wittgenstein's philosophy. Of course, this a very simplified picture and there are a lot of in-between and mixed positions concerning determinacy or indeterminacy of law.

The strong conception of semantic objectivity is based on the realistic semantic theory. It assumes that the meaning of the terms is entirely independent of the subject who interprets them. Verification of the meaning is based on the evidence – transcendental criterion.[198]

Such an approach, called the 'pictorial theory of language,' has been strongly criticized by Kripke,[199] mainly because of the way it states meaning. The 'pictorial theory' is also strongly connected with the classical theory of truth, which holds that the truth of the sentence in a given language cannot be consistently defined within that language. The confirmation of the meaning is made by empirical verification. This suggests that semantic objectivit y in the realistic version is limited to descriptive statements only.

---

198 See Jules L. Coleman, Brain Leiter, 'Determinacy, Objectivity, and Authority,' in *Law and Interpretation*, ed. Andrei Marmor (Oxford: Oxford University Press, 1995) 248–252.

199 See Saul Kripke, *Wittgenstein on Rules and Private Language* (Oxford: Harvard University Press, 1984) 68–80.

The semantic consideration in law centres on specific types of legal statements: norms and normative propositions, ascriptive statements, and descriptive and evaluative statements. Norms have a prescriptive character and cannot be classified as true or false. Normative propositions could be treated as descriptive but only with regard to a normative system.[200] The prescriptive character of legal facts also makes it much more complicated to apply the classical theory of meaning to the legal discourse. According to the specific character of law, statements can be both descriptive and prescriptive, making the problem of reference more complicated. When we justify ascriptive statements, we rely not only on empirical research but also on non-legal norms; for example, when somebody was doing something in good faith.[201] This is not just a matter of description but also of evaluation done in a direct way by recalling or referring to values and through interpretation. The next problem is how to determine a word's reference when it is based on values. It would be necessary to make cognitive assumptions in the sphere of ethics, which could be very controversial. I will leave this direction outside the scope of this work.

The next arguments about indeterminacy of law are hard cases, which can be characterized as disagreements about the reference of the terms. Disagreement shows us that there are no shared criteria about the meaning of certain words, that is why it is a hard case, and one could argue that the words here have no reference.

Taking into consideration these reasons, the realist approach has to be questioned as to whether it is fully applicable to legal discourse. Another argument for rejecting semantic realism is that its usage is constrained by its rigidity of meanings.

The semantics of legal discourse seems to be non-referential in the above spheres at least and that is why is it worth to considering the antirealist approach.

Antirealist semantic theory proposes that the meaning of a sentence is given by its assertability conditions; that is, the conditions under which the sentence can be asserted.[202] This approach is influenced by Wittgenstein's philosophy[203]. The claim is that there are no objective facts that can create or determine

200 See Eugenio Bulygin, 'Objectivity of Law in the View of Legal Positivism,' *Analisi e diritto* (2004) 221.

201 See Józef Nowacki, Zygmunt Tobor, *Wstęp do prawoznawstwa* [Introduction to Jurisprudence] (Warszawa: Oficyna a Wolters Kluwer, 2007) 180.

202 See Coleman and Leiter, 'Determinacy, Objectivity, and Authority, in Law,' 249.

203 Ludwig Wittgenstein, *Philosophical Investigations* (Oxford: Blackwell Publishers, 1997); Bogusław Wolniewicz, trans., *Dociekania Filozoficzne* (Warszawa: PWN, 2000).

meaning and that language is not determined at its very basic level. What a sentence means cannot be adduced by pointing to some facts. The thesis of the antirealist approach was later developed by Kripke and came to be known as Kripkesteinism, a sceptical interpretation of Wittgenstein. I will elaborate this approach later on in the separate chapter.

According to the minimal version of semantic objectivity, the meaning of a term is fixed and accepted by a majority of the relevant community. The majority decides the right meaning of a sentence in a certain situation. Such an approach is sometimes called linguistic communitarianism.[204]

According the modest version of semantic objectivity, the meaning of 'what is right is what seems right under ideal epistemic conditions, which has the main determining influence.'[205]

2.3.3.1. Kripke-Putnam Semantic Theory

In law, there is an attempt to apply a so-called new theory of reference, known as the Semantic of Kripke-Putnam, or K-P semantic. Some authors find this theory the most suitable in law for the interpretation of legal statements. One of the authors[206] stresses that K-P Semantic is not part of the antirealist approaches and points out many differences:

K-P semantic rejects traditional theories of reference and intuitive conceptions of meaning in favour of a causal theory of meaning. Its main characteristic is summed up by Putnam's slogan: 'meanings are not living in our mind,'[207] by which he is saying that meanings are not dependent on the subject. Undermining traditional semantics, K-P rejects the correspondence theory of reference, whereby the meaning is based first on looking for criteria for the content of the concept and then looking for objects in reality represented by these criteria. In other words, K-P semantics rejects the traditional relation between thoughts and objects. K-P also rejects the need to refer to the intention of speakers (so-called speaker's meaning) in order to determine meaning.

The main characteristic of this theory could be shown by indicating the direction of finding meaning, which goes towards conventional meaning, but not

---

204 See Coleman and Leiter, 'Determinacy, Objectivity, and Authority, in Law,' 253.
205 See Coleman and Leiter, 'Determinacy, Objectivity, and Authority, in Law,' 263.
206 See Nicos Stavropoulos, *Objectivity in Law* (Oxford: Clarendon Press, 1996) 201.
207 See Hilary Putnam, 'The Meaning of 'Meaning' in *Mind, Language and Reality: Philosophical Papers* (Cambridge: Cambridge University Press, 1975) 215–271.

speaker's meaning.[208] The first assumption of K-P semantic is to question the traditional content of the concept as a group of characteristic elements or properties that could be related to certain object in reality. When we identify an object as having the necessary features, we can claim that it is the 'designate' of this name. It means that names have corresponding objects that are rigid or fixed.[209] Lack of even one of the necessary features creates a situation where we cannot connect the name with the object.

Generally, K-P semantics is applicable to expressions designating concrete objects and their properties, which are mind-independent. 'K-P semantic makes for radical indeterminacy by conceiving every aspect of a concept's content as a substantive and thus open to doubts'[210]. So, the space for doubts is located between minds and objects in reality. Law's dependence on the mind and social practices makes the above framework fully adequate.

K-P semantics claims that it is our social practice of using certain names in the proper way over a certain period that decides which words are suitable for which objects. But still there is a problem of which existing practice to choose, and from what period of time? From the time when the texts were created or when they are interpreted? What is important to note here is that the practice itself has changed. As Stavropoulos says, 'The K-P framework of determining the content of the concept is not a mechanical exercise, but a complex theoretical procedure shot through with evaluative judgments.'[211] It means that the stress in the process of argumentation has moved from the interpreter to the text, and so from the speakers' meaning to the conventional meaning.[212]

One of the assumptions is also that, if there is no empirical object (fact) determining a certain reference, the content of the concept is set by the social practice of using it in a conventional way and not by objects existing in reality.

The application of K-P to law is criticized by some authors.[213] The first criticism is the potentially narrow spectrum of applicability of this theory because of its object dependent relation. This is visible in statements like 'equal treatment' or political concepts like liberty. In such cases, Stavropoulos claims that he is forced to make cognitive assertions; he comes back to the realist approach, not

208 See Marcin Matczak, 'Semantyka Kripkego-Putnama a język prawny,' Accessed 18 November 2015, http://pts.edu.pl/teksty/marmat.pdf.

209 See Saul Kripke, *Naming and Necessity* (Oxford: Basil Blackwell, 1980) 14.

210 See Stavropoulos, *Objectivity in Law*, 7.

211 See Stavropoulos, *Objectivity in Law*, 10.

212 See Stavropoulos, *Objectivity in Law*, 10.

213 See Endicott, 'Review book,' 21.

only on the ontological level of empirical objects in reality but also on the level of values. The second criticism concerns the whole range of doubts connected with different types of semantic theory that could be applied. Stavropoulos attacks the position that extends an interpretative semantic theory into a general semantic theory.[214] In my opinion, Stavropoulos seems to have fallen into the pit of failing to make the distinction between 'meaning and 'correct application.' This is the central problem that I am interested in, namely Wittgenstein's distinction between meaning and interpretation. Missing this distinction is what makes Stavropoulos application of K-P semantic so problematic. I will focus on it in the part of interpretation on Wittgenstein's philosophy in the last Chapter.

214 Endicott, 'Review book,' 21.

Chapter III Analysis of the Jurisprudence of the Court Rulings

3.1. Introduction

Reading court's judicature gives an insight into the way the term 'objectivity' is used by the courts. On the most general level one can say that the use of the term 'objectivity' in court's judicature regards making decisions. Decisions made by the courts, which are the result of the application of the law, in particular decisions regarding factual findings and interpretative decisions, are very often called objective. The exemplification of this are the situations of the very wide range of usages like: 'objective evidence,'[215] 'objective assessment of the convict behaviour,'[216] 'objective interpretative doubts' or 'objective good faith,'[217] etc. Also, the method of adjudication itself is called objective.[218] These aforementioned examples present a catalogue of different usages of objectivity in the court's decisions, which were subjected to further analysis in order to determine which understanding of the term 'objectivity' sis used in a given case.

The meanings of 'objectivity' that appear in the research sample have been classified on the basis of the methodology described below. As an effect of using such a classification it has been possible to highlight the most common contexts of occurrence of the use of 'objectivity.' However, to determine the meanings in use the first step consisted in identifying two types of situations, one in which the court itself explains how it understands the term 'objective,' and one in which the court does not provide an explanation of a given meaning. In the latter case a reconstruction of a given meaning of 'objectivity' has been made, taking into consideration first of all the closest linguistic context and then, if necessary, further contexts. For example, the category 'objectivity as identified with the truth' can be based on the fact that something is real or can be inferred by mathematical reasoning. Sometimes, however, the court did not provide such a justification and then a reconstruction of the usage has been made.

---

215 Judgement of the Constitutional Tribunal [Trybunał Konstytucyjny] of 13 July 2004, P 20/03, OTK-A 2004/7/64.

216 Decision of the Supreme Court [Sąd Najwyższy] of 29 September 2004, I KZP 18/04, OSNKW 2004/9/89.

217 Judgement of the Supreme Court of 4 October 2001, T I CKN 458/00, LEX no 52717.

218 Decision of the Supreme Court of 2 January 2003, III KO 59/02, LEX no 77010.

The meanings have been highlighted on the basis of an object-determined criterion, that is with respect to what the term 'objective' refers to in judges' decisions. In general terms, there are two main contexts of occurrence of 'objectivity:' one related to factual findings and one to the undertaking of judgemental decisions. They relate to, respectively, different types of facts, values and assessments. In practical terms, this means that all occurrences of the term objectivity in the research sample have been classified into a list of usages according to what they refer to. Subsequently, the list of meanings has been divided into clusters, according to the similarity of what they refer to.

As a result, the usages of objectivity that referred to brute facts and normative facts (and combination of the two) have been incorporated into the group of descriptive decisions, that is decisions regarding facts. Differently, uses of objectivity that, in the content of the judgements, referred to the assessment of the situation, together with evaluative judgement made by the court, have been classified as judgemental decisions.

The first context of occurrence, as remarked, consists of courts' decisions related to factual findings with regard to facts of different kinds. The scope of discussed facts encompasses both brute (empirical) facts, institutional fact, as well as combined, i.e. brute and institutional facts. For the purposes of the research, I have assumed a concept of fact differentiating brute facts from institutional facts, where facts that may occur only on the grounds of a proper legal institution are called institutional facts, while facts equivalent to complexes of empirical phenomena are called brute facts.[219]

The decisions of judges that were analysed regarding factual findings encompass at a large scale evidential findings related to phenomena of external world as well as decisions regarding subjects of law both in relation to their activities that can be observed and the subjects' internal world. A separate group that has been also included in the facts' group, was the 'objectivity' uses related to decisions regarding law, i.e. treating provisions of law or elements of the law system in a descriptive manner, as a type of determined objective fact hereinafter referred to as a normative fact.

At this point, it is necessary to stress that the stage of defining factual findings itself with regard to brute facts and institutional facts is a process combining both cognitive and judgemental elements, yet still usually it is regarded as purely

---

219 T. Gizbert-Studnicki, Przedmiot ustaleń sądu w procesie cywilnym, In: Krakowskie Studia Prawnicze, VII/1974, pp. 155–156. / *The subject of the court findings in civil proceedings, in: Krakow Legal Studies*

cognitive activity that is somewhat instrumental in relation to decisive elements.[220] The court, when defining factual findings, undertakes decisions related to a broader area of matters than, as it is commonly regarded, when making judgements only in relation to evidence assessment. First of all, it is difficult to consider the process of establishing the meaning of a (legal) language as a pure cognitive activity. Furthermore, both types of facts, brute and institutional, may be included in judgemental decisions and, therefore, this implies reference to some values.[221]

The second type of decisions that are called objective consists of judgemental decisions, mainly related to judicial discretion, where – as an assumption – the judge may (or, according to some theoretical standpoints, is obligated to) refer to his personal assessments. In particular, judgemental decisions undertook by the judge when referring to external criteria or given standards used as an external scale for assessments, has been referred to as 'objective.'

Within each type of decisions described above, descriptive decisions and judgemental decisions, it was possible to identify different usages of the term 'objective,' which can be classified as: A. subject- determined, B. object- determined and C. inter-subjectively determined. Taking this into account, the two groups of decisions can be subdivided into sub-groups depending on the usage of the term 'objective' they resort to, namely:

(1) descriptive decisions can be subdivided in 1.1) those in which the usage of 'objective' belongs to group B) (object-determined); and 1.2) those in which the usage of 'objective' belongs to group C) (inter-subjective determined);
(2) judgemental decisions can be subdivided in 2.1) those in which the usage of 'objective' belongs to group A) (subject-determined); and 2.2) those in which the usage of 'objective' belongs to group C) (inter-subjective determined).

In what follows, I provide details on the classification of the usages of objectivity.

---

220 Maciej Zieliński, 'Obiektywność ustalenia faktów jako element praworządności stosowania prawa' [Objectivity of establishing facts as the element of rule of law application], Ruch prawniczy [Legal Movement], Vol. 1 (1979) 32.

221 Provisions on keeping state or professional secret, or the principle of innocence pressumption, especially in the *in dubio pro reo* provisions, or provisions of the admissability of testimony denial etc., see Zieliński, Obiektywność w procesie…, 40.

3.1.1. Basic Meanings and Families of Meanings

The aforementioned determined contexts of the occurrence of the term 'objective' (A, B, C) in the situation of undertaking a decision by the judge indicate particular regularity with respect to the use of 'objectivity.' The classification of meanings according to the criterion of what the term 'objectivity' refers to, allowed to make another step to define the so-called basic meaning and families of meanings coexisting with them. As mentioned before, particular meanings of objectivity have been classified into the following categories: A. subject- determined, B. object- determined and C. inter-subjectively determined.

This classification is based on the arguments presented in the previous chapters in which different types of objectivity had been discussed, from both the theoretical and philosophical perspectives. Within the aforementioned groups I proposed to distinguish between the basic meanings of objectivity and their families of meanings.

Basic meanings, according to the A-subject-determined group includes epistemological judgements with the focus on eliminating engagement of a subject in the undertaking decisions, leaving it as 'neutral' in a given case, relying only truth that is provided from the outside, which is only used by the subject. While the B-object-determined group are epistemic statements on external – subjective reality, establishing a kind of 'truth' about the external world.

Finally, basic meanings from the C. inter-subjectively determined group similarly concentrate on the elimination of the engagement of a subject and at the same moment formulate judgement regarding external reality, yet the acceptance of a community is the source of the justification of this judgement.

Basic meanings have been differentiated by the basic functions that they fulfil, that is in the case of subjected- determined decisions – establishing a statement regarding reality that fulfils the role of truth regarding empirical reality and related to the sphere of law. In the case of object- determined decisions the function consisted in elimination of subjective factors and in the case of inter-subjective – rooting decisions in a public discourse. The difference between subject- determined and inter- subjectively determined usages of meanings consists in the criteria used to determine what is objective. Subject-determined meanings are those in which subjective factors that influence the subject undertaking a decision are eliminated, while inter-subjectively determined once are those in which common values, shared or accepted by the majority, are taken into consideration.

For the identification of basic meanings, the frequency of occurrence of a given term and the number of repetitions in the research sample was important.

To define a basic meaning, I considered tendencies repeated most often, that is the ones presenting the largest amount of repeated senses of usage of 'objectivity.' Differently, the catalogue of families of basic meaning classified the usages related more or less strongly to the basic meanings, but appearing less frequently in the research sample.

Families of meanings have been distinguished on the basis of the type of justification linking the use of a given term to the main meaning. For example, in the group of object- determined meanings the main meaning is 'truth,' and the family of meanings consists of some cases, including the following: real, as having empirical existence and valid, as based on mathematical reasoning. Therefore, it is possible to observe different types of justification of courts that claim truth, by saying that, e.g. a statement is objective because it is empirically, formally, scientifically or mathematically justified. The full list of usages of meaning and their families is presented in Table 1. Their detailed description is the core of this chapter.

3.2. Methodology: the Discourse Analysis

The research was carried out in the period 2009–2015. The original research was made on the basis of Polish case law published after 1st January 2000, accessed from the System of Legal Information *Lex* (Prestige Version). This database was at that time the largest and most widely used source of court rulings and the basic research tool used by lawyers and opinion leaders and is certainly a reliable information source.[222]

The procedure of selection of the relevant documents for the research implied an iterative search process. In particular, the following steps were followed:

(1) a keyword search on 'objectivity' and 'object*' (in Polish: '*obiektywny*' and *obiektywn-*). By this step it was possible to single out all the court justifications in which the term 'objectivity' was used. However, this returned a huge number of documents.[223] For this reason the choice

222 The *Lex* database contains all judicial decisions that have been published in official publications in Poland, for example: ONSA, ONSAiWSA, OTK, Biuletyn Skarbowy, Monitor Podatkowy, Monitor Prawniczy, OSA, OSP, Wokanda, etc. The *Lex* database is the biggest source for retrieving judicial decisions.

223 For example, as of 10 November 2013, the dataset Lex returned 89.073 results. In the period 2004–2011 the database was supplemented by few thousand rulings per month. See Marcin Kokoszczyński, Grzegorz Wierczyński, *System informacji prawnej w pracy sędziego* (LEX/el. 2011), chapter 5.

Table 1: classification of meanings of 'objectivity'

A. The subject-determined camp of objectivity
Main meaning: objectivity as neutrality
Family of meanings/type of justification:
1. Free of subjective influence: not following personal prejudices or personal interests
2. Independent: free of influences from the external world (media, public opinion, etc.)
3. Confirmed by an external viewer: higher instance of the court, the specialist, etc.
4. Equal treatment: full recognition, without preferences of one over another
5. Based on external criteria: identified with legal rules

B. The object-determined camp of objectivity
B1. Main meaning: objectivity as Truth
Family of meanings/type of justification:
1. Real: empirical existence, material truth
2. Formal method: based on logical, mathematical reasoning
3. Degree of application: universality, fullness

B 2. Main meaning: objectivity as based on Authority of Law
Family of meanings/type of justification:
B.2.1. Based on its own authority:
1. Self-confirmation
2. Set by the court/Institutional confirmation
3. Set by legal bodies of different types (prosecutor, etc.)

B.2.2. Based on the objectivity of law itself:
1. Defined by the legislator or by legal rules
2. In accordance with legal order
3. Legal doctrine
4. Judicature of the court

C. The intersubjective-determined camp of objectivity
Main meaning: objectivity as intersubjective
Family of meanings/type of justification:
1. Common acceptance
2. Validity based on rationality
3. Shared by many, by the majority, or other wider group

was narrowed down to decisions where 'objectivity' appeared only in the courts' justifications, and was not mentioned by the prosecutor, the parties, or listed in the part of the legal act as a legislator's usage.

(2) The second step consisted in checking, among the first 100 results from the search, whether any meanings of objectivity were repeated in similar contexts or used in similar ways. This brought to preliminary classification of usages by the Courts, by identifying some keywords that

could accompany the appearance of the word 'objectivity,' for example 'objective judge,' 'objective legal order,' 'objective truth.'

(3) This brought to a refined search, from which all meanings according to repeated senses were grouped in the way described in the following section. Because of the large number of judicial decisions that nonetheless remained, the present work does not contain all the examples from the research, but only a selection of the most representative ones in order to illustrate their mechanisms of usage of the term 'objectivity.'

Let me remark that legislators word their own messages by making use or abuse of 'objectivity.' I will not analyse this problem in details, but it seems important to note here that the law creators, or at least the authors of law, have the intention of framing the law to be applied in an objective way. For example, from *Lex* it appears that, in 2009, there were around 180 Polish statutes using the term objectivity.

Most of the uses are grouped according to their repeated meanings, which are specified by context. There is also separate group where the term objective appears to have been used for persuasive reasons rather than to denote any specific meaning. I will present all groups of meaning of objectivity in the following contexts, both those which accord with common intuition and those that can be classified as representing a meaning specific to legal discourse. This classification may help to verify the hypothesis on whether there is a specific meanings of objectivity that could be characteristic for the legal discourse.

Despite the great diversity of examples, it is possible to observe certain trends and one of the most prevalent was the way the courts applied objectivity in the situation of evaluation. The most common trend, that actually has recently developed during is to apply objective standards in a situation of judicial discretion, evaluation of facts and justifications of evaluative statements of the courts.

3.2.1. Critical Discourse Analysis

To carry out the research proposed in this book, I adopted a methodology following the Critical Discourse Analysis (CDA henceforth), in particular as developed by Norman Fairclough, who based his analysis on the works of Michel Foucault.

Why is this approach relevant to my analysis? According to Faucault,[224] the discourse is a representation of knowledge which is structurally linked with

224 Michel Foucault, *The Archeology of Knowledge and The Discourse on Language* (London and New York: Vintage Books, 2010).

power, domination and reproduction and social hierarchy. That is why the rules constituting 'the truth of the discourse' determine the way we think and speak about reality and we behave accordingly constituting it.

However, although doing the 'archeological work' in the linguistic structures of legal discourse aiming to reveal hidden power relations, domination or reproduction of social inequality is important to the project, this is not neither the only nor the main aim. First of all, I aim to demystify the practices of the judges through the analysis of how they think about the law. In addition, I want to investigate how they are creating the law and what are the consequences for the subjects of law. In other words, I go beyond the search of hidden power relationships, by identifying new elements in the structure of legal discourse, that is other reasons contributing to the (re)production of a non-transparent structure of the legal discourse.

The most useful approach, from a methodological point of view, was the Anglo-Saxon reception of the ideas of M. Foucault by N. Fairclough,[225] in particular, the adoption of his 'three- dimensional model.' According to this model, the relevant dimensions of CDA are the description of the text, its interpretation and explanation. The first dimension analyses the text as the representation of the given discourse in a given time and place, asking questions such that: which words were used in the text? What are their connotations? Which role do they play in the discourse? How are they used (i.e. in which context)? Which is their meaning (e.g. positive, negative)? Are they ideologically contested?

The second dimension regards the interpretation of the text in the relationship with the discourse, providing access to discursive practices, indicating internal and external institutional relations, involvement of human aspects, inter-textual relations, from where/how given words take their meanings and what was included and not included to the text. Finally, the third one tries to answer questions such as: 'why are given words used in the text, and how do they correspond to the structures of discourse?' This step mainly serves to disclose hidden power relations which correspond to social structures and the inequality they imply, and to perform the emancipatory function of the research.[226]

Last but not least, one should clarify the need of the adaptation of CDA to jurisprudence. As legal discourse is definitely an example of the discipline which have created its object through positivist institutionalization and it is perceived

225 Fairclough, N. (2001). *Language and power*. Pearson Education.
226 Fairclough, *Language and power*.

as (openly) political.[227] For this reason several contributions within the critical approach were already proposed.[228]

3.3. From the Analysis of the Jurisprudence of the Court to Classification of the Meanings of Objectivity

In this section I provide a detailed description of the classification, as obtained from an analysis of the jurisprudence of the Polish courts. In particular, I follow the structure presented in Table 1.

3.3.1. The Subject-Determined Camp of Objectivity (A)

In what I define the Subject-Determined camp of objectivity, I identify as the main meaning: 'Objectivity as Neutrality/Impartiality,' with its family of meanings:

A1. Free of subjective influence: not following personal prejudices or personal interests,
A2. Independent: free of influences from the external world (media, public opinion etc.),
A3. Confirmed by an external viewer: higher instance of the court, the specialist, etc.,
A4. Equal treatment: full recognition, without preferences of one over another,
A5. Based on external criteria: identified with legal rules.

'Impartiality' or 'neutrality' which are often use as synonymous in legal discourse is a principle holding that decisions should be based on external criteria not on the basis of prejudices, bias, or preferring the benefit of one person over another for improper reasons.[229] Such a definition binds two aspects together:

227 Adam Sulikowski, 'Perspektywy zastosowań metod Krytycznej Analizy Dyskursu w badaniach nad prawem: kilka uwag' [Some remarks on the prospects for applying the research approach of Critical Discourse Analysis to the study of Law], *Wrocławskie Studia Erazmiańskie. Studia Erasmiana Wratislaviensia*, Vol. VIII (2014).

228 See more, Rafał Mańko, 'Critical Legal Theory in the Central and Eastern Europe: in search of method,' *Acta Universitatis Lodziensis. Folia Iuridica*, Vol. 89 (2019) 5–14.

229 Zbigniew Łyda, 'Bezstronność arbitra a zakaz zainteresowania w sprawie,' [Impartiality of an Arbitrator and the Ban of Interest in the Case] *Państwo i Prawo* No. 2 (1996) 4.

(1) the attitude of agents as free of emotions and prejudices,
(2) the way judgments are formulated, considering all relevant and substantial circumstances of a particular case.[230]

From the practical perspective, one can say that impartiality is used in the context of when a decision must be taken by a person who is not directly involved, not engaged personally, or has no own vested interest. In legal context, it means that impartiality is regarded both as a feature of the judge and as a feature of the procedure.[231]

When analysing the Polish court rulings, it is possible to find all the meanings of objectivity and impartiality mentioned above. So, on the one hand, an objective judge is 'characterized as not following her prejudices' (A1), meaning that a judge had not earlier made up his mind on the subject,[232] or a court or the legal bodies undertook activities with particular own positive or negative approach.[233]

---

230 Tomasz Gizbert-Studnicki, 'Podstawy argumentacji prawniczej,' [Foundation of legal argumentation] *Acta Universatis Wratislaviensis* No 1772 Prawo CCXLIV, Wrocław (1995) 36; Ota Weinberger, 'Objectivity and Rationality In Lawyer's Reasoning,' in *Theory of Legal Science*, ed. Aleksander Peczenik (Dordrecht: D. Reidel Publishing Company, 1984) 217 ff.

231 Tobor, 'Bezstronność sędziego,' 3.

232 Judgement of the Supreme Court, 10 July 2001, II KKN 538/98, OSNKW 2001/9–10/80: 'Such an opinion would not be justified in any way, as the cited circumstances – without indicating their relationship to the currently considered case – cannot be reasonably accepted as sufficient for assuming that the judge had earlier made his mind on the subject, was suggested a solution or was prejudiced, and thus cannot be accepted as a sufficient base for undermining their objectivity.'

233 Judgement of the District Court [Sąd Okręgowy] in Ostrołęka, 22 May 2014, II Ka 109/14: 'It should be noted that the principle of objectivity, expressed in article 4 of the Polish Criminal Proceedings' Code, and the violation of which is complained, consists in the prohibition of adopting by the court a given view on the case before the evidential proceedings are finished on the hearing and presenting the parties with a view that the court already has its own version of the event, the responsibility for which it is to adjudicate. Lack of objectivity may be found in situations in which the proceeding bodies undertook activities with particular own positive or negative approach, prejudice and decisions made in the course of the proceeding have been biased or when the subject of the assessment and deliberations of the court had not been the whole evidential material accumulated in the case' (see also judgement of the Supreme Court, 16 February 1978, IV KR 4/78).

On the other hand, the court regards objectivity as ensuring the adjudication will be 'free of any influences from the external world' (A2), such as public opinion or mass media.[234] This ensures the impartial application of law.

A lack of judicial objectivity as impartiality can occur when the judge during the proceedings does not treat participants of the trial equally, favouring one party over the other, in a way that could be recognized by a party and the external viewer. It could be the case that for example a judge and a party of the proceeding are friends or even acquaintances.[235] However, if the doubts as to the objectivity of the judge were expressed only by a party, and as 'a party subjectively construes judges' attitude' this complaint was 'insignificant for the evaluation of the situation.' The only significant argument, according to the court, is justified for example by 'objective circumstance,' meaning 'facts.' The complaint by the party is recognized as subjective feelings or subjective interpretation of the facts. The question in this case, is how to make the claims of the party objective since they are subjective just by their positioning? Only objective facts confirmed by both parties or an outsider might confirm that the parties of the proceedings have not been treated equally by a judge. The quoted examples demonstrate that the provision of arguments by the parties of judicial proceedings and by the court has a

234 Judgment of the Supreme Court [Sąd Najwyższy], 21 January 2003, III KO 59/02, LEX No. 77010: 'Excessively broad interpretation of text of art. 37 Code of Criminal Procedure might lead to enfeebling the trust as to the independence of particular courts and their capacity to adjudicate objectively. Thus special situations, that might affect the liberty of adjudicating or create belief that there are no conditions for considering the case in an objective way, might justify the application of provisions defined in art. 37 of the Code of Criminal Procedure.'

235 Judgement of the Constitutional Tribunal [Trybunał Konstytucyjny], 13 December 2005, SK 53/04, OTK-A 2005/11/134: 'In view of the judicature of the Supreme Court, the fact that a judge and a party to the proceeding are friends or even acquaintances as well as that fact that during the proceedings a judge favours one party over the other, may constitute basis for excluding such judge from further proceedings. However, the way a party subjectively construes judges attitude is insignificant for the evaluation of the situation. What is of decisive character are facts i.e. all objective circumstances, that might testify that the parties to the proceedings have been treated by a judge in a diverse way and that might result in doubts (both on the side of the party as well as an outsider) as to the objectivity of the judge. As is shown in the judicature of the Supreme Court, the provisions of Code of Civil Procedure on excluding a judge are to serve for the purposes of removing such doubts and for creating 'the guarantee of impartial judiciary' (decision of the Supreme Court of 4 December 1969, case file No. I CZ 124/69, Lex Polonica data base.' Cf. also: decision of the Supreme Court, 7 November 1984, case file No. II CZ 117/84, ibid.).

different value. Specifically, the court, due to its privileged institutional position is entitled to express judgments, which they call objective, without presenting arguments enhancing their stance. On the other hand, the party of the proceedings regarded as the biased one, so that it could be hard or so that their arguments could be considered, must construct the argumentation referring to confirms their stance by external instances. As a result, this which is called objective in the mouth of a judge may sound as an arbitrary court because it is not enhances by the complex argumentation. The same kind of utterance from the position of the party of the proceeding requires 'objectification and enhancement of their stance.'

Impartiality is also identified with the perspective of 'an external and independent viewer' (A3). Although recognized as partial, due to its positionality, it is possible to accept this as objective because of the individual's lack of personal involvement. In a similar way, objectivity can be delivered by the independent position of the adjudicative body. An example of this is when a higher administrative body takes the decision as a controlling instance over a lower administrative body[236]. The supreme position of an administrative body which is authorized to adjudicate should guarantee independence and through this objectivity.

Such a construction of objectivity is principally formal, procedural and embedded in the foundation of institutional hierarchy of legal system. Attributing the feature of objectivity to the way legal body functions is institutional in the sense that it is arising from the fact that is situated hierarchically higher.

It could be said more precisely that this is rather a condition that allows a given legal body to be objective or to act in an objective way. Identifying institutional capability to act objectively with the fact that it acts objectively is to affirm that every action of this legal body by definition works in an objective way. This can open the doors to objective but also arbitrary statements which can be a consequence of power relation in a hierarchical legal system.

The decision is objective when it is taken upon full recognition of evidence, 'without preference of certain evidence over another' (A4). All kinds of evidence,

236 Judgment of the Supreme Administrative Court, 1 June 1998, II SA 534/98, LEX No. 41763: '(...) Finding that a decision is invalid is an extraordinary control measure applicable in case of especially gross violation of law. Objectivity of control performed under art. 156 of the Code of Administrative Procedure is provided by the fact that the body authorized to adjudicate, if a decision is invalid, is the supreme administrative body.'

for and against, must be taken into account without supremacy of one over the other,[237] and considering all circumstances both in favour and against.[238]

It is also possible to find the meaning of objectivity understood as impartiality that represents the same idea as introduced above but in a broader sense. An impartial decision is described as being 'taken upon objective criteria'[239] however what objective criteria means is defined 'by the knowledge and life experience of the judge'[240] (A5). However, criteria of life experience and knowledge of the judge to be identified as objective must be 'fully and logically explained in the justification of the judgement.'[241] These seem to be very personal and

---

237 Judgment of the Supreme Court, 11 February 2002, II KKN 475/99 LEX No. 53038: '(...) in order to make the criteria of evaluation of evidence shown in this case, including in particular the exert opinions in graphology, were applied by the court in a uniformly objective way, i.e. without indicating supremacy of one piece of evidence over the another.'

238 Judgement of the District Court [Sąd Okręgowy] in Białystok, 17 July 2012, II AKa 118/12: 'Maintaining objectivity, the requirement to which no justified doubts may be raised as it has been met by the adjudicating Court, should be expressed by taking into consideration circumstances that support both in favour and against the accused. The order should be treated as a general directive that is one of the main principles of criminal proceedings.'

239 Judgement of the District Court [Sąd Okręgowy] in Białystok, 21 January 2013, VIII Ka 1016/12: 'The normative content of article 7 of the Polish Criminal Proceedings' Code contains the principle of unimpeded evaluation of evidence what in any case is not equal to randomness of such evaluation. It is an assessment that has to regard objective criteria (logic, knowledge, life experience) and is subjected to procedural control in an appeal procedure and the body in the justification of the proceeding's decision has to explain its standpoint.'

240 Judgement of the District Court [Sąd Okręgowy] in Kraków, 11 December 2014, IV Ka 60/14: 'the plea regarding lack of objectivity of the Regional Court [Sąd Rejonowy] is groundless. The judge of the Regional Court, hearing the case in question and delivering the charged judgement fully maintained objectivity, has not been biased (...) Regarding the plea based on article 7 of the Polish Criminal Proceedings' Code, it should be indicated that the belief of the court about the reliability of some evidence and lack of reliability of others remains under the protection of the aforementioned provision, as long as it is preceded by revealing during the main hearing the entirety of the case, and is an expression of the consideration of all circumstances both in favour and against the accused and conforms with knowledge and life experience, and at the same time it had been fully and logically explained in the justification of the judgement.'

241 Judgement of the District Court [Sąd Okręgowy] in Kraków, 11 December 2014, IV Ka 60/14.

individualized criteria and, as much as the judges are subject to a similar training during their education both in the way of ruling and non-engaging their individual perceptions, it seems difficult to regard these criteria as objective in making decisions. The discourse fulfilling the conditions of transparency would label these criteria totally conversely: as subjective because they come down to a personal way of the application of gained knowledge and the reliance on life experience.

The literature stresses that there is a sense of talking about impartiality only when it is necessary to take decisions or when there is any possibility of being partial. For instance, when the subject taking the decision could decide in a partial way, but impartiality is demanded from him. On the contrary, there is no sense about talking about impartiality when there is no chance to be so. For example, when a legal decision requires just a simple application of a legal provision which is clear or does not demand interpretative measures.

One author defines impartiality as, 'partiality in the right direction,'[242] because when a judge must take the decision, the values are chosen by him and in this sense, he has to be partial. This is the sense of partiality in the 'right direction.' Such a definition stresses the impossibility of being impartial and that the main aim of institutional impartiality is the protection of trust through shaping the legal consciousness of legal subjects. In addition, this example shows that impartiality is only considered in the situations where plurality/diversity of values are involved. To deliver an illustration I refer to a case in which an administrative power is characterized as objective when it follows and 'realizes values for the common good.'[243] The expression 'values for the common good' is an evident example of a general clause where a potential discretion might be exercised. What it means is that the interpretation will be based on an evaluation, which value in this certain concrete case would be recognized as realizing or following the common good. Therefore, the application of such a directive is detached from objectivity or impartiality in a direct sense, but it is only the way present a given choice of value as the right one.

A new perspective of dealing with impartiality, present in both the court rulings and the jurisprudential literature, distinguishes between so-called

---

242 Tobor, 'Bezstronność sędziego,' 3.

243 Patrycja J. Suwaj, *Gwarancje bezstronności organów administracji publicznej w postępowaniu administracyjnym* [Guarantee of impartiality of public administration bodies in public administration proceeding] (Wrocław: Kolonia Limited 2004) 10.

objective impartiality[244] and subjective impartiality.[245] This typology is also known as impartiality *sensu largo* and impartiality *sensu stricto*. Both relate to the person of the judge. The first one means that the impartiality of the judge cannot be questioned from an external viewpoint because impartiality is protected by a list of external criteria formulated by the legislator. If judges break from the listed conditions, their impartiality can be 'reasonably questioned.' One of the safeguards of impartiality formulated by the legislator is the judge's duty to disclose details of personal and family financial and business interests. Impartiality *sensu stricto* means that only the judge in person knows whether or not there are any motives that can influence his or her process of taking an impartial decision. This cannot be verified by anybody else from an external point of view. Such a situation can happen when judges permit their own personal prejudices to influence their judgments. Take political preferences, for example. A feminist judge might take a decision in favour of women, whereas a male judge with a different political leaning might take an opposite decision in the same case. It is also stressed in the literature, though not very often considered when considering judges' impartiality, that not only personal bias but also corporate bias can influence judges' decisions. They mostly express their own corporate values, which are the products of their position in the society as part as the ruling establishment.[246]

To conclude this section, it is worth highlighting that sometimes the principle of impartiality is directly identified with the principle of objectivity and sometimes the legal doctrine makes some distinction between the two. Some authors claim that the principle of impartiality is in reference to the parties on trial and the other participants. This finds its justification in a very narrow linguistic interpretation. With regard to this perspective, the principle of objectivity, as much broader a concept, is in reference to the decision or the case itself.[247] But as one author stresses, the notion of impartiality relates to the situation when a person

---

244 Decision of the Constitutional Tribunal [Trybunał Konstytucyjny], 6 May 2005, Ts 42/05, OTK-B 2005/3/150: '(. . .) As the composition of court which adjudicated on granting compensation to the appellant included a judge-official receiver, who had previously submitted evaluation of the work of appellant as a receiver and a petition as to the amount of his remuneration, thus such court did not – in the opinion of appellant-fulfil the standard of objective impartiality.'

245 Ibid.

246 Paul Kelly, 'Impartiality: a philosophical perspective,' in *Judicial integrity*, ed. Andras Sajo and Lorri Rutt Bentch, (Dordrecht, Netherlands: Brill, 2004) 17–42.

247 S Stanisław Waltoś, *Proces karny. Zarys systemu* [Criminal Procedure. An Outline of the system] (Warszawa 2002) 220.

must decide between different solutions, that is, when they have the discretion of deciding in favour of one solution over others.[248] This implies that impartiality could be both a feature bound with the person taking decisions and with the decision itself.

The aforementioned analysed meanings of objectivity as impartiality enter the category of understandings of objectivity, which determine the subject. Impartiality is then understood as constraints imposed on the person of a judge so that they do not indulge in undesirable external pressures and so that they are not governed by their own personal preferences, which could lead into some undesirable direction. The formed procedure of impartiality/objectivity is to constrain a judge so that any potential situations of exceeding their position and follow the rule of equal treatment of the parties in a trial and to make decision based on law, not in an arbitrary or emotional way. The statutory definition of the rule of impartiality has mainly a negative nature or it formulates negative premises of impartiality, stating when a judge is not impartial.

However, what emerges from case law is the image of a positive formulation of impartiality, defining when the attitude of a judge is impartial – objective. These are the situations, in which a judge makes decision based on life experience and their own knowledge and it justifies a decision in a reliable way referring to all issues raised in this case. The image of applying objectivity – impartiality in the analysed decision-making sample oscillates between two approaches, which I labelled above as negative and positive, or non-involvement/non-emotionality and the inclusion of subjectivity. The negative definition of impartiality states that the elimination of the situation of partiality eventuates in this that a judge could rule in an uninvolved/unemotional way. On the other hand, the image of impartiality, which results from case law, adding the statutory formulation of impartiality/objectivity is ruling based on life experience, or involvement of subjectivity in making a 'partial' decision but 'in a right direction' because as a judge has to make a final decision, which due to the value of their beliefs deserves protection.

As a result, we have, in one set, the decisions which range between non-emotional and uninvolved attitude based on the myth of 'view from nowhere' up to the decisions subjectively involved, transparent but justified and non-arbitrary.

In this view, there appears the meaning of impartiality/objectivity as well as the one confirmed by: an external observer, objective facts or higher hierarchical

---

248 Zbigniew Łyda, 'Bezstronność arbitra a zakaz "zainteresowania w sprawie,"' *Folia Philosophica* No. 15 (1997) 47.

instance. The way of justifying impartiality provided by the court, or the justification from external and uninvolved perspective is the evidence for 'view from nowhere.' The metaphor of La Fontaine's Carafe indicates that each perspective is involved towards which the position of a genuine impartiality is impossible to be carried out. No facts, external observers or higher instance do not speak for themselves, but they are formulated from their own subjective position, which is simply not revealed. As it may be seen, the narration, in which this image of impartiality/objectivity is formed on the possibility of 'view from nowhere' is based on the premises as if law was not a part of the interpreted world.

The image of applying objectivity – impartiality in the analysed decision-making sample oscillates between two approaches, which I labelled above as negative and positive, or non-involvement/non-emotionality and the inclusion of subjectivity. The negative' definition of impartiality states that the elimination of the situation of partiality eventuates in this that a judge could rule in an uninvolved/unemotional way. On the other hand, the image of impartiality, which results from case law, 'adding' the statutory formulation of impartiality/objectivity is ruling based on life experience, or involvement of subjectivity in making a 'partial' decision but 'in a right direction because as a judge has to make a final decision, which due to the value of their beliefs deserves protection.

As a result, we have the discrepancy between the non-emotional and uninvolved attitude based on the myth of 'view from nowhere' up to the decisions subjectively involved, transparent but justified and nonarbitrary. In other words, impartial decisions are both uninvolved and involved in a controlled way, non-arbitrary and transparent but also based on the mythological narration of view from nowhere, as a result of it – arbitrary ones.

3.3.2. The Object-Determined Camp of Objectivity (B)

In what I define the Object-determined camp of objectivity, I identify two main meanings, 'Objectivity as Truth' (B1) and 'Objectivity as based on the authority of law' (B2). The corresponding family of meanings for B1 are the following:

B1.1. Real: empirical existence, material truth,
B1.2. Formal method: based on logical, mathematical reasoning,
B1.3. Degree of application: universality, fullness.

For the main meaning B2, instead, I identified two sub-meanings, 'Objectivity based on its own authority' (B2a) and 'Objectivity based on the objectivity of law itself' (B2b) with their own families or meanings, defined in the following way:

B2a.1. self-confirmation,
B2b.2. set by the court/Institutional confirmation,
B2c.3. set by legal bodies of different types (Prosecutor, etc.),
B2b.1. defined by the legislator or by legal rules,
B2b.2. in accordance with legal order,
B2b.3. legal doctrine,
B2b.4. judicature of the court.

The justifications provided by the court via the expression 'objective,' which are included in the object-determined camp of objectivity, comprise mainly a family of meaning related to truth. The family of meanings of objectivity referring the authority of law is a particular example of the usage included in this group. All these meanings that could be explained in relation to the different kind of objects to which objectivity refers to belong to the object-determined camp. The role of objectivity here is mainly to constitute some kind of truth about the world, which appears for the objects and the object itself does not fulfil any role, except for the description of existing reality. The very object is the central element of objectivity. The controversy of this perspective was discussed by the standpoints on the occasion of philosophical debate between realism and antirealism.

In light of the analysed examples, the subjective reference is the following: the family of truth comprises meanings such as 'real' and 'truth' as basic meanings and clearly manifests itself in the principles of material truth in penal law, which expresses the meaning: 'adequacy with reality,' which mainly means the confirmation in empirical facts. The remaining applications demonstrate different methods of the access to what is regarded as truth or as a real thing, for example the scientific methods leading to establish truth such as logical or mathematical reasoning. The remaining cases concern rather a bigger or lower reference to the coherent truth such as, e.g. the definition based on the most thorough or even holistic view providing almost universal perspective. Similarly, the thing concerns the meaning referring to formal judicial truth, which is the weakest version of truth, which may be fiction at least, however based on the consent of the parties.

The group of the object – determined camp of objectivity is mainly represented by meanings related to two notions that are very close to each other, 'true' and 'real.' The first is used mainly with regard to statements; the second confirms the empirical existence of certain states of affairs that something happened in the past.

The problem of truth in law is broadly discussed in jurisprudential literature[249] and could be approached from several perspectives. To make the problem

249 Anna Pintore, *Law without truth*, see translation of Anna Pintore, *Il diritto senza verità*

of truth in the context of law more evident it is necessary to clarify how 'truth' can be contextualized. One can distinguish between truth of law and truth in law. The first perspective deals with such questions as: can law be true or false? How can legal norms be true?[250] As we have a diversity of conceptions of law and conceptions of truth, this question remains very ambiguous.[251] The second perspective could be approached through a question such as: what does it mean to say that a proposition of law is the truth? There are several possible answers: they are true if they accord with certain institutional facts, they are true if they accord with a principle of morality, or they are true if there is a convergence in interpretative assumption about law.[252]

The second perspective, dealing with the possibility of truth in law, also belongs to issues dealing with past events, in criminal trials, for example. In the analyses conducted here, it is just the perspective of truth in law that will serve as the frameworks for the quoted examples.

Here, I just want to give some examples that identify objectivity with truth, as this is a popular tendency in the court rulings. One of the examples is the truth principle in criminal law,[253] or so-called principle of objective truth[254] or principle of material truth (both expressions describe the same situation). It

---

(Torino: Giappichelli, 1966) in Anna Pintore, *Law without truth* Vol. 11 (Deborah Charles Publications, 2000); Patterson, *Law and Truth*, 182.

250 If law is a body of norms and if those norms (conceived as sentences, meanings or suchlike) are entities belonging to the universe of directives, then truth is not a predicate that applies to the law: just as illness is not applicable to numbers, Pintore, *Law without truth*, 4.

251 See more, Pintore, *Law without truth*, 8.

252 Patterson, *Law and Truth*, 3.

253 Judgement of the Supreme Court, 21 January 2008, III KK 403/07: '(. . .) In the event when it refers to a person accused of act defined in art. 233 § 1 of the Penal Code, responding together with a person whom the questioned testimony refers to, it may be problematic to make statement of fact on the behaviour of the 'main' accused, and thus to know the actual course of events. Thus, one of the principal rules of penal procedure – the principle of objective truth – is at risk.'

254 Judgment of the Constitutional Tribunal, 16 January 2006, SK 30/05 OTK-A 2006/1/2: '(. . .) The lack of two-instance procedure and the principle of objective truth, as a basis of procedure in front of the Constitutional Tribunal justify the inclusion of the evaluation presented by social organization in the procedure on control of constitutionality.' See also Guidelines of the Supreme Court of 25 June 1953, C. Prez. 195/52, OSN 1953, item 95, PiP No 10 (1953) 68; follow: Witold Brodniewicz, *Postępowanie cywilne w zarysie* [*Civil Procedure in an Outline*] (Warszawa: Lexis Nexis, 1983) 49.

is important to stress that this principle considers objectivity and truth as one and the same because they can be fully identified with each other. This example shows that the identification of these two principles is commonly recognized in legal discourse to express adequacy with reality. The term 'principle of objective truth' was employed by Principle of Suggestions to the Legal Interpretation of the Polish Highest Court.[255] The term 'objective' has/plays the role of stressing the uncompromising character of this procedural principle and at the same time it assesses the possibility of cognition of the material truth.[256] As contemporary jurisprudential literature indicates, the formulation of the principle has the logical fallacy *reductionem ad absurdum,* because it is not possible to distinguish between truth of the real and the unreal, especially within the paradigm of the classical theory of truth.[257] Adding the adjective objective to the notion of truth raises the question about the possibility of any other kind of truth. One can claim that describing truth as objective has the function of distinguishing it from the formal conception of truth, which is characteristic for civil law procedures. The formal conception of truth does not focus on what really happened, but what both opposing parties admit to take as true. This difference gives a much better grasp on making typological distinction between the material and the formal conception of truth. It is worth noting that since law is considered according to the classical theory of truth, there is no real necessity to stress the objective character of truth. In this context, the main question about truth in law is how it is possible to establish true, or at least acceptable accounts of past events? The argument here will be that, even in criminal law that operates with the conception of so-called material truth, a certain conception of coherence is essential to the process of proving what was done, or what has happened, namely 'narrative coherence.'[258] To find out what really happened, the institutional legal facts, means to comprehend past events as series of actions or acts linked together under some common purpose and values within a normative framework.[259]

---

255 Guidelines of the Supreme Court of 25 June 1953, C. Prez. 195/52, OSN 1953, item 95, PiP No. 10 (1953) 68; follow: Witold Brodniewicz, *Postępowanie cywilne w zarysie* [*Civil Procedure in an Outline*] (Warszawa: Lexis Nexis, 1983) 49.

256 Michał Waligórski, 'Gwarancje wykrycia prawdy,' [Truth identification conditions] *Państwo i Prawo* No. 8–9 (1953) 256–257; Jadwiga Klich-Rump, *Podstawa faktyczna rozstrzygnięcia sądowego w procesie cywilnym* [The actual merit of a judicial decision in a civil lawsuit] (Warszawa: Wydawnictwo Prawnicze, 1977) 111–115.

257 Jerzy Wróblewski, *Sądowe stosowanie prawa* [The Judicial Application of Law] (Warszawa 1988) 198.

258 MacCormick, *Rhetoric and The Rule of Law*, 215.

259 MacCormick, *Rhetoric and The Rule of Law*, 216.

What should be stressed here is that the empirical truth only relates to statements that are considered as stating propositions to which a certain interpretation is ascribed.[260] So, the interpretation of the meaning should be in accordance with the world. In the light of what has been said, it is still controversial to make truth claims in law. In addition, it is important to point out the limitation of material truth in situations where it has to be balanced against other values, like the protection of privacy, the protection of public interests, or protection of medical confidentiality.

In the light what has been said, the examples from judicial decisions, quoted below, are based on a bit naive assumption that truth is confirmed in fact and that the indication of fact is sufficient to establish the truth, and certainly to regards it as truth in court records. The most numerous group of meanings of objectivity/truth is represented by the examples based on the assumptions of correspondence of truth theory, which are treated as self-emerging with truth not requiring any justification, in a naive realistic view.

In this part of this section, I would like to introduce a set of examples extracted from the Polish courts including the Constitutional Tribunal, which deal with objectivity in reference to 'truth' and 'real' meaning in the aforementioned context (B1.1). The example of the meaning of 'truth' can be exemplified by the following fragment of court's rulings in which one may read: 'Allowing persons to complete the bar exam whose professional abilities are not objectively verified, because they do not have the appropriate legal training (as trainees at the bar), limits the possibilities of the amount of supervision they can do in their job.'[261] In this case the court referred to the situation in which the facts had to be confirmed by defining if given people applying for taking the examinations possess the required documents certifying their professional qualifications or not.

Regarding the second meaning of objectivity, namely its reference to it is important to stress that this meaning is used to confirm the empirical character of an event. It is used in the sense that something exists objectively, it really happened, it has its own entity independent of anybody's will or consciousness, or at least of the speaker's will or consciousness. The following example extracted

---

260 MacCormick, *Rhetoric and The Rule of Law*, 68.

261 Judgment of the Constitutional Tribunal [Trynbuał Konstytucyjny], 19 April 2006, K 6/06, OTK-A 2006/4/45: '(. . .) Moreover, admitting for a professional examination for barristers persons whose objective professional skills have not been verified, and who have not undergone apprenticeship, limits the possibility of supervising such persons' proper performance of their profession (especially immediately after registering in the register of barristers).'

from one court's rulings illustrates this usage: 'The deciding criteria about judges' lack of objectivity are facts, that is, objective circumstances that could prove judges treated participants in the trial differently. This kind of fact may create doubts both in participants' and in the external viewer's eye.'[262] Another example of this type says, 'the effect of a banking transaction is objectively verified on basis of the documents.'[263] In both cases, the courts were looking for criteria of to confirm the real dimension of events in the past.[264]

The next meaning of objectivity/truth is based on formal, logical, mathematical type of reasoning (B1.2), which still represents object-determined types of meanings. This understanding of objectivity used in court rulings basically relies on an understanding reached by applying a method that does not allow any intervention of the subject. In simple terms, objectivity refers solely to the object and subjectivity is identified with any situation where the subject is involved. This example shows the objective method based on the mathematical counting. The Court says, 'the objective method of deciding the salary of judges is based on the principle of the valuation of wages in the relation to the average salary in the public sector in the economy.'[265] As the objective method indicates, it is possible

---

262 Judgment of the Constitutional Tribunal [Trynbuał Konstytucyjny], 13 December 2005, SK 53/04, OTK-A 2005/11/134W: '(...) The facts are of decisive character here, i.e. all objective circumstances, that might testify that the parties to the proceedings have been treated by a judge in a diverse way and that might result in doubts (both on the side of the party as well as an outsider) as to the objectivity of the judge.'

263 Judgment of the Constitutional Tribunal, 21 March 2006, K 13/05, OTK-A 2006/3/31: 'As long as payment of the subsidy depends on strictly accounting operations, the result of which is subjectively verifiable on the basis of the documents referring to employment and degree of disability, there is no question of any kind of power solution to be imposed by a body, let alone – of imposing sanctions against employees. It needs to be emphasized here that the act does not provide for a procedure of appeal against a negative decision of the Fund, which has been omitted by the petitioner.'

264 Judgment of the Voivodeship Administrative Court [Wojewódzki Sąd Administracyjny] in Wrocław, 8 November 2011, II SA/Wr 587/11: 'The Voivode pointed out also, that the appellation body pursuant to the principle of unconstrained evaluation of evidence resulting from art. 80 of Code of Administrative Procedure is not bound by any particular power of evidence of such evidence means as investor's declaration and evaluates evidence collected in the case as a whole in order to determine the actual state of affairs in the case pursuant to the principle of objective truth provided for in art. 7 the Code of Administrative Procedure.'

265 Judgement of the Constitutional Tribunal, 14 March 1995, K 13/94: '(...) Articles 14 and 15 of the above-mentioned act are also contradictory to art. 1 of the Small

to count what the salary of judges should be and there are no discretional elements in this process.

The next example also demonstrates the objective method, 'in establishing incomes, because they based on the declarations of the incomes of the household and this declaration is based on counting the social insurance payment.'[266] In this case there is also no place for subjects' decisions. The subject's role is only to count according to a certain pattern, which is not dependent on his will, and it is provided as external standard. The effects should be the same, no matter who is doing the calculations. In other words, subjects are just a kind of tool for setting aims. The similar situation is in the subsequent example, where the court refers to a measurement of distance between two designated points in space, indicating that the application of Euclidean geometry is the most objective method to conduct the operation.[267]

The next example of meaning of objectivity belonging to the family of truth is 'universality' and 'fullness' (B1.3). The example derives from the Constitutional Tribunal, in which it says that the objective method is represented not only by a formal but also a material approach. 'The running of law needs other methods than those which Tribunal Court is using. It is not enough to use the analysis of

---

Constitution which introduces the principle of separation of power and the independence and sovereignty of the judiciary, because they abolish retroactively the objective method of shaping remuneration of judges (the principle of indexation of pay with relation to average pay in the sector of national economy enterprises) and introduce the prognostic-negotiation method, which does not provide for such guarantee.'

266 Judgment of the Constitutional Tribunal, 18 January 2000, K 17/99: 'In the opinion of the General Public Prosecutor, the criteria of establishing income assumed in the provision we appeal against, have been objectified, as they refer to declaration on achieved income by the members of the household and to declaration constituting basis for social insurance contributions, and only when these persons are not subject to insurance an assumption was made that a person conducting business activity has income which is not lower than the lowest basis for social insurance premium binding for insured persons on the basis of separate regulations.'

267 Judgment of the Voivodeship Administrative Court [Wojewódzki Sąd Administracyjny] in Poznań, 1 December 2011, IV SA/Po 1044/11: 'Moreover, in the court's opinion, as the district council in the resolution passed pursuant to art. 12 item 2 of the Alcoholism Prevention Act in case of lack of clear definition of the manner in which to measure the distance between the protected facilities and alcohol selling points, it seems justified to adopt the following interpretation: such measurement should be done in the simplest, most objective and one could say – most obvious way (in view of Euclidean geometry), i.e. in straight distance.'

language and different types of legal reasoning based on legal logic. It is necessary to employ empirical examinations that are obligatory to objective evaluation of social facts. To social facts which are the consequences of legal regulation brought into force.[268]

This fragment suggests that neither language interpretations nor legal reasoning, with its logical references, are sufficient to guarantee the values of objectivity and certainty. In addition, empirical data is required to create a full picture of the situation in order to make the evaluation more objective. This meaning is the closest to coherent truth, which is determined on the basis of more complex criteria, comprising an active position of subject. The court, establishing the objective/real state of affairs, indicates that we need to consider the entire set of factors, so that the broadest and fullest image could be created. In the example demonstrated below, taking into consideration the consequences resulting from the application of a given regulation, is according to the court, the best way so that its objective/real meaning of a legal regulation could be obtained.

According to this usage of objectivity, the fuller the picture is, the more objectively the picture can be seen. As the court says by another occasion, 'to objectively evaluate how the NFZ legal act was working, it has to be taken into account what consequences have followed this legal act.'[269]

Also, this example presents objective evaluations as based on considering the whole context, approached by a holistic view as far as possible. According to it, the more holistic the depiction, the more objective it becomes. So, according to this position, the content of objectivity requires a wide-angle perspective, as the broader view is closer to the truth.

The second type of justification indicated by the court via the expression 'objective,' which was included in the object-determined camp of objectivity, is objectivity based on authority of law (B2). This is a special meaningful group, which was isolated in the research as a special (peculiar) meaning, which functions solely in a legal discourse. And it is related to the nature of a legal discourse. This meaning was included in the object-determined group of meanings because the court justification was demonstrated in the way as if the subject did not have any impact on the ruling procedure, and the sphere of objectivity appears to be

---

268 Judgment of the Constitutional Tribunal, 7 January 2004, K14/03, votum separatum: '(. . .)functioning of law requires other methods than those used by the Tribunal. Therefore, linguistic analysis and various types of reasoning based on legal logic are not enough. One needs to turn to empirical research necessary for objective evaluation of social facts that are to be the consequence of the existing legal solutions.'

269 Judgment of the Constitutional Tribunal, 7 January 2004, K14/03, votum separatum.

pre-decided by law. The 'objectivities' based on authority and presented in the analysis integrate into the object-determined meaning because, as in the case of a family of meanings related to truth, the subject does not have any impact on the truth 'self-revealing to them.'

This specific legal narration, which I mean, writing that this family of meanings of objectivity is characteristic for law, is related to reaching for authority of law as the highest and final argumentative instance. The reference to authority of law is then one of the basic premises constituting the objectivity of a given solution in the examples provided in this section. Law in this view is presented as a non-deliberative phenomenon and essentially as non-argumentative as well, but rather as complete and arbitrary. This non-deliberative argument about the highest power of persuasion, which cannot be appealed, does not additionally provide any transparency because it does not provide any justification except for the statement that law is objective.

On the other hand, referring to authority of instance making decisions, which makes it objective, is a situation in which the reference is made to the self-created authority by self-confirmation, with the use of the institutional power of authority. This meaning seems to be characteristic, particularly for the judicial discourse, not only because the positionality of a judge (the location of a judge in a judicial discourse) is determined by the quality of their judgements, which is revealed as a tendency to lack of transparency and arbitrariness, but it refers to the arguments which I call 'legal' ones in this chapter. These arguments refer to authority of law itself or the institutions representing law, which in the argumentative cases applied, have the attribute of objectivity, solely because they belong to legal order. As a result, it seems that authority of law attributed by law to itself, through the attribution of the features of objectivity to the elements of a legal discourse results in the naturalization of a legal discourse by treating law as belonging to pre-interpretative/non-interpretative order.

When it comes to the practice of usages, they deserve special attention because of their unique meanings. It is possible to observe that they very often provoke astonishment because they contradict our common intuitions and our usage in common language.

I argue that these meanings are the effects of an open texture process, which is also characteristic for the practice of law, and that this special context creates special meanings. I will present groups of meanings that are singled out from Polish judicature and then I will devote more attention to each of them, making further comments concerning their usage. Two legal senses of objectivity deserve special attention – objective judgments/evaluations and objectivity of legal facts – and these are discussed in separate chapters. I have chosen these two meanings because of their very significant character in law and legal practice. In the final part of the book I deal with the most basic ontological level of how legal facts are set (Chapter 5.) and with the issue of judicial discretion as well (Chapter 4.)

The subcategory which opens up the group of meanings rendered by law on the basis on its own power or authority (B2a), is the one that uses self-confirmation tactic (B2a.1). I will start with the example extracted from the justification of a Supreme Court decision: 'Objective evaluation is made by the court as the court adequately referred to the collected evidence and evaluated it meticulously and comprehensibly.'[270]

This short fragment shows how the objective evaluation was made and which conditions were necessary to make the legal evaluation objective. The Court has made the evaluation and then ascribed the property of objectivity to it. Objectivity belongs to a group of terms that have very strong presupposition about neutrality, suggesting independence from the subject's individual approach to the case, or the subject's personal attitudes, so making objectivity an immanent feature of the evaluation 'results in neutralizing it.'

What is interesting in this case is that the Court named its own action as 'objective.' It was done well and rightly. The Court indicates that there is a right way of evaluating and, in this instance, the highest court supports the evaluation made by the lower court. By using the word 'objective,' it ascribes to the process of evaluation elements that are not obviously ready-made but refers to values that are hidden behind the right answer.

A similar example comes again from the Polish Supreme Court examining a verdict made by the lower court. It says, 'In this justification of the verdict, the Court claims that Regional Instance Court carried out legal proceedings in a correct way and that the collected evidence was evaluated objectively and thoroughly. That is why the Supreme Court takes the stated facts and the legal arguments gathered in the justification made by the Regional Court as its own (. . .).'[271] These two examples are representative of a certain tendency that exists in Polish case law, when the Supreme Court, or a higher court, decides to accept the ruling of a lower court, call it objective, and then fully agree with it.

What is characteristic in these two examples quoted above is the fact that the 'objective' evaluation made by the court was not justified in any way. It seems, however, that the very use of the adjective 'objective' is treated as the justification in itself as a formula indicating the objective state of affairs. The use of

270 Judgement of the Supreme Court, 23 of May 2000, II UKN 551/99.
271 Judgment of the Supreme Court, 15 June 2005, II PK 276/04.

argumentative power of objectivity couples with, in this case, the institutional authority of court, which allows for self-confirmation with a strong demand for truth.

In the analysed examples, the court does not use the expression 'evaluation,' it does not make an evaluation in the strict sense but of the description touched with evaluation or it shares or accedes to a view of the lower instance court based on factual and evaluative premises, then the status of this court as 'objective' one is controversial because: it contains the elements of evaluation in itself, which remain covert, it results in lack of transparency or the evaluation made by lack of justification is more arbitrary.

Stronger examples come from other court justifications, where the central problem is focused on the possibility and necessity of hearing further evidence. The Court refuses to admit further evidence from the defence on the grounds that they will have nothing meaningful to say and it will not be objective. The Court deliberates, '(. . .) hearings of parties are applied in the situation when there are no other kinds of evidence delivered by the parties that makes the situation clear. The principle of the Court is to decide whether or not the evidence of the witnesses is important for making clear the facts of the case. This is the objective evaluation of the Court.'[272] This is in opposition to the subjective judgment of the defence who was asking for admission 'of the witnesses' statements as evidence.'

This example also demonstrates that except for the strategy of self-confirmation of its position as the objective one, the court assists in announcing its stance by the very organization of the court suit in which it has a privileged position towards the parties. The nature of the activity of the participants of the trial, or the objective court and the subjective stances of the parties, is the derivative effect of the trial organization. The features of the activity are assigned secondarily to them in relations to the position occupied, not on the basis of the content-related justification. As a result, the parties must make a double effort to demonstrate that their 'inherently' subjective stance is worthy of consideration, and the court, using its institutional status of being objective – as in the similar examples – does not make any justification of its stance. It is so evidently objective that we may see it with the naked eye.

The discussed example demonstrates that the inequality of locating the participants of the trial is behind the qualification in defining own judgments of the court as objective ones and the stance of the parties as the objective one.

272 Judgment of the Supreme Court, 13 April 2005, II PK 258/04.

A further example of self-assertion of objectivity by the Court is the characterization of the moral attitude of the defendant as subjective. The Court says that the positions of the defendant are just the presentation of a subjective internalization of values. At the same time, the Court names its own position as 'objective legal evaluation.'[273] It is worth stressing that both the Court and the defendant are evaluating the same legal situation. Hence, what matters is the position from where the judgment was taken, not the merit.

In addition, the activity of the party is qualified as a moral sphere of evaluation and the courts includes its evaluation in the legal sphere, naming it 'the objective legal evaluation.' In the very judgment the court writes, however, that 'The use of a general clause by the legislator always leads to entrust the final evaluation to the ruling court, while – which is evident – this evaluation should be made with the use of relevant criteria. Simultaneously, this evaluation will always remain individualized, referring to specific circumstances, they will constitute, however, the basis of a jurisdictional decision of the court. As it is relevantly emphasized in literature, a notion of 'proper behaviour,' similarly to the notion of 'principles of community life' or 'established customs' are worded with content in specific situations.[274]

While the court states that it makes an objective legal evaluation, it simultaneously admits that it makes the evaluation within a discretional judicial authority, evaluating whether the activity of the party is contrary to good practices. The application of a general clause is the move beyond the designated legal standards so that the court could make its own evaluation of a situation, based on its own experience and the awareness of social reality. The argumentation based on subjectivity and objectivity is misleading in this case because the evaluations of both the court and the party are subjective. Based on such an assumption the court would have to reveal its evaluation and subsequently justify it. The reference to the objectivity of the evaluation by the court exempts it from

---

273 Judgment of the Supreme Court, 26 September 2002, III CKN 213/01: 'The belief of the appellant in the last resort appeal that their action 'does not violate any ethical-moral norm' must not be effective. This statement may be at most regarded as the demonstration of the subjective understanding of moral norms by the respondent, which does not influence the objective legal evaluation. What results from the court's justification is that it regarded as the circumvention of the law, contrary to good practices, which was based on omission of advertisement prohibition of specific goods by hiding it under the form of a permitted advertisement. This view of the Court should be supported.'

274 Judgment of the Supreme Court, 26 September 2002, III CKN 213/01.

the disclosure of the evaluation, the justification but also it exposes the court to a potential polemic.

In a different court's justification one can find a repetition of the mentioned above way of thinking. The court writes: 'The effect of the criminal process is based on the truth, in realizing justice and is objective itself, contrary to the subjective expectation of the parties.'[275] Keeping in mind such a point of view, one could reach the conclusion that the positions of the parties would be always subjective, and the position of the Court would be always objective in virtue of their positions within the organization of legal world. Likewise, when argumentation is examined one could also reach the conclusion that the law treats itself and its products as 'objective.' The expressed attempt of the court to justify its stance based again on the attribution of a feature of objectivity to the activity of the court is an expression of self-affirmation but not argumentation. The stance of the party, is, on the other hand, regarded as subjective or unjustified expectations. We may, then, treat the fragment above, as an expression of rhetoric, however, it indicates the possible assumptions made by the court.

The Court of Appeal, in the same judgment, referring to the interpretative stance of the Supreme Court, which is applied in the justification of the case in question, states that the understanding of the key term by the Supreme Court is the objective understanding, on the other hand, the understanding, proposed by the parties, fits into the subjective ground. The objective understanding suggested by the Supreme Court, refers to its linguistic field, which is regarded in the subject literature as a controversial attitude. The linguistic clarification is a set of many different possibilities, which the person making an interpretation, e.g. reaching for dictionaries to establish the meaning of a colloquial language,[276]

---

275 Judgment of the Court of Appeal [Sąd Apelacyjny] in Katowice, 15 May 2008, II AKa 13/08, LEX nr 447031, Biul.SA Ka 2008/3/4, KZS 2008/9/41, KZS 2008/9/42: 'The written motives of the stance expressed by the Supreme Court undoubtedly prove that the notion 'will reveal' within the meaning of the regulation indicated above preserves its linguistic meaning both in the subjective ground – both from the offender's perspective as well as in the objective ground – from the perspective of the body appointed to prosecute crimes.'

276 The dictionary meaning is not 'given' once and for all. It is changeable, formed by the contexts of use and it enters the dictionaries from such a use – in accordance with the preferences of the author of a dictionary, who selects the contexts and creates meanings based on them. The dictionary descriptions are created in this way. Hence they differ in various dictionaries. Cf. Zygmunt Tobor, Piotr Żmigrodzki, Agnieszka Bielska-Brodziak, 'Opis semantyczny leksemów w słowniku ogólnym i jego doniosłość prawna' [The semantic description of lexemes in a general dictionary and its legal

reaching for legal definitions to establish the meaning of a language of the law and eventually for meanings suggested by the doctrine and case law (which provides many opportunities within the so-called legal language). These meanings may be in conflict and they are conflicting, which is revealed within the contexts created by specific cases/situations.[277] Additionally, social changes, as an additional factor influencing the change of context, and because of this the meaning of a given expression, is the subsequent argument indicating lack of objectivity of the meanings of the interpreted expressions. The argumentation of court, indicating, that the suggested meaning of a given expression of subjective, seems to be based on ascribing the features of the meaning of a given expression to the attitude of the position taken in a trial. In case of the stance expressed by the Supreme Court we have a detailed explanation of different understandings of the interpreted notion. The court referring to the stance of the Supreme Court qualifies them into objective and subjective, implying that subject is inappropriate.

As the analysed examples indicated, the way in which opinions, judgments, and decisions perceived as subjective are treated is not surprising. They are commonly eliminated from the discourse as arguments not deserving to be considered because of their insignificant character. In this way, arguments of opposing parties are eliminated. However, when one looks closer and deeper at the character of arguments given by the two parties, one realizes that almost all of their arguments have to be subjective in some sense. This point of view is the consequence of the contradictory character of the legal process; the parties on trial deliver arguments and evidence to make their own position stronger and more convincing or persuasive. Keeping in mind such a point of view, one could reach the conclusion that the positions of the parties would be always subjective and the position of Court would be always objective in virtue of their positions within the organization of legal world. Likewise, when argumentation is examined one could also reach the conclusion that the law treats itself and its products as 'objective.'

The attribution of the objective point of view to court and the subjective one to the parties, even if we want to treat them as an expression of solely the court

significance] *Język Polski* 88/1 (2008) 3–13; Agnieszka Bielska-Brodziak, Zygmunt Tobor, Słowniki a interpretacja tekstów prawnych [Dictionaries and interpretation of legal texts] *Państwo i Prawo* 5 (2007) 20–33.

277 Agnieszka Bielska-Brodziak, *Interpretacja tekstu prawnego na podstawie orzecznictwa podatkowego* [The interpretation of a legal text based on fiscal case law] (Warszawa: Wolters Kluwer, 2009) 23–87.

rhetoric, expressing the willingness to enforce its argumentation, demonstrates what covert assumptions function in the way of the functioning of courts.

Other examples where the law delivers the value of objectivity on its own authority can be derived directly from the Polish case law (B2b), like the situation when the court refused to admit the evidence submitted by the party, which is within its discretion, claiming that it is its 'objective evaluation.' Some shorter but meaningful examples from the court rulings are where the courts use phrases such as: 'objective criteria defined by the legislator'[278] or 'objective because it's based on the legal rules' (B2b.1),[279] 'objective because it's set by the court' (B2b.4),[280]'objective because it is set by the prosecutor's institutions/bodies,'[281] 'objective because it is in accordance with objective legal order' (B2b.2)[282] (which is defined in one justification as 'procedural and substantive norms'[283]).

In all the above examples, one can observe that the Court makes assessments on very strong ontological premises based on 'objective legal order,' 'objective legal rules' and 'the objective activity of legal bodies.' The problem in all above quotations is that they are used as descriptive statements with a strong ontology behind them. They presuppose that law belongs to pre-interpretative order, which is defined once and for all in a 'proper' and real way. Such a view is the closest to the most radical doctrines of philosophical realism, which ignores the entire tradition of legal hermeneutics or any antirealistic stances (see Chapter 1). The controversy of such idealistic premises in relation to the character of law is outside the scope of this monograph, as do not discuss metaphysical objectivity of law.

The way of justifying decisions presented in the afore-mentioned example with the use of argument from objectivity, reveals the court logic, which is based on the reflection of the structure of a trial situation, in which the court is in the situation of making decisions from the position of 'neutrality' and 'objectivity,' and as a result from the position of a claim for validity and the parties are always biased and subjective, which condemns their argumentation to a

---

278 Judgment of the Constitutional Tribunal, 29 November 2007, SK 43/06.

279 Judgment of Voivodeship Administrative Court in Szczecin, 23 April 2009, I SA/Sz 104/09, LEX *No.* 502682.

280 Decision of the Supreme Court, 15 December 2006, III CZP 112/06, LEX No. 260365.

281 Judgment of the Court of Appeal in Katowice, 15 May 2008, II AKa 13/08, LEX No. 447031.

282 Decision of Voivodeship Administrative Court in Poznan, 21 October 2008, II SA/Po 656/08, LEX No. 504611.

283 Judgment of the Supreme Administrative Court, 13 December 1999, IV SA 1671/99.

weaker position. In addition, the reference to the objectivity of all which is 'legal' enhances not only non-discursiveness of an argumentative situation, but as a result it makes it a priori, based on hierarchism and authority. Such conclusions may be drawn based on the way in which the argumentation is demonstrated, or the analysis of solely justifying decisions, not knowing substantial premises for making such decision, which is emphasized in the subject literature as two different possible paths of argumentation known as the decision-making context and the context of justification.[284]

The subsequent effect of referring to arguments on objectivity in a style of a hierarchical trial organization, or the attribution of the judge's position and legal principles or legal order of a feature of objectivity is the fact that the court defends norms included in the system more than the interests of the entities applying for protection.

The examples of judgments belonging to a group of the application of objectivity 'based on the objectivity of law itself' in three subgroups, will be discussed below, which are as follows: referring to the objectivity of legal sciences (legal doctrine), the objectivity of legal rules and the contents included there and the objectivity of a judge's activities.

The first judgment analysed provides the example based on authority of legal sciences: The objective is defined as confirmed by 'legal doctrine,' courts rulings, the pattern in case law that resembles some tendency.[285]

---

284 Following the logic of the separation of decision-making context from the justification of decisions, the analysis included in this chapter concerns the way in which the court justifies and not what values the court was guided by while making them. 'The justification of decisions formed ex post does not constitute the demonstration of perception, which really led to make the justified decision. The demonstration of the justification is to indicate not that the decision was made but whether it is legitimate, that is if there exist the reasons which advocate their acceptance (regardless of the fact if they had a real impact on making it).' Tobor, 'Bezstronność sędziego,' 10.

285 Judgment of the Constitutional Tribunal, 12 May 2005, SK 13/05, OTK-A 2005/8/9: 'The rule of definiteness of criminal law does not exclude the use of indefinite or evaluative expressions by a legislator if their designates may be defined (of the Constitutional Tribunal of 23 January 2003, reference file of documents K 2/02). The very penal code uses numerous indefinite expressions, which solely aim at marking a qualified form of crime. It suffices to indicate art. 218 § 1 of penal code – saying about 'malicious' influence, art. 304 of penal code – saying about 'forced location,' art. 311 of penal code – 'significant meaning,' where the use of such expressions determines the very criteria of a penal act. The meaning of those phrases is not however set in a legal vacuum, which could cause uncertainty, but is determined via analysis of the doctrine output, and especially of court judicature, which authoritatively removes the existing

As it was already mentioned in a different context example from the Polish Constitutional Tribunal talks about 'objective vagueness of the legal rule' and 'objectively high vagueness of legal rules.'[286] In this instance, they mean that the fragments of certain legal rules are perceived as vague for everyone because of some rational reasons. However, the Tribunal is stating that 'The meaning of those phrases is not however set in a legal vacuum, which could cause uncertainty, but is determined via analysis of the doctrine output, and especially of court judicature, which authoritatively removes the existing objective doubts.'

As we may observe based on this case, doubts are solved by legal science, which acts as an argument from authority. We may take into account the fact that legal sciences abound in frequently diverse concepts from each other as well as in understandings of legal notions and treating only some of them – the ones which are used frequently and gained recognition of practice – may be regarded as non-context-related. This is not the popularity of use nor authority of legal sciences or the context of use that should decide about the selection of meaning. Understanding objectivity in this case comes down to building the justification of the selection via authority of legal sciences and the acceptances of a given meaning by an interpretative community – in this case the court discourse and the discourse of legal sciences. The force of an argument from authority acts with its fulgent power, particularly strongly where other stances, which are not so popular, remain unrevealed and covert. Moreover, the style of judicial justifications is constructed in such a way that it does not demonstrate a broader

---

objective doubts.' It does not suffice the very negligence of a declaration to state a fraud, but willfulness of action or negligence of a taxpayer or a payer is necessary. It means that, e.g. erroneous activity related to tax obligation, in accordance with art. 10 of Penal and Fiscal Code, will not be qualified as fraud. The construction of a justified error, e.g. from objective vagueness of tax law regulation excludes penal and fiscal liability. This regulation should be used with the inclusion of objectively high degree of vagueness and imprecision of Polish tax law. The multitude of tax regulations, as well as their changeability and objective vagueness, requires the proportional use of penal and fiscal sanctions. It is constitutionally unacceptable to shift into a taxpayer not only an economic risk related to faulty use of vague tax regulations but also a risk of criminal liability (The statement of the Constitutional Tribunal).

286 Judgment of the Constitutional Tribunal, 12 September 2005, SK 13/05, OTK-A 2005/8/9: 'The meaning of those phrases is not however set in a legal vacuum, which could cause uncertainty, but is determined via analysis of the doctrine output, and especially of court judicature, which authoritatively removes the existing objective doubts.'

array of possibilities, which could be taken into account but it builds a justification for this solution, which was selected by a judge for this purpose.

The next example of the use of objectivity in the discussed group of meaning is a situation of the reference to the objectivity of law itself, and in particular the situation in which legal act indicates objective criteria.[287] A fragment of the statement by the Constitutional Tribunal is quoted in the decision of the Constitutional Tribunal related to the interpretation of art. 60 of the Constitution, which states that: 'The Polish citizens enjoy full civil rights and are entitled to the access to public healthcare on identical basis.'

The Constitutional Tribunal states that regulations of law, in accordance with the constitutional requirements are to have the objective nature, which means in the case discussed that the regulations should define 'uniform' criteria of selection of candidates for public duty (in this case the selection of policemen). In this case it is understood as the implementation of the equality of chances of candidates applying for the afore-mentioned positions, as non-discriminatory criteria, not excluding candidates by differentiating criteria. The objective criteria used for a specific case may turn out to be objective, or non-discriminatory – non-excluding or not fulfilling these features, just after their application. The theoretical considerations on equality (here understood as objectivity) of the same criteria were repeatedly discussed in the literature as a debate of consequentialist ethics with ethics of care. As an example, one may suggest a discussion in terms of ethics of care,[288] indicating that each subject due to its individual otherness will position itself towards the same criteria, which often results in injustice. E.g. the entire group of subjects due to its otherness may not fulfill the feature mentioned in the regulation and because of this it may have an excluding, discriminatory nature. Such understanding of objectivity as uniform criteria for all, being an expression of universalization and rationalization of subjects and conventionalist thinking, remains insensitive to the final effect, or actual justice of legal entities with diverse status.

---

287 Decision of the Constitutional Tribunal, 22 November 2011, K 10/10: 'The Spokesman quoting the Tribunal's judicature, emphasized public legal status of policemen and their service. He also cited the opinion of the Tribunal on art. 60 of the Constitution which requires the act to define the objective criteria of selection of candidates for public duty and which should regulate the rules and procedure of recruitment in such a way as to provide the observation of the principle of equality of chances of all candidates.'

288 See more, Virginia Held, *The Ethics of Care: Personal, Political, Global* (New York: Oxford University Press, 2006).

The next case of this group of meaning is provided by the example, in which the obligation from the legal act is defined as having objective character.[289] In this case, the court says that tax duty as regards civil law activities has been defined in the provisions of the act and has objective character. More precisely wrote that 'tax obligation on civil law transactions was defined in the regulations of the act has objective nature.' This argument was written in the argumentation line justifying the necessity to pay tax from the advance collected in a defined amount, which was not paid by the party because they stated that there exist the circumstances to pay this tax in a lower amount (exemption from tax on civil law actions). The court rejecting the arguments of the party and indicating that payment obligation has objective nature because it results from the regulations forms law image as objective and not being subject to interpretation. In this regard, all contents included in the regulations have objective nature, also these which the party refers to. In addition, the argument applied from objectivity has a rhetorical overtone because it emphasizes absolute character of tax obligation, which concerns all and which cannot be evaded.

The next example provides a case on judicial objectivity, however in other context than the afore mentioned, discussed judicial objectivity in terms of neutrality or impartiality.[290] A judge, in accordance with the fragment analysed, cannot act for their own rights, they must be objective in social assessment, they are to use competence norms in such a way, act in accordance with regulations of law so that they would be perceived as objective by the so-called rational entity. The verification of the perspective of a rational entity is characterized as the perspective of a moderately intelligent person, a moderately educated person, not

289 Judgment of the Voivodeship Administrative Court in Wrocław, 16 November 2011, I SA/Wr 717/11: 'Tax duty as regards civil law activities has been defined in the provisions of the act and has objective character.'

290 Judgment of the Court of Appeal in Wrocław, 27 October 2011, II AKa 261/11: 'The judiciary is not contained within the borders of its functions and does not act for its own rights. It should be constructed and have its competence norms shaped in such a way and use them according to law in such a manner as to remain – in public opinion – objective, reliable, competent, impartial and just. From this perspective it is not decisive, if the adjudicating judge finds himself impartial or if the parties or participants to the procedure do not question his impartiality (which may arise from various reasons and motivations or from simple unawareness or ignorance of qualifications), but if in relation to a given set-up of the procedure created by given factual circumstances, one might remove the doubts and convince any averagely educated, averagely intelligent or reasonably thinking member of the society not directly interested in the result of the trial, that in such set-up the judge could be and was impartial.'

interested personally in the result of the trial. The objective perspective is identified here with the view from the outside, however such a construction is closer to the idealized 'view from nowhere,' which rather resembles the 'divine' position not having any perspective. The attempt to subjectify a single perspective of a judge by depriving them of positionality and subjectivity is a resort to an unauthorized idealization. As it was described alongside other examples (vide judicial discretion), a specific person, with their own assessments and judgments, representing their own, positioned perspective is behind a rational and average person, who is a judge as well.

3.3.3. The Intersubjective-Determined Camp of Objectivity (C)

In this part of the chapter I introduce the meaning of objectivity that corresponds to intersubjectivity (C). In particular its main meaning is: 'objectivity as intersubjective,' while its family of meanings is defined as follows:

C1. Common acceptance,
C2. Validity based on rationality,
C3. Shared by many, by the majority, or other wider group.

In the jurisprudence literature 'intersubjectivity' is understood as commonly valid, valid for everyone, or something that a rational human being could accept.[291] The term 'common' corresponds with the intuition that objectivity is something that is common for everybody. Just as subjective is identified with something that is individual, objective is identified with something that belongs to the 'community or it is shared by others.' It is something that everybody can agree on and that will be accepted by the majority. The term objectivity as 'commonly valid' is widely used by the courts once a judge decides to accept a given 'standpoint' and looks for a justification accepted by the legal interpretative community. We may provide many examples illustrating the opposite tendency, in which the court rejects a given standpoint claiming that they are exclusively individual standpoints, which are not shared by the majority. The scheme of negating individual standpoints is commonly applied here since they are individual, subjective (C1).

291 Tomasz Gizbert-Studnicki, 'Podstawy argumentacji prawniczej,' [The basisc of legal argumentation] *Acta Universatis Wratislaviensis* No 1772 Prawo CCXLIV, Wrocław (1995) 36; Ota Weinberger, 'Objectivity and Rationality In Lawyer's Reasoning,' in *Theory of Legal Science*, ed. Aleksander Peczenik (Dordrecht: D. Reidel Publishing Company, 1984) 217 ff.

The next example is the reference to objectivity – the intersubjective community based on reason and rationality (C2). The latter type of justification, except for the indication of some common area, also provides acceptance criteria of what is common via a common measurement of rationality (C3). However, within this standpoint, we have different types of examples, from general clauses with the most prevalent 'bona fides in the objective meaning,' or reference to standards shared by discourse participants appointed by a measure of rational subject, to the examples objectifying general clauses in a way, which may be called 'weak,' referring only to common acceptance criteria or rationality.

In the first quoted example (C1), the court says that, 'interpretative doubts must have an objective character, they cannot be doubts of only one person who is carrying out the interpretations'[292]. In another example, courts explain to the party, who raised interpretative doubts related to the fragment of the interpreted legal rule, how to make criteria objective, they should be 'based on references to the wider group of participants and their feelings (which) is commonly practiced and serves for the acceptance of social norms of behaviour (tradition).'[293]

In both cases, interpretative doubts are to be understood as shared by other people, the best by majority of legal subjects who are recipients of the vague legal rule. Such an approach raises doubts, mainly due to the fact that the definition of interpretative doubts – whether they should be taken into account or not – is not a result of a democratic approach, in which numbers are calculated, but arguments, which point to a new context justifying the occurrence of a new meaning or also lack of acceptance for such a situation. We need to take into consideration that language has a public nature and if interpretative doubts constitute a new meaning and are comprehensible and shared by others, then they are intersubjective. Linguistic meaning is always intersubjective or incomprehensible, which is derived from Wittgenstein's argument about the impossibility of a private language and a communicative function of the language itself. It would

292 The decision of the Constitutional Tribunal, 25 February 2006, K 48/04: '(. . .) The reported doubts should simultaneously be of an objective character, i.e. they should not be exclusively doubts of the petitioner as regards the interpretation. For the procedure on interpretation of the judgment, the principle of *clara non sunt interpretanda* is applicable.'

293 The judgment of the Supreme Court, 11 March 1997, III CKN 33/97: '(. . .) That is why the evaluation criteria must be subject to objectification, i.e. one needs to take into consideration the feelings of a larger group of participants and the generally assumed and deserving acceptance norms of conduct (custom, tradition, etc.) Motivation of the perpetrator of the violation is not without significance here.'

be more advisable to say, in the analysed case, that doubts are incomprehensible in terms of other language users or they are not shared by them. The reference to lack of objective nature of interpretative doubts, although expressed in academic language, does not have much in common with it because it does not touch upon a core of the problem of interpretative doubts in language terms (lack of their objective nature, as discussed in the previous chapters).

Another example, this time extracted from the decisions of the Polish Constitutional Tribunal talks about 'objective vagueness of the legal rule' and 'objectively high vagueness of legal rules.'[294] In this instance, the Tribunal means that the fragment of certain legal rules which are indeterminate might be perceived as vague for everyone because of some rational reasons. These are however, according to the Tribunal, removed by the analysis of the doctrine output, and especially of court judicature, which authoritatively removes the existing 'objective doubts.'[295]

This example of a rational justification, which removes objective interpretative doubts, illustrates a specific judicial rationality on built authority of judicature

---

294 The judgment of the Constitutional Tribunal, 9 August 2005, SK 13/05: Opinion of Constitutional Tribunal: 'The principle of the specificity of legal provisions does not exclude however the usage of indeterminate phrases or evaluations, if their designates may be defined the judgment of the Constitutional Tribunal of 23 January 2003, case file No. K 2/02). The Penal Code itself uses numerous indeterminate phrases which do not aim exclusively at designating the aggravated crimes. It should suffice to cite art. 218 § 1 of the Penal Code which mentions 'malicious infringement,' art. 304 of the Penal Code – 'compulsory circumstances,' or art 311 of the Penal Code – 'crucial importance: where the use of such phrases determines the very fulfilment of a penal act. The meaning of those phrases is not however set in a legal vacuum, which could cause uncertainty, but is determined via analysis of the doctrine output, and especially of court judicature, which authoritatively removes the existing objective doubts. Therefore, unreliability of a declaration is not sufficient to pronounce a fraud, one needs to prove intentionality of action or negligence of a taxpayer or payer. This means, that e.g. acting in error as regards the text of tax duty pursuant to art. 10 of the Penal and Fiscal Code cannot be qualified as a fraud. The construction of a justified error resulting from e.g. objective vagueness of a provision of tax law excludes the penal and fiscal liability. This provision should be applied taking into consideration the objectively high level of impreciseness and vagueness of the Polish tax law. Multitude of tax law regulations, their changeability and objective vagueness require proportional application of penal and fiscal sanctions. The Constitution does not allow for shifting the economic risk related to erroneous application of tax provisions as well as the risk of penal liability to a taxpayer.'

295 The judgment of the Constitutional Tribunal, 9 August 2005, SK 13/05.

and doctrine, which creates lists of interpreted contexts of particular fragments of legal texts ready to be applied by courts. A low clarity of an argument, observable on this example, supports the transfer of common acceptability into arguments being of major importance due to the recognized authority, in this case attributed to them by law itself. As the result we can see, the meaning of objectivity as intersubjectivity may cover understandings such as 'what is common,' 'shared by others,' 'commonly accepted,' 'valid for everyone' with or without specifying the criterion or the reasons of such acceptance. On the argumentative level they are not equal and cannot be treated as synonyms, as they represent different level of justification, specifying (or not) the source of such an acceptance.

They correspond with acceptance by the majority or everybody within a certain group and may not have a rational justification but a justification of power. That is why it is possible to conclude about the graduated character of intersubjectivity, that might have stronger and weaker justification. The importance of this remark lies especially in the wide practical usage of this term, with the connotation of intersubjectivity.

The analysis of general clauses was discussed in a separate chapter. The examples of the application of the judicial discretionality will be demonstrated here, which refer to intersubjectivity, acceptability based on a criterion of rationality and their derivatives (C2). Not discussing the examples of bona fides, as they were discussed in a separate chapter. I will refer to what is important in terms of intersubjectivity, or the roots of their community dimension.

Firstly, I will refer to the clause of bona fides in the objective and subjective meaning[296] as it constitutes the most popular example of such understanding of the application of objectivity in the sense of intersubjectivity, which is based on rational criteria, recognized as a common feature of the participants of the social world, which their apply in their behaviour. The justification for the search of objective patterns allowing for the evaluation is sought in the historical conditions of an expression of *bona fides* originating from Roman law. It is emphasized in the literature of Roman Law that it initially expressed the definitions of a state of consciousness of a buyer, however with time *bona fides* was being discussed in the subjective meaning to define the level of consciousness of a subject. As a result, a construction of *bona fides* occurred in the objective meaning (mainly in contract law), pointing to duties whose performance, in a relatively occurring

296 Ewa Rott-Pietrzyk, 'Klauzula generalna racjonalnego podmiotu,' [The general clause of a rational subject] in *Klauzula generalna rozsądku w prawie prywatnym* [The General Clause of Common Sense in Private Law] (Warszawa: Wydawnictwo Beck, 2007).

circumstances, could be expected from honest people. It was indicated that despite individual difference among subjects, what is common should be taken into consideration, or the need to manage the so-called objective rationality,[297] who determined basic and fundamental value with reference to the opinions, views and beliefs commonly accepted by all reasonable (rational) people[298] or particular social groups.[299] As it can be seen then, rationality was treated widely, as a tool, which subjectively indicated values, principles and moral norms, which should be applied by all people. Reason as a criterion of objective features was which all people accept, and what is more – they use them. Romans considered the 'institution' of the so-called objective rationality because reason served for objective evaluation, which values and moral norms should be regarded as fundamental and suitable to be included while adjudicating based on bona fides.[300] This criterion is simultaneously related to a demand of preserving objectivity in courts. The fundamental values and principles comprise these which are commonly respected 'among all people.'

As the brief reconstruction of the clause of 'bona fides in the objective meaning' indicates, it is profoundly rooted in intersubjectivity, understood as shared and accepted by members of a given community. Apparently, the context of rationality in a modern pluralist society of the culture of civil law changed and the objective evaluation by referring to values is not justified (because there are many of them, various ones), but rather to the procedure based on rationality, which determines a technique we agree with, and through that we accept its result. However, the historical outline, presented above, demonstrates the

297 Arystoteles, Etyka nikomachejska [The Nicomachean Ethics] (Warszawa: Wydawnictwo Naukowe PWN, 2008, 1098 b 10, 114 b and subsequent ones.; J. Finnis, Prawo naturalne i uprawnienia naturalne [Natural law and natural entitlements], trans. Karolina Lossman, (Warszawa: Dom Wydawniczy ABC, 2001) 315; Paweł Łabieniec, *Prawo rozumu. O teorii prawa naturalnego J. Finnisa* [About natural law theory by J. Finnis] (Łódź: Uniwersytet Łódzki, 2004) 124 ff.

298 Wojciech Dajczak analysing bona fides in Roman law, sees benefits in continuous considerations over 'objective rationality' to define the contents of bona fides. See Wojciech Dajczak, 'Problem "ponadczasowości" zasad prawa rzymskiego. Uwagi w dyskusji o "nowej europejskiej kulturze prawnej,"' [The problem of timelessness] *Zeszyty Prawnicze*, Vol. 5 Issue 2 (2005) 21; Idem, *Dobra wiara jako symbol europejskiej tożsamości prawa* [Bona Fides as a Symbol] (Poznań: Księgarnia św. Wojciecha, 2006) 23.

299 Cf. Wiesław Litewski, *Jurysprudencja rzymska* [The Roman Jurisprudence] (Kraków: Wydawnictwo Uniwersytetu Jagiellońskiego, 2000) 124.

300 Ewa Rott-Pietrzyk, 'Klauzula generalna racjonalnego podmiotu.'

community embeddedness of *bona fides* as objective rationality, which is present in the practice of other general clauses as well.

Here I will mention the examples of other general clauses, which refer to objectifying criteria, or to the argumentation of a rational subject, which may be applied to each participant of legal affairs (C3). The following clauses may provide the example, in which the court with the application of the argument from objectivity: determined if the objective standard of due diligence was applied (objective measurement of diligence),[301] if the intention to wielding a thing was based on objective criteria[302] or serious reasons occurred[303] or objective difficulties[304] or objectively existing danger.[305] In the first example the court, evaluating

301 Decision of the Supreme Court, 4 November 2011, I CZ 119/11: 'The premise of lack of guilt in not observing the deadline is subject to evaluation considering the objective measurement of diligence that might be required from a party taking proper care of its interests, considering also default caused even by the slightest negligence. Such standpoint should be understood as well grounded in judicature (cf. inter alia decision of the Supreme Court of 11 December 2008, case file No. IV CZ 102/08, unpublished; decision of the Supreme Court of 25 April 2008, case file No. I UZ 1/08, unpublished; decision of the Supreme Court of 17 April 2008, case file No. I CZ 19/08, unpublished, resolution of the Supreme Court of 10 January 1956, case file No. IV CO 58/55, OSNCK 1956, No. 4, item 106).'

302 Judgment of the Supreme Administrative Court, 10 November 2011, I FSK 13/11: 'Assumption that a given natural person – by selling plot of land designed for construction purposes – acts in the capacity of a taxpayer conducting business activity (as a salesperson), needs to be supported by proving that such activity is of a professional character, and that it is constant (repeatable activity and intention supported by objective proofs of its continuation).'

303 Decision of the Supreme Administrative Court, 22 September 2011, II GZ 424/11: 'The circumstances that might result in justified doubts as to the impartiality of a judge in a given case must be real, not potential. The very fact that a party merely suspects or that they have lost their faith in judge's impartiality resulting from subjective feeling of a party, is not enough. It is necessary to point out significant reasons, that would objectively cause loss of faith in judge's impartiality.'

304 Decision of the Supreme Administrative Court, 14 September 2011, I OZ 666/11: 'One has to assume thus, that the legal representative of the petitioner is right when he indicates objective difficulties that would require lodging cassation appeal within 7 days really, which result from application of art. 87 § 4 of the cited act that obliges one to perform delayed activity simultaneously with the request for reinstating the deadline.'

305 Decision of the Court of Appeal in Katowice, 30 November 2005, II Aka 281/05: 'Reckless endangerment is not only a situation, after all, in which the offender causes certain occurrences that become dangerous for these goods (e.g. they set a fire,

proper care of a subject, made it through the prism of the understanding of this notion rooted in judicature. On the other hand, 'the intention of wielding a thing,' 'serious reasons,' 'objective difficulties' and the 'existing danger in the objective meaning should constitute these ones, which are externalized, physical, empirically confirmed because they are possible then to be verified by everyone. Thereby, the rationalized general clauses gain intersubjective, universal dimension. In all the afore-mentioned examples in which the court made an evaluation, referring to objective criteria, which were to implement the intersubjective dimension, only the criterion of what is acceptable by 'everyone' from rational through commonly observable – physical, have the empirical confirmation and are based on authority of law.

---

start an avalanche) or creates an immediate danger of their occurrence, but also such when in a place where danger objectively exists they bring legal goods, which were not placed in the danger zone, so they were safe before.'

Chapter IV Objective Judgments and General Clauses

4.1. The Notion of General Clauses in the Context of Judicial Discretion

The first words in Judge Barak's book 'Judicial Discretion' say, 'Judicial discretion is for the most part a mystery to the general public, to the community of lawyers, to the teachers of law, and to the judges themselves.'[306]

How could this be so? What are the reasons for such a statement? What are the sources of the problems with general clauses?

In this chapter, I deal with the problem of general clauses from the point of view of their objective character. One of the reasons behind the 'mystery of general clauses' is the conflict between their evaluative character and the ambiguous nature of objectivity. Both these elements have to be clearly understood for the construction of objective general clauses. I aim to show the questionable status of objectivity of general clauses.

I will examine why applying general clauses has claims to objectivity, to what extent such claims are justified, and why 'objective general clauses' appear to be controversial. First of all, I will introduce some definitions of general clauses from jurisprudential literature and the doctrine of law, and then examine specific examples of 'objective general clauses' extracted from Polish court rulings.

General clauses are of interest to both theorists and practicing lawyers, though their approaches to how they should be understood and applied are commonly very different and even seem contradictory at times. Unable to find any one clear accepted opinion, I will introduce several understandings from the jurisprudence and the Doctrine of Law and then contrast these with what happens in legal practice. In doing so, I will show the reasons behind the construction of 'objective general clauses' and, at the same time, shed more light on the elusive meaning of objectivity as applied to law.

General clauses can be roughly characterized as a special type of judicial discretion. When Ronald Dworkin characterized judicial discretion, he stressed that, 'the concept of discretion is really only at home when someone is charged with making decisions that are subject to standards set by a particular authority

306 Aharon Barak, *Judicial Discretion* (New Haven and London: Yale University Press, 1989) 3.

(..) it always makes sense to ask: 'discretion under which standards' and 'discretion under which authority'?'[307] Sometimes 'discretion' is used in a weak sense, simply to say that the standards must not be applied mechanically by officials but demand the use of judgment.[308] General clauses are discretions under the authority of law and they demand judgments in the process of their application.

This approach indicates two important elements: subjection to the standards of authorities and demanding the use of judgments. These two elements form the framework by which I will consider the possible objectivity of general clauses.

In jurisprudential literature it is possible to find very different presentations of general clauses. One example says that general clauses, also referred to as 'standards,' are identified with legal rules (or parts of them) that are not precisely formulated and have terms and concepts that have no clear core. They are not formulated by the legislature in a way that lends itself directly to application.[309] The task of specifying the content is left to legal practice, that is, the courts. The question is what the character of their application is.

Leszek Leszczyński variously characterizes general clauses as referential clauses and redirecting clauses, which are also vague and blurred terms.[310] They refer to criteria such as principles or rules of good standards, good faith, principles of fairness, public interests, well-being of the child, important reasons, and justified reasons. In other words, they can be characterized as referring to standards outside written law, and they may refer to facts and to values and norms as well. Different types of general clauses can be distinguished, depending on whether they refer to customs or evaluative criteria. General clauses include also all expressions that are considered as vague.[311]

General clauses that refer to evaluative criteria do not form a homogenous group. It is possible to distinguish between expressions that demand only estimations and those that demand using a system of values from outside the law in their application. An example of the former is 'important reason.' These expressions, sometimes called referral expressions, are composed of two

307 Ronald Dworkin, 'The Model of Rules,' in An Anthology of law and legal theory, ed. Dennis Patterson (Oxford: Blackwell 2003) 56–57.

308 Dworkin, 'The Model of Rules,' 57.

309 Stefan Grundmann and Denis Mazeaud, ed., *General Clauses and Standards In European Contract Law: Comparative Law, EC Law, Contract Law and Codification* (The Hague: Kluwer Law International, 2006) 3.

310 Leszek Leszczyński, *Tworzenie generalnych klauzul odsyłających* [*Setting up of General Referral Clauses*] (Lublin: UMCS, 2000) 7–39.

311 Leszczyński, *Tworzenie generalnych klauzul*, 7–39.

elements: a description of facts (circumstances, reasons consequences, etc.) that have to be confirmed as having actually happened, and an evaluation to determine if the fact is important, specific, or appropriate, etc.[312] The latter are sometimes called 'real general clauses' and include expressions such 'good faith,' 'public interest,' etc.

Józef Nowacki, characterizes general clauses as so-called 'vague terms' (blurring expressions) that are included in legal texts as evaluations that have to be done outside the written law.[313] The basic question he asks, which is especially important when examining their objective character, is whether legal rules really refer to good standards, good faith, principle of fairness, public interests, well-being of the child, important reasons, justified reasons, etc. or are such claims not justified?

He argues in a very convincing way that every referral has to be to somebody or to something that exists. But there is nothing already made to refer to in the process of application of general clauses. Legal bodies must take decisions on whether certain actions were 'in good faith' or 'what is good for a particular child.' There is no set of rules to indicate which reasons are important in a particular concrete case. One cannot refer to principles or rules outside the legal system because there are no such ready-made rules. In all types of general clauses, the evaluation is based on a hierarchy of values that is accepted but not revealed. That is why evaluations can differ widely from each other in the way they are carried out.[314] And that is why it is so difficult to see how general clauses could be objective.

A sharp distinction must be drawn between the two types of general clauses above. The second group, which refers to principles or rules outside the legal system, is identified by the judicature as a set of moral principles; for example, norms regulating social relations or public morality, which are the most popular in the Polish legal system. They can be understood in two ways: situational and normative.

Situational general clauses are understood as nothing but situational morality, which means that every act of moral choice has a creative character.[315] This idea of the creative character of morality is at complete variance with the idea of

312 Leszczyński, Tworzenie generalnych klauzul, 7–39.

313 Józef Nowacki, 'O przepisach zawierających klauzule generalne,' [About Rules Contain General Referral Clauses] in *Studia z Teorii Prawa* (Kraków: Zakamycze, 2003) 140.

314 Nowacki, 'O przepisach,' 140.

315 Nowacki, 'O przepisach,' 145.

objectivity. Every creative act is subjectively dependent and arbitrary and, in this sense, cannot be classified as objective under any strong form of objectivity.

Normative general clauses, sometimes called principles, moral norms or social norms, are understood as nothing else but normative morality, that is as an 'ethic of norms' or an 'ethic of principles.' Here, morality is understood as a set of rules or principles, as a command or interdiction formulated in a general and abstract way. This means that in a particular situation there is an obligation to act in the way the norm containing the general clauses indicates. These types of general clauses are based on the evaluation of the legal body, who will decide as a last resort instance whether the 'norm will be applied or not.'[316]

In summary, general clauses are commands for authorities applying law to make an evaluation. This characterization suggests that subjects applying law that includes general clauses are forced to make an evaluation.[317]

In light of the above, it is justified to conclude that the application of general clauses relies upon making evaluations and it cannot be free of it. But when it comes to applying general clauses in practice, it often becomes problematic to state if the evaluation has actually been made. These doubts come from many examples extracted from the Polish court rulings that refer to 'objective general clauses.' If we accept that the application of general clauses is an evaluative activity of legal subjects, the use of this expression seems hard to understand. Nevertheless, the so-called 'objectification of general clauses' is not only common in court rulings but it can also be found in jurisprudence.

Krzysztof Pietrzykowski suggests 'good faith and norms regulating social relations or public morality are by their own nature objective notions.'[318] What is more, the practice of law goes even further to formulate the objectification of general clauses.[319] This position is supported by examples extracted from case

---

316 Nowacki, 'O przepisach,' 157.

317 Nowacki, 'O przepisach,' 162.

318 Krzysztof Pietrzykowski, 'Nadużycie prawa podmiotowego w prawie cywilnym,' [Misuse of Right in Civil Law] in *Nadużycie prawa*, ed. Hubert Izdebski, Aleksander Stępkowski (Warszawa: Liber, 2003) 125; I am qouting: S. Grzybowski, 'Struktura i treść przepisów prawa cywilnego odsyłających do zasad współżycia społecznego,' [The Structure of the Civil Law Norms Reffering to Norms Regulating Social Relations] *Studia Cywilistyczne* No. 6 (1965) 48–49: 'Principles of community life are intrinsically an objective term. Regardless of this, based on Supreme Court judicial decisions and doctrine statements we may formulate several rules appointing the use of art. 5. These rules aim at further objectification of measures placed in this rule.'

319 Pietrzykowski, 'Nadużycie prawa,' 125.

law, where it is very popular to create 'objective criteria' when applying general clauses in the justification process of legal decisions. Concepts such as 'objective good faith,'[320] 'fairness in objective meaning,'[321] 'objective legal gap,'[322] 'violating

320 Judgment of the Supreme Court, 15 November 2006, I BP 12/06: 'The text of social norms is not defined. Taking into consideration that the Republic of Poland is a democratic state of law, implementing the rules of social justice (art. 2 of the Constitution of the Republic of Poland), it needs to be remembered that reference to social norms is a reference to the idea of rightness in law and to generally accepted values in the culture of our society. Generally speaking, one may assume that the social norms are the basic norms of ethics and honesty (...). Provisions of art. 5 of the Civil Code and art. 8 of the Civil Code allow for refusal to protect an entity that executes its right contradictory to the social norms or social-economic purpose of such law. Such contradiction is defined as a violation of the subjective law. The phrases used in art. 5 of the Civil Code and art. 8 of the Civil Code as undefined phrases do not reflect the nature of the violation of law, thus they refer to principles of rightness, good will in objective meaning, or to the principles of honesty binding in private law relations. That is why for the evaluation, if the claim for protection of the subjective law lodged in labour law case is not contradictory to the social norms, one may use the judicature of the Supreme Court referring to art. 5 of the Civil Code (corresponding to art. 8 of the Labour Code). Each subjective right exists within the borders marked by the text of art. 5 of the Civil Code. This provision is applicable when the conduct of the authorized person is not in conformity with the objectively understood and generally accepted moral norms, but contradicts such norms.'

321 Judgment of the Voivodeship Administrative Court in Łódź, 18 March 2008, II SA/Łd 57/08: 'The limited amount of financial means designated for social aid is a notoriously known fact. It does not, however, exempt the bodies form the duty to pursue exhaustive findings. It is not enough to just cite in the justification of the decision the provisions of the act on social aid without referring to the detailed analysis of the evidence justifying the refusal to grant the aid that has been applied for. Thus referring to the limited amount of financial means and listing who and for what purposes is granted such means in the first place, does not meet the requirements that need to be fulfilled in a justification. While explaining the refusal to grant means the body should name the amount that it has had in a given month for such aid, indicating the amount that has already been granted and for what purposes, what the situation of the person receiving aid has been, and what the average amount of the aid has been. The justification should convince the person who did not obtain the aid that the decision – even if unfavourable – is just and in conformity with law. The detailed motives of the decision should convince of its objective rightness.'

322 Judgment of the Supreme Administrative Court, 4 June 2008, II OSK 268/08: 'In case of use of fireworks in a public place the following may be applicable: art. 51 of the act of 20 May 1971 Code of Violations (Dz.U. [Journal of Laws] No 12, item 114, as amended – hereinafter referred to as 'Code of Violations'). This provision makes the

personal goods in an objective sense,'[323] 'objective pattern of reasonable victim,'[324] 'objective social interests,'[325] and 'objective special circumstances'[326] have all been used to support judges' decisions

Another phenomenon found in the court rulings is 'objective evaluation.' Court rulings refer directly to 'objective evaluation of proofs,'[327] 'objective

---

liability for violations conditional on the statement that the offender's act was a prank. Such act may be in particular the use of pyrotechnic materials and agents disrupting public peace, order, quiet hours or committing immoral act in public place. The prank resulting in a situation defined in this provision results in the liability defined in art. 51 of the Code of Violations. That is why there is no the so-called objective legal loophole necessary for issuing regulations.'

323 Resolution of the Supreme Court, 3 August 2007, I PZP 7/07.

324 Judgment of the Supreme Court [Sąd Najwyższy], 14 November 2008, II PK 88/08 emphasized that the character of Petitioner's pleadings and appeals indicated the subjectivity of her evaluations. It concluded that for claiming that a certain behaviour means mobbing one needs to create and objective pattern of reasonable victim.

325 Judgment of the Supreme Administrative Court [Naczelny Sąd Administracyjny] 31 January 2006 II OSK 475/05: 'By virtue of a judgment of 28 July 2004, case file No. II SA/Ka 1458/02 the Voivodeship Administrative Court dismissed the complaint of Zabrze Association of Traders to the decision of the Voivode of Silesia of 21 May 2002 on refusal to admit the social organization to the participation in the procedure concerning the construction permit. In justification the court stated that by virtue of the decision of 2 April 2002 the Mayor of the city of Zabrze did not admit the Zabrze Association of Traders to participate in the administrative procedure on granting construction permit for construction of 'G' Shopping centre in Zabrze. The court of I appeal found that the association should have been admitted on grounds of an objective social interest of legal nature and not only factual character.'

326 Judgment of the Supreme Administrative Court (until 31 December 2003) in Warsaw, 22 March, II SA 2169/99: 'In the court's opinion in view of the actual state of the case presented in detail in the historic part of the justification, none of the situations defined in art. 71 item 1 of the act on public procurement of 10 June 1994 takes place. The necessary construction works of the lacking facilities that were to contain technical base, i.e. laundry and kitchen of the Municipal Hospital in Y. are neither additional orders as defined in art. 71 item 1 point 1 nor unique works that can be obtained exclusively from a particular contractor (art. 71 item 1 point 3); also there are no objective, special economic or social circumstances that could not have been perceived by the ordering party and which require immediate completion of the order (art. 71 item 1 point 6) and what we deal with here is just a consequence of a faulty, wrongly organized investment process.'

327 Judgment of Voivodship Administrative Court in Łódź, 14 January 2009, I SA/Łd 899/08: 'Tax law by refraining from the obligation to precisely clarify the matter and objective evaluation of evidence, which caused to base the solution on erroneous

evaluation of the behaviour of an employee in a situation where victimization is considered,'[328] 'objective and rational evaluation is not possible without substantial justification of the evaluation,'[329] and that 'objective evaluation can be made on the basis of complete materials and a holistic view.'[330]

This is how one court defines the application of the general clause of 'justified interests': 'to recognize the interests as justifiable, it should be based on the objective evaluation of the situation and not on arguments by individuals trying to convince that they are the injured party or that they have been unfairly treated.'[331]

Elsewhere, the court says: 'if the decision of the lower court was right, the process of judging should have been done objectively,'[332] which is understood as being impartial when taking decisions.

---

factual arrangements, resulting in unsubstantiated assumption that the invoices issued in October and December by 'C' S.G. company as a subcontractor and the invoice of 29th Oct 2009 No. 2/2004 issued by a plaintiff in favour of 'B' LL were documenting the activities, which actually did not take place.'

328 Judgment of the Supreme Court, 14 November 2008, II PK 88/08: 'If an employee perceives specific behaviour as mobbing, then the acceptance of his opinion is dependent on the objective evaluation of these manifestations of behaviour in the context of revealed factual circumstances.'

329 Judgment of the Supreme Court, 22 April 2008, II UK 215/07: 'The evaluation is similarly of the dogmatic character that work was done 'for a very high remuneration.' The disadvantage of both these statements is in the first place lack of precision in defining an accepted solution basis (the circumvention of the act or contradictions with principles of community life) and its aftermath, because both premises of invalidity from art. 58 § 1 and 2 of Civil Code, referring to other legal and non-legal norms, require content-related justification of such evaluations. In connection with such relinquishment or lack of argumentation, we need to observe that the statement of the first instance is within rational and objective assessment that the applicant's remuneration did not considerably differ from remunerations she was receiving from her former employers.'

330 Judgment of the Voivodship Administrative Court in Warsaw, 4 March 2008, IV SA/Wa 1149/07: 'Only exhaustive collection and analysis of the entire evidence will allow for its objective assessment.'

331 Judgment of the Voivodship Administrative Court in Wrocław, 24 January 2008, IV SA/Wr 630/07: 'The recognition of the party's interest as appropriate should result from the objective evaluation of the situation, but not from one's own conviction based on a sense of harm, inequality or not understanding a difficult factual situation by the institution.'

332 Judgment of the Supreme Court, 1 October 2007, IV KK 232/07: '(. . .) Assessing the appropriateness of deciding by the Court of first instance, the entire evidence must be included, but not selectively some parts of evidence and circumstances resulting

In another example of the application of 'justified interests' the court says, 'Protection of the justified interests of the third persons should be based on the objective evaluation of following legal rules.'[333] In the next example, the court formulates a certain opinion about the interpretation of an advertisement and presents it as an 'objective evaluation of the average viewer of the advertisement.'[334] One can read further: 'If violation of the personal good takes place, it is

from it, preserving objective approach in assessments, and one's stand point appropriately justified in a written justification, in which elaborate considerations should be mentioned, as for the potential recognition of the act the defendant is accused of, and committed on 23 June 2004, the act of art. 190 § 1 of Penal Code against J.M, as the act co-penalized prior to the act of art. 157 § 2 of Penal Code.'

333 Judgement of the Supreme Administrative Court, 10 July 2007, II OSK 1032/06: 'The protection of justified interests of third parties, which are mentioned in the discussed regulation, should be based solely on the objective assessment of following current regulations, in particular within technical-construction requirements and projecting norms, building and maintenance of building object, in accordance with the requirements of contemporary knowledge. To assess, whether the justified interests of third parties have not been infringed, it is necessary to consider whether a given construction object meets technical-construction conditions and whether it will not cause the worsening of sanitary conditions or nuisance for the community. Meanwhile, Voivodship Administrative Court limited itself solely to quote the discussed regulations, without indicating what the alleged infringement of the interests of third parties is based on, which prevents from the instance inspection of the appeal against the judgment. It simultaneously constitutes the infringement of the regulation of art. 141 § 4 Act on proceedings before administrative courts, based on not explaining the legal basis of the decision of Voivodship Administrative Court.'

334 Judgment of the Court of Appeal in Warsaw, 4 May 2007, I ACa 668/06: 'Advertising film promoting O.M. beer is an independent piece with the meaning of the copyrights, consisting of several dramatized documentary scenes, the brief analysis of which confronted with completely different conclusion and recapitulated product advertisement. The plaintiff's motion is unauthorized, concerning the cause – by the aforementioned described fragment concerning a dancing fun with the participation of Baśka and her partner and the subsequent, after a scene in a toilet, caption 'She did not have a cool bust' – of a stream of thought associated with a song by B., personally author Robert G and his potential errors related to the female partner's physical valours, and as a result about 'interest transfer' which he aroused as a popular person on the advertised product. The court of second instance shares the standpoint that the indicated fragment of a song should be assessed as inspiration causing distant and ambiguous associations and lack of basics to assume that Robert G. recommends a product O.M. beer. In any case, the objective assessment, of an average viewer and a purchaser of the indicated products is presented in such a way. Its point of reference

not decided by the subjective evaluation of the person looking for protection, but by an objective evaluation of the reaction of the reader to certain information (in the journal).'[335] In this case, objective evaluation is ascribed to the perspective of an external viewer.

From the analysis of the above examples, there appears to be two prominent attitudes in the way general clauses are treated. On the one hand, judicial practice and legal doctrine make claims that objective criteria have to be applied on the grounds that they refer to something that is commonly accepted, or that is commonly shared, like certain values or norms of behaviour that could be confirmed from the perspective of an external viewer. On the other hand, there are very strong opinions that characterize general clauses as a direct command to make an evaluation. The most radical claims state that general clauses are objective by their own nature, but which conditions justify a legal evaluation to become objective in itself seems to be a complete mystery.

However, the above authors explain general clauses, they understand objectification as reference to moral or social norms. However, J. Nowacki shows, in all types of general clauses, we always deal with the evaluation process because they do not refer to something that is ready made. Judges choose certain criteria or values in the act of evaluation or directly evaluate themselves.

So how do we explain problems with the application of general clauses? What is it that judges do when they apply general cases in deciding cases, citing objective criteria as the basis for their decisions? When one assumes that the application of general clauses demands making an individual evaluation, the picture becomes more complicated. When certain types of values are involved, the public character of law demands the moral system employed to be revealed. Judges should justify how their decisions are reached. This is why they try to support and gain acceptance for their decisions by constructing external, objective criteria. But they also use 'objective criteria' as tools to make right decisions. What I want to find out is whether or not the process of objectification replaces evaluation. This will be done in Section 2 below, where I have selected a few examples from case law to shed more light on this problem.

---

is standpoints of unchangeable authentic valours of this drink, but not the analysis of particular anecdotes.'

335 Judgment of the Court of Appeal in Poznań, 11 January 2007, I ACa 833/06: 'The subjective assessment of a person searching for protection does not decide about infringement of personal interests, but the objective assessment of the reaction, which given information causes in a recipient.'

The next questions concern the role of objective criteria in the process of applying general clauses. Do they help to avoid responsibility for the evaluation? Do they really support the evaluation process and make it less subjective? Or are they just a kind of mystification, which creates the impression that this part in the process of applying law also relies on independent and objective constructions?

After looking closer, one could claim that the process of objectification is the outcome of the applying law rather than an independent evaluation process. The question also is, why it should be entirely independent? Not every case needs to be evaluated in an objective and non- personal way. This is particularly relevant in cases of private law.

The next argument could be based around the aim of the general clauses, especially those where the legislator puts general clauses in the legal rules because he wants a certain case to be evaluated individually but with certain values involved. Here the objective, non-personal treatment would even be against the aim of the general clauses. At very least, it seems necessary to reveal how the process of building supporting objective criteria is achieved. It seems to me that the mystery of applying general clauses lies at the point of applying objective criteria, because this is where the evaluation process is moved one stage higher simply by electing so-called objective criteria.

4.2. Some Examples from Justifications of Legal Decisions

4.2.1. General Clauses and the Objective Point of View

To provide a picture of how general clauses are applied, I introduce the following case[336]: The Court had to state whether the norms regulating social relations had been violated in a case where the plaintiff claimed that the defendant, an undertaker, conducted a funeral ceremony in an inappropriate way. The defendant claims that the undertaker wanted it to finish quickly so that he could attend to the other business. As a consequence, not all the mourners were able to pay their last respects. The Court had to establish whether or not the general clauses of public morality were violated. To evaluate this case, the Court sought public opinion to represent an objective point of view. The Court asked other people attending the funeral if they also felt that a violation of good standards of behaviour had occurred. However, the opinions of the other mourners were not taken into account in their final evaluation. The Court's justification claimed that the mourners' points of view were subjective, because they were mainly the members

336 Judgment of the Supreme Court, 23 October 2003, VCK 311/02, LEX no 82272.

of the plaintiff's family. From this ruling, we can see that the Court considered that the opinion needed to come from an independent, external viewer or impartial observer in order to be objective. Alternatively, the defendant would have to agree with the plaintiff's point of view – in which case, the view accepted by both parties represents the objective position. It would appear that the assessment was made from the formal point of view concerning the source of the opinions and did not take into account the content of such opinions.

The important question in this case is how the guarantee of an objective point of view could be built on an opinion regarding the feelings of others who are not in the same emotional state as the plaintiff? It would be quite reasonable for an independent observer, say, to have no particular feelings about the funeral precisely for the reason that they had no personal interest. In this case it seems that the special emotional situation of the plaintiff needed to be taken into account, as it is unlikely that anybody else could feel the same as someone who lost a close member of his family. This situation didn't need objectification at all and highlights the weakness in trying to apply objectivity in universal way. To quote from Judge Barak, 'the objectification may weaken the human element in the decision.'[337]

This example also shows the power of using the adjective 'objective.' Opinions or evaluations described as subjective are eliminated from legal discourse even when they seem quite reasonable. This means that, in legal discourse, personal and, in this sense subjective, opinion should be deferential to objective opinions. But to counter this, the creation of an objective opinion's status should be transparent, clear and justified. The importance of this process is justified because the objective opinion is automatically accepted, taken as valid, treated as the last argument, and is no longer disputable.

To come back to the examined case, it is worth commenting on the final decision of the Court. The objectification of general clauses of public norms helped in building argumentations against the violation of public norms. In this case, it meant that the plaintiff's claims were rejected.

In another very similar situation, the Court stated, 'The plaintiff argue that somebody's action does not have legal consequences if no legal norms have been violated but only moral ones. However, such positions could be at best be qualified as a subjective understanding of moral norms, which have no meaning with regard to objective legal evaluation.'[338]

---

337 Aharon Barak, *Judicial Discretion* (New Haven and London: Yale University Press, 1989) 129.

338 Judgment of the Supreme Court, 26 September 2002, III CKN 213/01.

In the above quote, the Court's position seems to present an objective process of decoding objective moral norms, which is only possible for the Court to do from a legal position. The Court made reference to morality understood objectively, which could be the manifestation of normatively interpreted morality based on certain norms or rules, which are the consequences of access to a certain type of morality.[339] This position, when one explains its roots, could be accepted as justified, but nevertheless it is highly controversial on the map of epistemological and ethical positions. Comments on the impossibility and idealistic character of such a perception of morality and the process of its cognition were presented in Chapter 1.

The legal decision above could be said to belong to a group of justifications where the position of the plaintiff was disqualified on the grounds that it is only a subjective position. Following this style of thinking, arguments from either party could always be said to have a subjective character because they have the aim of protecting or forwarding their own position. What seems sure in this context is that when the Court names its own interpretation 'objective' this immediately makes their decision stronger and gives it authority.

In another decision, the Polish Supreme Administrative Court states that, 'norms regulating social relations are an objective measure of evaluation.'[340]

4.3. General Clause as Individual Measures

I will introduce just a few examples of general clauses that offer contradictory explanations to those presented above. In this group are the general clauses that relate to making individual judgments and evaluations. For example, I have presented the notion of objective meaning, but one can find also 'good faith in subjective meaning.'[341]

Below are just a few of many examples illustrating contradictory interpretations of general clauses relating to individuals making judgments and evaluations.

In this example, I use the Court's own words, 'general clauses have to be applied individually according to circumstances of each single case; the court evaluates concrete situations and, through this, judicial discretion is exercised.'

In the literature, this kind of approach is known as 'general clauses in situational meaning.'

339 Nowacki, 'O przepisach,' 153.

340 Judgment of the Supreme Court, 1 April 2004, II CK 130/03.

341 Judgment of the Supreme Court, 6 April 2000, III RN 150/99.

To quote the Court again: 'When a legislator places general clauses in legal rules, it means that he entrusts the final evaluation to the Court and it is obvious that this evaluation should be made using appropriate criteria. At the same time, the evaluation remains particular to the concrete circumstances because it will be the based for the final decision of the Court. Jurisprudential literature rightly stresses that the notion of 'good standards' or principles of norms regulating social relations are filled up with different contents in each particular concrete situation (. . .).'[342] This example shows that objective criteria are used, but as a kind of form, which indicates only the frame of what has to be fulfilled. But still, what is 'objective' in applying general clauses?

In one justification, the Polish Constitutional Tribunal says, 'The notion of 'unfair benefit' is an abstract notion and a vague term. This element makes it impossible to objectively evaluate the criterion, which is the basis of the claim. It also makes the control decision-making process impossible.'[343]

---

342 Judgment of the Supreme Court, 26 September 2002, III CKN 213/01.

343 Judgment of the Constitutional Tribunal, 8 July 2008, P 36/07. The litigated regulation also causes – according to court – doubts concerning the compatibility with the rule of reliable legislation, resulting from art. 2 of the Constitution. The term 'unjustified benefit' occurring in the content of this article is a general and underspecified notion, which excludes the possibility of the objective assessment of criteria, underlying a claim, as well as the inspection of the decision by judging institutions based on its content (. . .) The clauses contain the element of individualized assessment of current state, while the burden of formulating the assessment *ad casum* and the appropriate legal results for its definition are ceded by the legislator on court or other institution applying the law. This pragmatic feature of general clauses is connected with their semantic property, based on under specificities of expressions used in their content (S. Grzybowski, Struktura i treść przepisów prawa cywilnego odsyłających do zasad współżycia społecznego, 'Studia Cywilistyczne' 1965, Vol. XXXII, 32–33). The general clauses serve to make legal regulations more flexible, they prevent from their 'overlegalization' (see judgments of the Constitutional Tribunal, 7 December 1999, file No. K. 6/99, the Opinion of the Constitutional Tribunal ZU No. 7/1999, item 160; 17 October 2000, file No. SK 5/99, the Opinion of the Constitutional Tribunal ZU No. 7/2000, item 254) and they facilitate the application of law in the way comprising the special circumstances of a given case. Due to that the Constitutional Tribunal takes the view that the use of the general clauses by a legislator meet the conditions of appropriate enacting of law in a legal state (compare a decision of 7 June 1994, signature K. 17/93, the Opinion of the Constitutional Tribunal in 1994, item 11 and the aforementioned judgment of signature SK 5/99). The charge of infringement of the rule of good definiteness of law may be regarded as justified only when if it was impossible to assign the expression used in the general clause the content corresponding to the Constitution or also if there was a consolidated jurisdiction approach,

The Tribunal continues, 'General clauses contain individual evaluations and the burden of formulation of these evaluations is in the hands of the courts, according to the will of the legislator. This pragmatic feature of general clauses is combined with their semantic vagueness.'

These arguments favour the thesis that general clauses cannot be characterized as objective. However, in a further part of their justification, the Tribunal looks for any other previous usages of 'unfair benefit' in order to 'find a meaning.' The Tribunal looked for a prior meaning which has been used in legal practice as an established judgment practice, as meanings used in the rulings of other courts. In this case, the court says that it is impossible to find objective criteria to carry out the evaluation, but it still looks for other firm meanings established by legal practice or earlier cases. The latter could then be used as a pattern (see Section C below) to determine points of reference from which they could create objective criteria.

4.4. Models and Patterns of Behaviour as an Objectification Process

Another 'objective' context is when the court chooses to make an evaluation using objective models or patterns of behaviour.

In all these situations, in which evaluations have to be made and in order to make this possible, the court creates 'objective criteria.' Objective criteria are treated as patterns, which can indicate what is good or bad in particular situations. They are a kind of measure, which enables the court to determine an individual situation in relation to the general pattern. In most cases, such patterns are created specifically for the needs of a particular concrete situation and according to the circumstances of the case. Consequently, the final effect is dependent on what kind of pattern is chosen. The pattern will be called 'objective' and 'external' and it will be the point of reference for the court's decision. As you

---

conferring this expression a non-constitutional meaning (compare the judgment of the Constitutional Tribunal of 19 Feb 2008, signature P 48/06, the Opinion of the Constitutional Tribunal ZU No. 1/A/2008, item 4). Considering the charge formulated in such a way, the Tribunal decided to analyse whether the clause of 'unjustified benefit' has meaning grounded in the practice of enforcing law and if this clause is given the content in accordance with the Constitution. Only the establishment that there is a fixed jurisdiction approach giving this expression the non-constitutional meaning will necessitate the opinion about the incorrectness of art. 1 item 1 of the act of 21 June 1990 with art. 2 of the Constitution.

can see, again the situation is not free of individual choice or free of evaluation, because the chosen criteria will decide whether a situation pertaining to a certain case will be treated positively or negatively.

In practice, the Court's reasoning looks as follows: where an evaluation is necessary, an objective model is created according to certain rules. A model is built keeping in mind the concrete situation to be evaluated. The main aim is in making a comparison between the concrete situation and an already built objective model. What is in accordance with the model is correct or objective, what does not follow the model is classed as a subjective behaviour or action.

Examples of such models extracted from decisions of the Polish courts include: 'objective diligent recipient,'[344] 'objective measure of care,'[345] 'objective pattern of proper care,'[346] 'what is the objective cruelty/abuse measure of an average victim,'[347] 'evaluative norms about objective character working in a morally healthy part of society,'[348] and the well-known construction of 'reasonable person' in tort law. Here, the Court directly says, 'a pattern of proper diligence has an objective character. Its legal usage in practice is based on the choosing the model that sets out the optimal way of acting in a socially accepted way in certain situations and then this is compared with the concrete behaviour of the person in question.'[349] All references to an established judgment practice are treated in

344 Resolution of the Supreme Court, 11 October 2001, I KZP 23/01.

345 Judgment of the Supreme Court, 8 January 2008, I UK 172/07.

346 Judgment of the Supreme Court, 11 December 2003, II CK 315/02.

347 Judgment of the Supreme Court, 11th Feb 2003, IV KKN 312/99: '(. . .) The essence of crime of cruelty is based on qualitatively different behaviour of a perpetrator than on ordinary insult or violation of bodily integrity of the harmed person. The objective assessment should be decisive in case of approval of 'cruelty' as behaviour causing mental suffering of a victim, not just in a subjective perception of a victim. Cruelty cannot be regarded as perpetrator's behaviour which does not cause any serious moral suffering for the victim nor in a situation when there is a mutual 'cruelty' between the accused person and the harmed person.'

348 Judgment of the Supreme Court, 20 July 2000, I PKN 737/99, OSNP 2002/43.

349 Judgment of Supreme Court, 23 October 2003, V CK 311/02. The provision of art. 355 § 1 of the Civil Code obliges the debtor to fulfil an obligation with appropriate care, namely such care generally required in the relations of a given kind. The pattern of appropriate care has an objective character. Its practical application is firstly based on selecting a model, establishing an optimal modus operandi in given conditions, appropriately specified and socially approved, and subsequently on the comparison on the debtor's behaviour with such behavioural pattern. Not only does the incompatibility of the debtor's behaviour with a model decide about the fact that based on specific circumstances an obliged person may be charged with lack of appropriate care

a similar way and described as 'objective,' for example: 'objective indication,'[350] 'objective criteria,'[351] etc.

4.5. The Concept of 'Reasonable Person'

> 'When the judge describes a reasonable person, in most cases he is thinking of himself.
> Yet nothing could be further from the truth'[352]

The concept of reasonable person is broadly commented in jurisprudential literature. I would like to introduce the concept with some statements from international law and the Polish Court rulings. Finally, I will make a comparison with the construction of 'reasonable person' in the common law tradition.

---

in fulfilling obligations, but also possibility and duty conditioned by life experience to predict relevant consequence of behaviour. The measure of the debtor's behaviour, the essence of which underlies in abandonment of appropriate care, cannot be formulated at the level of obligations impossible to be enforced, separated from experiences and specific circumstances.

350 Judgment of the Constitutional Tribunal, 7 February 2005, SK 49/03: '(. . .) This what is commonly defined as a facultative character of deciding about a financial compensation approved on the basis of art. 448 of the Civil Code – within a scope analyses in a complaint – does not assume court arbitration in the process of deciding about its adjudication. The opinion was approved in the judicial decisions of Supreme Court that while deciding about a form of compensation, an adjudicating court cannot proceed deliberately, but it is supposed to be guided by the objective indications – compare judgment of Supreme Court of 23 May 2002, signature IV CKN 1076/00, OSNC No. 9/2003, item 121). The judicial decisions based on art. 445 of the Civil Code established the criteria accepted in doctrine, which should be included by court, while judging about the justification of the decision on a financial compensation for detriment resulting from violation of personal interests indicated there (compare G. Bieniek, Komentarz do kodeksu cywilnego. Księga trzecia. Zobowiązania, volume 1, ed. G. Bieniek Warszawa 1999, 410–413), A. Szpunar, Zadośćuczynienie za szkodę niemajątkową, Bydgoszcz 1999, 81–82 and 215). These rules apply to the decision of such compensation in the situation indicated in the questionable provision. The decision whether in a specific case the adjudication of a financial compensation will be an appropriate form of compensation for harm experienced by a victim, belongs to court obligations. After deciding, however, about this issue in a positive way for a victim, court is obliged to adjudicate an appropriate amount of money.'

351 Judgment of the Voivodeship Administrative Court in Szczecin, 23 April 2009, I SA/Sz 104/09.

352 Barak, *Judicial Discretion* 125.

4.5.1. Reasonable Person in International Law

It is clear from the outset that the intensity of the concept of reasonable person differs considerably from one clause to another in different legal systems.

The concept of 'reasonable person' is sometimes directly identified with objective criteria. We can find this in civil law literature, not only in Polish law, but also in international law.[353] One of the most common contexts where this construction is used is in the interpretation of contracts. The construction of 'reasonable person' is used in all situations where any kind of lacuna appears. To show some examples, the construction of 'reasonable person' appears in the following legal acts:

- United Nations Conventions on Contracts for the International Sale of Goods (Vienna, 1980);
- Principles of European Contract Law – Parts I and II revised 1998 (Parts I and II revised 1998, Part III 2002);
- Unidroit Principles of International Commercial Contracts (Rome, 1994, 2004, 2010, 2016).

The Principles of International Commercial Contracts (UNIDROIT) deal with 'reasonableness' in the interpretation of statements and the conduct of parties making contracts. The construction of reasonable person is helpful when there is a problem with stating the common intentions of both parties. When such a problem arises, the meaning is ascribed according to the model of a reasonable person, which is based on the predictability of behaviour in certain circumstances.[354] Under the interpretation of intentions of parties making a

353 Article 8 of United Nations Conventions on Contracts for the International Sale of Goods, or the so-called Vienna Convention [1980], says about category of reasonableness; art. 1:302 and art. 5:101 par. 3. of Principles of European Contract Law; art. 4.1. and 4.2. of Principles of International Commercial Contracts UNIDROIT both from 1994 and 2004.

354 Principles of International Commercial Contracts UNIDROIT, art. 4.1. 'A contract shall be interpreted according to the common intention of the parties. 2. If such an intention cannot be established, the contract should be interpreted according to the meaning that reasonable persons of the same kinds as the parties would give it t it in the same circumstances.' art. 4.2. 'The statements and other conduct of a party should be interpreted according to that party's intention if the other party knew or could have not been unaware of that intention. 2. If the preceding paragraph is not applicable, such statements and other conduct should be interpreted according to the meaning that a reasonable person of the same kind as the other party would give to it in the same circumstances.'

contract, UNIDROIT says that the parties have to reach a common intention as the first step in the process of interpretation. However, as one author has stressed, in the situation of conflicts, which is generally when interpretation is needed, it is not possible to find out the common intention of both parties. They have a different, mostly opposite, views on how the meaning should be interpreted. If it were possible to set the common meaning, they would not come to Court and could reach agreement by themselves.[355] So, we can assert that in the situations of conflicts, establishing common intention is difficult, if not impossible, and other tools are needed in stating the intentions of the parties.

The line of interpretation of the contract in an objective way offered by UNIDROIT stresses that both the statements drawn from the contract and the conduct of the parties are interpreted in connection with the intention of parties. The most significant question to answer is why is this type of contract interpretation named as 'objective,' on which criteria and on what basis? Why do objective interpretations have been done when it refers to the intentions of the authors of the contract? Answering these questions is important because of the different points of view represented by other legal systems. UNIDROIT prescribes the status of objective to the interpretation based on the intention of author; most Polish court rulings seem to have the opposite view, but they still call it objective.

4.5.2. The Polish Example

Interpretation of contracts is one specific part of the problem of interpretation generally. The specific character lies mainly in that the parties that negotiated the contract were at the same time the authors and subjects of interpretations. Let us have a closer look at some examples extracted from the Polish Court's jurisprudence and the Polish legal doctrine to make this point clearer. The terminology of objective interpretation appears there very often and the approach to building definitions could be decoded on the basis of following quotations.

The picture given by judges is that, 'the objective interpretation of contracts shows the real sense, the meaning of the contract, which it is necessary to grasp when doubts of interpretation have appeared.'[356] The aim of objective interpretation is clearly indicated but it gives no real information of' what constitutes objective interpretation.

---

355 Ewa Łętowska, *System Prawa Prywatnego* [Private Law System] Vol. 5 (Warszawa: C. H. Beck, 2006) 25.

356 Judgment of the Supreme Court, 9 November 2001, III RN 145/00, OSNP 2002/19/450.

The next quote says, 'that objective interpretation is going to reconstruct the content of the contract on the basis of a linguistic examination.'[357] Here the burden lays on the method of interpretation, which must guarantee the objective effects. It means that the interpretation should be based on the words used in the contract, and not on the authors' intention nor on the interpreter of the contract. How is it possible to make an interpretation based on the literary meaning 'objective'? This question could be answered by the doctrine of textualism.

The position held by textualists is that judges should consider only the public meaning (the ordinary meaning of the language) of the statutory text. This is opposite the intentionalist approach to the process of interpretation. A very rough characterization of textualism says they 'look at the statutory structure and hear the words as they would sound to the mind of a skilled, objectively reasonable user of words.'[358] However, one has also to consider criticism against the possibility of textualism[359], especially the possibility of its 'objective' status. Many authors stress that interpretation always refers to the supposed intention of the legislator.[360] Three main arguments support this thesis:

- The analytical argument from the notion of literal meaning.[361]
- The view stressed by linguists, who argue that differences in sentence meaning, utterance meaning and simple meaning simply do not exist. That is, sentence meaning as a combination of the meaning of the expression and certain syntax rules of the sentence without any contextualization is a complete fallacy in language.
- The argument from court rulings, when court explicitly states that the literal interpretation is not enough to set the meaning, and that the intention of the legislator, the aim of the statute must be taken into account.[362]

---

357 Ibid.

358 Frank H. Easterbrook, 'The Role of Original Intent in Statutory Construction,' 11 Harvard Journal of Law and Public Policy Vol. 59 (1988) 65.

359 Lawrence M. Solan, 'Learning Our Limits: The Decline of Textualism in Statutory Cases,' Wisconsin Law Review (1997) 2; William N. Eskridge Jr. and Philip J. Frickey, 'Statutory Interpretation as Practical Reasoning' Stanford Law Review (1990).

360 Stanley Fish, 'There is No Textual Position,' *San Diego Law Review* Vol. 42 (2005) 629.

361 Zygmunt Tobor, 'Iluzja wykładni literalnej,' in *Konstytucyjne uwarunkowania tworzenia i stosowania prawa finansowego i podatkowego* (Białystok: Temida 2, 2010) 194–201.

362 Resolution of Supreme Administrative Court, 20 March 2000, FSP 14/99, ONSA 2000/3/92: '(...) The linguistic interpretation cannot be constrained to search for a sense of particular words – to have a philological nature – but it should search for a genuine sense of particular sentences (their sets), which requires its combination with

An additional argument comes from examining the rulings of Justice Scalia, a key follower of the textual approach to interpretation. Analysis of his rulings clearly shows that an interpretation has an intentional character.[363]

That is why it is justified to say that the textualists' position could be approached in two ways: as a method of setting or understanding meaning, or as a method of setting intentional meaning. In the light of the introduced argument, it is very controversial to link textualism with objectivity and, though very common practice in court decisions, is entirely based on myth.

Another court ruling says 'objective interpretation is based not only on what comes out at the linguistic level but on grasping the contract's real meaning.'[364] This quote shows that the Polish approach is not coherent. This quotation does not represent the line of arguments that statutory interpretation has an objective character but goes behind it. To read further:

> Expressed in the quoted legal regulation, rules of interpretation are centred around two respected civil law values. On the one hand, there is the intention of the party taking legal action; on the other is the trust that is put in the parties as receivers of the contract. In relating to these values, the legal doctrine distinguishes between the subjective method of interpretation, which is focused on the intention and the will of the party which is making declaration, and the objective (normative) method, which accepts the point of view of the addressee.[365]
>
> So, the prevailing values are the protection of the trust of the addressee of the contract over the intentions and purpose of the author. Such an understanding of objective interpretation favours the certainty of legal relations and leads to the certainty of conduct in legal transactions.[366]

The Doctrine of Polish Civil Law further adds that the application of the model of reasonableness according to the addressee's interpretation is built with respect to the reasonable expectation and trust of the third person. Through this, the primary values of the interpretation of contracts are protected. This pattern should

---

a purpose of law regulations. The employer defines by words what he/she intends to achieve.'

363 Miranda MacGowan, 'Do as I do, not as I say: An Empirical Investigation of Justice Scalia's Ordinary Meaning Method of Statutory Interpretation,' *Mississippi Law Journal* Vol. 78 (2008) 129, Quote from Tobor, Iluzja wykładni literalnej, 4.

364 Judgment of the Supreme Court, 9 November 2001, III RN 145/00, OSNP 2002/19450.

365 Resolution of the Supreme Court, 29 June 1995, III CZP 66/95.

366 Ewa Rott-Pietrzyk, 'Wzorzec rozsądnej osoby jako kryterium wykładni oświadczenia woli,' [The pattern of reasonable person as a criterion of declaration of the interpretation of will] in *Studia z wykładni prawa*, ed. Czesław Martysz and Zygmunt Tobor (Katowice: Branta, 2008) 79.

also be built in relation to the specific situation of the recipient's expression of the will *in concreto.*[367]

Here we have three different explanations observed from the Polish Court rulings of how the concept of reasonable person is applied in reference to objective standards. One refers to the intention of the authors, one to the text, and one to the perspective of external viewer.

Summing up, an attempt of setting an objective interpretation (finding its real sense or meaning) of an expression of will is based on two elements: the literal meaning and the reading or decoding of the will from the point of view of receiver. These elements should support the value of assurance and confidence, also called the Principle of Trust. Realization of these values is very often at the core of argumentation in all evaluative cases.

It is also important to stress that, besides the objective method of interpretation, Polish legal doctrine also identifies a subjective and a combined method of interpreting contracts. The subjective method is focused on the will of the contracting parties, no matter how many contracting parties are involved. The combined method of interpretation joins both subjective and objective perspectives.[368]

This short typology has been introduced in order to make the comparison with objective methods used in other European legal systems.

4.5.3. English, German, and French Examples

Cultural diversity produces differences in many legal situations, caused by different underlying conceptions. An attempt of making comparison is possible under the condition that compared notions are understood in a similar way. In relation to objective and subjective interpretations of contracts, problems appear at the level of different understandings of these terms. The expressions 'objective interpretation' and 'objective approach to interpretation' are often understood differently.

The starting point in my analysis of the interpretation of contracts is the terminological assertion that 'the objective approach to interpretation is based on the meaning which appears from the text of the contract.'[369] This is the position

367 Rott-Pietrzyk, 'Wzorzec rozsądnej,' 77.

368 Rott-Pietrzyk, 'Wzorzec rozsądnej,' 76.

369 Annuck De Boeck and Mark Van Hoecke, 'The Interpretation of Standards clauses in European Contract Law,' in *Standard Contract Terms in Europe: A Basis for and a Challenge to European Contract Law*, ed. Hugh Collins (Wolters Kluwer,

represented by English Law. In contrast, the French style of interpreting contracts is focused on the will of the contracting parties and such a position is called as subjective. The German position is situated between French subjective and English objective approach. German contract law incorporates an 'objectified subjective approach'[370] and according to this 'the meaning is what a reasonable outsider would assume it to have been meant.'[371]

To make this topic clear, I have refrained from using terminology and categorization according to the objective-subjective pattern. It would be more clear to name French position as 'will-approach.' In the same category it is possible to place the position represented by UNIDROIT, which is also will-oriented but it fills the model of reasonableness by referring to objective criteria. This comparison shows how the terminology changes from the status of description to the level of prescription. This example proves we can no longer trust the descriptive character of 'objective terminology' because it has started to be values oriented but still with the strong presuppositions about neutrality or the rightness of the position taken. The 'objective' character is linked with 'will-oriented, text-oriented, and recipient-oriented methods of interpretation,' as well.

What is revealed through the above examples (French, English, German, Polish and those taken from International law) is that the character of the 'reasonable person' is not clear. This construction has the aim of being applied with reference to certain objective standards, but what is happening here is that objectification goes in contradictory directions. One is filled by the will of the contracting parties (UNIDROIT), one is found in the third-person, outsider's perspective (German law), one realizes it through the meaning of the text (English), and the last, Polish, example refers to the recipient's interpretation to protect values of predictability. All these examples are called 'objective' method of interpretation.

4.5.4. Common Law Tradition

To show an example extracted from common law tradition, it is worth recalling the concept of 'reasonable care under the circumstances.' This concept is based

2008) 209–219. Read more: Hein Kotz and Axel Flessner, *European Contract Law* (Oxford: Clarendon Press, 1997) 107–109.

370 See more, Mark Van Hoecke, 'Deep Level Comparative Law,' in *Epistemology and Methodology of Comparative Law*, ed. Mark Van Hoecke (Oxford and Portland, Oregon: Hart Publishing, 2004) 165 ff.

371 De Boeck and Van Hoecke, 'The Interpretation of Standards clauses,' 211.

on the ordinary reasonable person as a fictional entity, the so-called 'every person' or non-person.'[372] As one tort scholar wrote:

> he is not to be identified with any ordinary individual... Nor is it proper to identify him even with any member of the very jury who are to apply the standard... it is sometimes difficult to escape the conviction that the refinements which have been developed in instructing the jury on the application of personal standards are artificial and unreal, and quite beyond the comprehension of the average man in the box. The only possible justification lies in a basis of experience justifying considerable uneasiness about what any jury may conceivably do, which has led to an excess of precaution in the effort to give them proper guidance.[373]

Michael Johnson interprets this concept as follows: actually the defendant is required, to serve as an objective ordinary reasonable communicator of a warning or direction and the plaintiff is required to be an objective ordinary recipient of the warning. What this author finds interesting is that so-called objective standard of conduct matches up rather nicely with the outside observer or third person view of the communication process.[374] Firstly, this point of view presents the abstract idea of 'reasonable person,' which is very questionable when applied in practice simply because, once applied, abstract models lose their abstract character and involve values. Secondly, the perspective of an observer as the right position for a reasonable construction is also not value free. It only means that this third person applies different values, which I will later explain.

There are also opinions in jurisprudential literature presenting the construct of a 'reasonable person' as a probabilistic construction. Michael Johnson, wanting to make this definition more precise, argues, 'the concept of an ordinary reasonable person maps onto probabilistic thinking in a way that makes the data statistically relevant to the evidentiary concerns of the courts in product liability cases.'[375] So how could this problem be solved in the context of probabilistic nature of language? Because, language is commonly perceived as an intersubjective medium of communication, that is why we expect some common pattern to be available and understandable by a third person. This author suggests that the language expert is taking the third–person position, the position of the outsider. He claims that the term 'probable enough' refers to the absolute probability that

---

372 Micheal G. Johnson, 'Language and Cognition in Products Liability,' *Language in the Judicial Process* (1990) 300–301.

373 William L. Prosser, *Handbook of the Law of Torts*, 4th ed. (St. Paul: West Pub. Co, 1971) 150.

374 Johnson, 'Language and Cognition,' 301.

375 Johnson, 'Language and Cognition,' 302.

the intended interpretation will be comprehended by the recipient and to the relative probability that it will be understood within the interpretative community overall.[376] This explanation raises some doubts. The linguistic expert as the person from outside also makes an interpretation in a certain context and with a certain aim. He or she takes a certain point of view. That is why his or her exact position should be revealed. What kinds of values are assessed? And how is such third-person perspective identified with an objective position? Because of lack of any interests in the contract other than a linguistic one?

4.5.5. The Notions of Objectivity in Interpretation of Contracts: a Summary

In light of the practical usage, one can ask what does 'objectivity' actually mean? What is its goal? As mentioned before, as to objective interpretation identified with the pattern of the reasonable person, the meaning of objectivity is based on one the following solutions:

- the common will of contracting parties
- the interpretation of the receiver, the interpreter
- the linguistic content, what the text says,
- The third-person perspective, how an outsider would perceive it.

It could be argued that the differences present in different legal systems could be the consequence of different meanings of objectivity. So, it is necessary to make explicit what one wanted to reach by employing and applying the objective standards in the process of interpretation. What is its goal? I would like to analyse this by comparing examples from international law and Polish law. Let us start by considering both examples.

Both approaches agree that objective interpretation takes place when the values of predictability and certainty are realized, and this is considered to be its goal. The instructions proposed by UNIDROIT, to stress one more time, say that objective interpretation takes place when we interpret a contract, by which it means the statements in the contract and the conduct of the parties with reference to the intentions of its authors. The Polish legal doctrine says that objective interpretation is realized through reference to the subject(s) receiving the message, namely the person to whom this act of will /contract is dedicated to. The core difference is that one is from the point of view of author, the other is from the point of view of recipient, but both are called 'objective.'

376 Johnson, 'Language and Cognition,' 304.

This comparison allows us to draw the conclusion that two opposite tendencies are called 'objective.' Two different sentences cannot both be true at the same time, but maybe they can both be objective? It all depends on what we mean by objective. The examples we have looked at show how hard it is to grasp its meaning in an unambiguous way, but for sure it is not identified with truth.

An additional possible solution is that both options may be objective in a weak sense. The ambiguous character of objectivity allows for such a broad interpretation that both opposite tendencies can be called 'objective;' both protect the value of certainty and predictability, but in relation to different points of view. Certainty would be protected if contracting parties have the protection of their original will. On the other hand, it is also possible to argue that certainty and security are based on the common understanding of all participants in the conduct of legal transactions, thus making the third-person perspective an 'objective' viewpoint.

Taking a different point of view, we could deliver another argument. Let us look at the problem in terms of realizing values. Both examples realize the value of certainty and predictability, but one does this from the author's point of view the other from the recipient's point of view. We can infer from this that certainty and predictability cannot be realized in an absolute way, but must be reached with regard to relative interests. Such an answer confirms the assertion that the values of the legal system are not universal. This point meets Barak's reflections about reasonable person. These two ways are crossing here. Delivering examples that show different approaches to the same concepts of notion is the evident proof that the process of interpretation is the process of concretization in relation to different values. So, the application of the concept of reasonable person will look completely different in relation to which values are realized. So, Barak's conception of universalization or generalization using the concept of reasonable person has sense only when the values applied to this process are revealed. So, as we can see, the discussion has moved on to the level of values. So, the question that could deliver some final explanation is about the status of values. In the light of the above, the guarantee that a certain point of view is objective is only possible to accept with proper justification and by revealing the points of reference.

The above explanation has not delivered any arguments for taking an objective position in the interpretation process and presents very doubtful arguments on the nature of objective interpretation. Taking for granted that the interpretation would be value free in order to fulfil the conditions of objectivity is just the realization of a legal myth.

The conclusion so far is that objectivity as a universal concept does not work in practice. The way objectivity is used in law does not fulfil the function of common validity, but it is related to certain points of reference. We faced a similar situation when we looked at the relation between objectivity and truth (Chapter 1.). In spite of strong connotations, practical usage has shown that these two notions cannot be identified with each other.

4.5.6. Reasonable Person or Reasonable Man?

In order to give a flavour of the complexity of the problems concerning the 'reasonable person' concept, I will briefly describe the perspective given by the feminist movement. Feminist legal theorists[377] point out that behind the terminology of 'reasonable person,' very often the perspective of 'reasonable man' is assessed.[378]

Feminists in jurisprudential literature stress that the 'reasonable person' test in tort law assumes that there is only one view in society as to what should be classified as 'reasonable behaviour.' The problem arises in situations when reasonable behaviour differs according whether one is a man or women. It is especially visible in cases of sexual harassment. Women may feel threatened by a men's sexual comments, whereas the men may have not intended to be threatening. With regards to these kinds of cases where there is no universal standard of behaviour then the 'reasonable person' test is impossible to apply. There are two reasonable perspectives: men's and women's.

Furthermore, both the feminist movement and the Critical Legal Study movement point out that the vast majority of judges are men, and this is why the 'reasonable man' perspective prevails in judge's view.

These arguments further add to the controversial status of the 'reasonable person' test as an 'objective' and 'universal measure' in the process of application of law. As feminists rightly stress, even on the level of language expressed through legal terminology, the so-called objective perspective imposes a particular point of view as valid for everyone, creating a hidden element of violence against those who do not conform to the norm.

---

377 See more, Drucilla Cornell, *Imaginary Domain: Abortion, Pornography and Sexual Harassment* (New York & London: Routlege, 1995); Katharine T. Bartlett and Rosanne Kennedy, *Feminist legal theory: readings in law and gender* (Boulder: Westview Press, 1991); Patricia Smith, ed., *Feminist jurisprudence* (New York: Oxford University Press, 1993).

378 M. Chamallas, *Application Feminist Legal Theory to Women's Lives. Sex, Violence, Work and Reproductions* (Temple University Press, 1996) 810.

4.6. The Observed Aim of 'Objective' General Clauses

It is important to explain the most common aims when employing the terminology of 'objective judgments.'

(1) The adjective 'objective' is used as the guarantee of eliminating the arbitrary character in judgments. When the evaluation is objective, it means that it is not the result of an individual judgment. It is not subjective or, at least, other people will share the same subjective point of view.
(2) It is used as a reference by the jurisprudence of the court. It represents a traditional pattern that has been present since a certain time in case law and embodies the opinions shared by the majority of the community. This may explain why 'objective' is used as a feature of judgments but it does not provide a proper justification. It still leaves unanswered the question of what does 'objectivity' actually mean? Does the jurisprudence of the court really embody certain tendencies present in the community? When is it justified to talk about such tendencies? References to the tradition of interpretation and patterns of legal behaviour are certainly very practical and successful ways of making argumentation stronger. It represents a group of arguments based on the authority of the majority in which the court's point of view has to be taken into account because it is part of the legal reality. But, as suggested by many examples, there are opposite tendencies in case law and there does not appear to be a single completely dominant view. The extracts from the Polish court rulings concerning the general clause of reasonable person clearly demonstrate this.

4.7. From the Judges' Point of View

To change perspective, it is worth looking at how judges present their own way of thinking. Judge Barak has some interesting things to say on the matter. On the one hand, A. Barak has stressed the necessity of objectification, but he also points out its weaknesses and even the impossibility of reaching this position. The objective test is based on reasonableness, which has to be determined at the judges' discretion. But on the other hand, as Barak stresses, 'when the judge describes a reasonable person, in most cases he is thinking of himself. Yet nothing could be further from the truth.'[379] If we accept that it is impossible to be free of an

379 Barak, *Judicial Discretion*, 125.

individual perspective, what is presented as an objective or rational standpoint is the judge's process of rationalization when exercising judicial discretion.

What is the real role of rationalization? And what is the difference between objectification and rationalization, if any? Could the process of rationalization be treated as the process of translating or transforming what is subjective into what is objective? The important accent is between translating and transforming. Is it enough to call something objective by making it open to public view and giving it an explanation and a justification? It seems that, in many cases of applying general clauses or generally examined judicial discretion, the objectification process is just the description of how it was done.

This objectification in practical terms brings the necessity of transformation from subjective to objective, from personal or individual to common. So, the process of application of general clauses is more like a process of transformation than translation.

So how do judges reach an objective position? 'For the principle of the rule of law, the judge takes a distance himself, as far as possible, from giving preferences to his personal views over what justice demands.'[380] This quotation shows how important it is to make efforts not to be subjective but, as Barak himself indicates, this is still not objectivity. As Justice Frankfurter claims, 'To practice the requisite detachment and to achieve sufficient objectivity no doubt demands of judges the habit of self-discipline and self-criticism, incertitude that one's own view are incontestable, and alert tolerance toward views not shared.'[381] This opinion brings some new light to the problem and a new perspective on understanding objectivity in the context of discretion. What kind of objectivity are we discussing here? Is objectivity not just imposing a subjective view? And if it is possible to eliminate the translation from the subjective position into the objective reasonable view, does it mean that we need the view from outside? Or maybe we need empathy, not objectivity, in the judge's discretion? Maybe it is necessary to consider the subjective situation in a broader context? It would mean judges have to be open and not necessarily follow firmly held 'public and common shared standards or rules'?

The second meaningful observation is that the process of transition from 'judge' to court is the transition from 'subjective' to 'objective.' Reasonableness

---

380 Barak, *Judicial Discretion,* 126.

381 Rochin v. California 342 U.S. 165, 170, 172 (1952); See also Felix Frankfurter, *Of Law and Life and Other Things That matter,* ed. Philip B. Kurland (Harvard University Press, 1965) after: Barak, *Judicial Discretion,* 127.

is the objective subject's point of view. And the way to escape from the subjective perspective is to go through the common corridor of what is general and shared.[382] This is not only a metaphor, but also a legal reality. Courts do not make subjective claims and this requirement, which is also the style of official legal discourse, creates the commonly seen schizophrenia in the law's approach of objectivity. Courts making decisions in the name of law accommodate this amongst the universal values that are identified with the values represented by certain society where court is judging. As Barak claims, 'a judge has to look for such values (universal) and avoid imposing subjective ones on society.' This decision-making practice could work in societies that are homogenous and have clear and widely shared values. But this style of thinking is not acceptable in new types of societies where there is no common agreement on the level of values. In pluralistic, post-secular societies, referring to public, universal values is highly controversial.[383]

Finally, I will consider why the confusing construction of general clauses is so often applied to court rulings, taking into account how this process looks from the judges' point view.

A partial explanation for the sources of the confusion in legal practice could follow from the widely held opinion, echoed in both the jurisprudential literature and the legal doctrine, that general clauses refer to something that is already made. But, as it has been shown in this chapter, there are very strong arguments against this.

The second argument based on the character of public discourse whereby the judge's decision is taken in the name of the court. However, this justification does not explain why in all that cases when an evaluation could be or even should be made. The argument is presented as an impartial and objective process. Jerome Frank claims, that when the judges decide cases basing their decisions on the 'law' (statutes, precedents, objective legal criteria, or objective general clauses) that this is only 'window dressing' for their decisions.[384] This phenomenon could be explained as rationalization and the accomplishment of legal mythology. All the examined examples in this chapter only confirm this thesis. What is more, what J. Frank suggests is that basing decisions on law, or on objective standards,

382 Barak, *Judicial Discretion*, 38.

383 Jurgen Habermas, Notes on the post-secular society, accessed November 22, 2015, http://www.signandsight.com/features/1714.html.

384 Brain H. Brix, 'Transaction Introduction,' in Jerome Frank, *Law and the Modern Mind*, (New Brunswick: Transaction Publisher, 2009) XV.

is upholding the artificial vision of an ideal judge. Instead of this 'the rational alternative is to recognize that judges are fallible human beings. We need to see that bias, prejudices, and conditions of attention affect the judges' reasoning as they do for the reasoning of ordinary men.'[385]

385 Frank, *Law and the Modern Mind*, 156.

Chapter V Objectivity of Legal Facts

The main aims of this final chapter are to find out how legal facts can be objective, to determine exactly what it means for legal facts to be objective, and to discover when and under what conditions it is justified to call them 'objective.' I shall introduce first the different conceptions of legal facts and then examine the relation between legal facts and statements about legal facts.

My enquiry is on two levels: the semantic and the semantic-pragmatic. The first is based on the typology of legal facts by J. Wróblewski, which represents an analytical approach. From this, I will analyse how legal facts (or more strictly the statements identified by legal facts) could be objective on a semantic level. Using Wittgenstein, and Kripke's interpretation of Wittgenstein's theory, I will further explore whether the meanings of statements about legal facts could be objective.

The semantic-pragmatic approach is based on the conception of institutional legal facts in a narrative and normative context developed by N. MacCormick. I will also question how institutional facts could be objective on the grounds of this theory.

Also, in this chapter, I examine examples from Polish courts to illuminate the differences between legal theory and legal practice.

The term 'fact' is troublesome enough in common language but, as the jurisprudential literature shows, getting to grip with facts and legal facts in law is even more problematic and faces many controversies. At one extreme, there is the conception that a 'fact is something which goes without saying.'[386] This manifests itself in common language expressions like 'everyone knows what a horse is,' 'facts need no deliberation,' and 'facts say everything about themselves.' At the other extreme, facts are treated as ambiguous expressions of reality that are dependent on the paradigm of interpretation of reality.[387]

The first approach expresses the realists' vision of reality, albeit in quite a naive version, based on the assumption that what we perceive is 'true' reality. In other words, what we observe or perceive is identified with something that is empirically real. However, this in itself is a paradigm of interpretation of reality. It says that we do not need any special notions to act as intermediaries between

---

386 See Patrick Nerhot, 'Introduction' in *Law, interpretation, and reality: essays in epistemology, hermeneutics and jurisprudence*, ed. Patrick Nerhot (Dordrecht, The Netherlands: Kluwer Academic Publishers, 1990) 2.

387 See Patrick Nerhot, 'Introduction.'

perception and reality in order to grasp it, because what we perceive is already true reality. Hence, we could say that there are not two different types of theories that try to explain what facts are, but one single approach based on the assumption that we need a paradigm of interpretation to understand facts.

The theory maintains that the paradigm of interpretation of reality dictates, or is interrelated with, the paradigm of facts. In the legal world, we have legal rules and principles that constitute the paradigm of interpretation, which in turn indicates how to interpret brute facts according to their institutional network or how to create new constitutional facts.

Before going deeper, a general ontological assessment needs to be made. First of all, one could say there are two types of facts that can be distinguished in the world: brute facts and institutional facts. This typology is based on John Searle's distinction between brute facts and institutional facts in his theory of institutional rules.[388] The next important step is guided by Ascombe's work. She illustrates the distinction between institutional and brute facts with the following example: the event of going to the grocer and buying something implies that the client will be given a bill. 'The set of events is the ordering and supplying of potatoes; something is a bill, only in the context of our institutions.'[389] This is the way she explains the core of institutional facts, which exist only in certain contexts. So, the bill, as an institutional fact, would lose its meaning outside the grocery shop. This is the same framework of concepts that make up the foundation of the institutional theory of law by N. MacCormick and Ota Weinberger, which I will adopt in my analysis of objectivity of institutional legal facts.

Reality that exists in time and space is built with empirical facts; we can say these are brute facts or even strong facts. These types of facts are entirely independent from human minds or human activity.

Institutional facts exist but, unlike brute facts, cannot be perceived solely on a physical or psychological dimension. Facts such as contract, marriage, money, culture, knowledge, literature, parliament, sports, and games exist but they need special rules in order to institutionalize them. These rules give the meaning to institutional facts. The existence of institutional facts depends partly on brute

---

388 John R. Searle, *Speech Acts* (Cambridge: Cambridge University Press, 1969) 50–53.

389 Gertrude Elizabeth Margaret Ascombe, 'On Brute Facts,' in *Ethic, Religion and Politics. The collected Philosophical Papers of G. E. M. Ascombe*, Vol. 13 (Oxford: Basil Blackwell, 1981) 23.

facts, empirical events, or behaviours, and partly on rules. That is why according to MacCormick such facts are dependent on human activity.[390]

The next important feature of institutional facts is that they cannot be grasped or framed descriptively; they must always have a normative element. From the words alone, we could not understand what it means for people to get married, greet each other, or play chess.[391] We also need to know the normative element to grasp the meaning.

On this basis, it is already possible to indicate two arguments against the claimed objectivity of institutional facts. First of all, they are depended on human activity, because people create them, design them and decide about their meaning. Secondly, they are not descriptive, because they are mainly composed of normative and ascriptive elements.

That is why two types of statements have to be formulated: descriptive ones, which describe and explain relations; and normative ones, which are formulated on the basis of values, preferences, and aims or goals. The main difference between these two types of facts is that brute facts are descriptive and exist in a particular space and time, while institutional facts as abstract concepts are potential and not directly related to a particular time and space. Institutional facts are a kind of ideal entity; they exist as abstract notions. To make institutional facts real, institutional rules and brute facts are needed.[392]

5.1. The Definitions and Various Types of Legal Facts

There is a lot written about legal facts in the literature and there have been many attempts to categorize them. To make things clearer, I will very briefly review the different conceptions and definitions of facts and the ways in which they are interpreted. This will help us move further in answering the question about their objectivity.

It is not possible to give one general answer for the question about objectivity of legal statements, mainly because of the diversity of types of statements in law.

Some authors, who consider legal facts to be objective, define them with the following kind of statements: 'a true proposition about the law,'[393] 'any statement

390 Neil MacCormick, Ota Weinberger, *An Institutional Theory of Law. New Approaches to Legal Positivism*, (Dordrecht, The Netherlands: Kluwer Academic Publishers, 1986) 24.
391 MacCormick, Weinberger, *An Institutional Theory*, 24.
392 MacCormick, Weinberger, *An Institutional Theory*, 24.
393 See Rosati, 'Some puzzles about objectivity of law,' 276.

of what the law requires on some point.'[394] The first definition seems to be controversial because of the questionable status of a true statement in law. The second one could be taken as the starting point, but it is necessary to make the meaning of 'what the law requires' more precise to avoid potential controversies. Although it is not possible to give one general answer, mainly because of diversity of types of statement in law, it is meaningful to go deeper into the types of statements that express what the law requires and say which of them could be objective and which could not. So, what should we take into account when interpreting legal facts? What are the necessary elements for the category of legal facts? The answer to these questions depends strongly on whether we consider them on a semantic level, where law is identified as a linguistic phenomenon, or take a broader view, taking law in a semantic-pragmatic context?

Taking the first assumption that considerations about facts are made on the level of language, I will carry out further analyses on the semantic level to see if this can yield any answers to the question about the objective meaning of legal facts.

Let us consider a typology of legal facts in relation to the types of statements in which they are represented in order to state which ones could be objective. I will start by presenting the definition of legal facts proposed by. J. Wróblewski. He defines a legal fact as a fact worded in legal language; its existence is based on legal norms and it is the subject of argumentation in the process of application of law.[395] This definition leads us to the conclusion that certain types of legal facts are dependent on the richness of the legal language. It is important to mention here that both procedural and substantive norms have an influence on the choice of facts that will be the subject of investigation by the court. The facts have to be important facts appropriate to the nature of the case; that is, facts described by the hypothesis of a norm. The norm then is the basis of the decision in the case. In other words, legal facts are extracted from legal norms, thus being normative facts. It is also possible to say that the way of looking at the facts is through the notions that are contained in legal norms. Legal facts could not exist apart from this relationship because of their connection with legal language. That is why there are such types of facts described in what follows.[396]

---

394 See Coleman and Leiter, 'Determinacy, Objectivity, and Authority, in Law,' 598.

395 See Wróblewski, *Sądowe stosowanie prawa*, 172, also Jerzy Wróblewski, *The Judicial Application of Law*, ed. Zenon Bankowski and Neil MacCormick (Dordrecht, The Netherlands: Kluwer Academic Publishers, 1992).

396 See Wróblewski, *The Judicial Application*, 137–149.

5.1.1. Facts Determined Descriptively

Facts determined descriptively are designated by terms in the legal language. They are proven in a way that correlates with their description. They are verified like every existential statement in a particular domain. For example, 'employer,' 'vehicle,' 'contract,' 'marriage,' 'commissioner,' 'legal capacity,' and 'tree.' The quantity of these facts depends on the vocabulary of legal language.'[397]

There is also a difference when descriptive legal facts depend on whether they are determined in a simple or in a relational way. A descriptively determined fact is a simple fact when it is simply an existential statement. For a relational fact, it is necessary to assess its consistency with a defined rule, as with 'valid act,' 'observation of rules,' and 'act contrary to the statute.' Relational facts are complex, composed of the conjunction of relational statements, 'x is consistent with rule R' and the existential statement 'x exists in spatiotemporal dimension.'[398] Another way of classifying descriptive legal facts is as events, processes, and subjects of law.

5.1.2. Facts Determined by Evaluation

Facts determined by evaluation, extracted by judgments, have their sources in those parts of legal norms which are based on evaluation, For example, statements like 'justified interest,' 'moral jury,' 'right reason,'[399] 'fair interest of taxpayer,' 'acting in good faith,' and 'well-being of the child.' In all these examples, a positive or a negative evaluation has to be made. There is a process of prescribing values to the objects that are not intrinsically good or evil. In order to recognize the point of reference it is useful to distinguish between 'simple' and 'instrumental' evaluations. The former is based on assigning values on a positive to negative scale. In practice, it is just imposing a set of beliefs about good or evil. This process just refers to 'pure' values. This simple kind of evaluation is based just on psychological experience. The instrumental evaluation is subordinate to the aim served by the evaluation as a whole. It does not mean that this process has lost its evaluative character; the evaluation is just moved to the higher level – to the level at which values are realized.

So, the evaluation is based on relativization with regard to another hierarchy of values. For example, 'fair interest of tax the payer according to a rational

397 See Wróblewski, *The Judicial Application*, 137.
398 See Wróblewski, *The Judicial Application*, 143.
399 See Wróblewski, *The Judicial Application*, 138.

legislator' is considered with regard to the rational legislator's hierarchy of values. So, even when the process of evaluation is based on external criteria, it is still not free of values. They are simply on one level higher, because they refer to the hierarchy of values composed or represented by the rational legislator.[400]

The features of facts determined by evaluation are also complicated because of the problematic character of values. It seems to me that it is first necessary to consider whether they are based on assumptions related to either the cognitivist or the non-cognitivist approach to values.

Wróblewski assumes a non-cognitivist position and this influences his consideration about facts.[401] This makes it impossible to consider facts in terms of true and false. Only descriptive facts are proven descriptively; evaluative facts are dependent on defining their values and characteristics. Wróblewski claims that evaluative facts should be treated as highly controversial linguistic statements: one states the existence of the object of evaluation and defines this object as 'having a value.' For example: 'important reason' and 'behaviour under strong emotion justified by circumstances.'

There are also terms which are not clear and are hard to qualify according to any one criterion because sometimes they are treated as descriptive, sometimes as evaluative. The expression 'strong affection'[402] is one such example. Facts like 'right' have no semantic reference.[403] They are sometimes described in jurisprudential literature as pure institutional facts.[404] Other examples of facts with no semantic reference are: juridical persons, money, etc. These kinds of facts are based on certain assertions connected with the law's[405] context.[406]

5.2. Objective Legal Facts according to the Polish Judicature

According to the above qualifications of legal facts, it seems quite difficult to think about objectivity of legal facts. But there are a great number of statements

---

400 See Józef Nowacki, 'Domniemanie dobrej wiary,' [Presumption of Good Faith] *Studia Iuridica Silesiana* No. 5 (1979) 123.

401 See Wróblewski, *The Judicial Application*, 139.

402 See Wróblewski, *The Judicial Application*, 139.

403 See Karl Olivecrona, *Law as fact*, (London: H. Milford, Oxford University Press, 1997) 246.

404 See Tomasz Gizbert-Studnicki, 'Przedmiot ustaleń sądu w procesie cywilnym,' [Object of court findings in civil procedure] *Krakowskie Studia Prawnicze* VII (1974) 154.

405 This is exactly what Wittgenstein says about the condition of assertability as fixing meaning.

406 See Olivecrona, *Law as fact*, 250.

in the Polish judicature about the legal facts as being objective. Polish judges very often write about 'objective legal facts' in their justifications, facts extracted both by description and by evaluation. Again one is faced with a dualism between theoretical approach, which denies or shows difficulties connected with the objectivity of legal facts, and the practical approach represented by the court rulings, which treat the objectivity of legal facts as nothing controversial.

Let us have a closer look at some fragments from the case law to examine their statements about objective legal facts, and then we will draw some conclusions on whether their approaches seem justified.

5.2.1. Facts Extracted by Description

In this group, it is possible to consider very different examples. One can find both 'easy' and 'hard cases.' The following fragment pictures a typical example of the former. The court says, that 'the transportation tax should be paid by every lorry weighing between 3.5 and 12 ton.'[407] There is an objective measure that qualifies which lorries are subject to taxation. The criterion is precisely determined and known *a priori*. There is no possibility of the subjects influencing the measure and in this sense the fact is objective.

An example of a more difficult case can be found in a dispute about the definition of pecuniary damage. There were two different interpretations of pecuniary damage between two different courts in the same cases.[408] Both were called objective in the sentencing by two different courts. The First Instance Court argued that objective pecuniary damage is only *damnum emergens*, and the High Court said that objective pecuniary damage is the sum of *damnum emergens* and

---

407 Art. 8 point 1 of the act of 12 January 1991 on Taxes and Local Fees: Art. 8 The following are subject to means of transport tax: 1) lorries of the gross vehicle weight over 3.5 t and below 12 t; the Judgment of the Supreme Administrative Court in Warsaw of 20 July 2004, FSK 154/04, Tax Monitor 2004/9/2: In the justification of the cassation appeal the General Public Prosecutor claims that damage to property is both the actual damage (*damnum emergens*) as well as loss consisting in 'preventing the expected profits from property (*usufruct cassation*).' The General Public Prosecutor also indicates that 'damage to property is an objective fact and exists as long as the loss to property has not been completely offset.' Thus, it is impossible to alter the amount of damage by intention of the parties expressed in an agreement, court or bank settlement; the parties may merely express their resignation to pursue the offset of loss, which does not however affect 'the legal and penal existence of the effect, i.e. property damage.'

408 Decision of the Supreme Court, 7 June 2001, V KKN 75/01, LEX no 51843.

lucrum cessans. Both courts introduced justifications in favour of their theses, but it still remains questionable as to whether pecuniary damage can be an objective fact. If it is objective, which definition is right? The definition of Higher Court because this court is more authoritative within the Polish legal system?

5.2.2. Facts Extracted by Evaluation

There are lots of examples of ascribing objectivity to these kinds of legal facts. They are mainly general clauses, which are defined as a command for evaluation.[409]

I introduce the example of the general clause that somebody acted in 'objective good faith.' In this case, it is situational understanding of the general clause, meaning it has to be with regard to the specific circumstances of the case. This understanding of general clauses is identified with morality in the situational meaning. Accordingly, every moral choice is treated as a creative action.[410] Such an understanding of this general clause assumes a creative understanding of morality, which is highly controversial in a judge's style of reasoning, especially when the argumentation is related to common standards of behaviour.

What the analysis of the objectivity of legal facts says to us is, that even facts that qualify as descriptive are controversial when they act under the banner of objectivity.

In spite of the highly controversial status of objectivity with regards to legal facts and the difficulties with justification, statements about objective legal facts are widely found in the court rulings. A possible conclusion that could be drawn is that courts use such statements for facts of a different character, mainly to assert that facts are objective in the same way they are in common language, as if were descriptive.

5.3 Narrative and Normative Coherence of Law

The explanation of the duality of objective legal facts and their questionable status could be delivered by the theory of narrative and normative coherence in law.[411]

As suggested by N. MacCormick, there are two different tests of coherence in law: normative and narrative coherence. Normative coherence has to do with

409 See Nowacki, 'Domniemanie dobrej wiary,' 123.
410 See Nowacki, 'Domniemanie dobrej wiary,' 124.
411 Neil MacCormick, *A Theory and The Rule of Law. A theory of Legal Reasoning* (Oxford: Oxford University Press, 2005) 214–237.

'the justification of legal rulings, or normative proposition, most generally in the context of the legal system, conceived as a normative order.'[412] Narrative coherence has to do with 'justification of findings of facts and the drawing of reasonable inferences from evidence'[413] The lack of either normative or narrative coherence 'involves a failure to make sense.'[414]

MacCormick explains normative coherence with the following example. There is a house where all inhabitants are allowed to make their rooms untidy on Mondays, Wednesdays, and Fridays, but they must tidy them up on Tuesdays, Thursdays, and Saturdays. Sundays are strictly observed as a day to rest. It is possible to have, and to observe, such house-rules but what sense does it make?[415] As MacCormick comments, there is no sense.

Narrative coherence is 'a test of truth or probability in the questioning of facts and evidence where direct proof by immediate observation is unavailable.'[416] This category is necessary for almost every legal decision because they are nearly all based on past facts.

Narrative coherence is a form of justification that is made with intelligibility and explanatory principles in mind. True propositions about perceived events are compensated by other propositions that fit the explanatory schema.

What makes legal narrative special is the peculiar character of legal time and its connection with the idea of action. Lawyers perceive a series of events in analytical time; they reconstruct what has happened in the real time.

Human activity has a temporal character and it always exists in a particular context. Our capacity to understand depends on our seeing 'how particular acts belong in larger activities or projects.'[417] As Kant showed, our minds comprehend any particular moment as one in a series of moments in time. That is why the time-bound character of all human experience makes narrative coherence fundamental to the process of obtaining access to past facts and making judgments about them.[418]

Coherence is understood as 'the property of a set of propositions which, taken together, make sense in its entirety.'[419]

---

412 MacCormick, *A Theory and The Rule of Law*, 189.
413 MacCormick, *A Theory and The Rule of Law*, 189.
414 MacCormick, *A Theory and The Rule of Law*, 189.
415 MacCormick, *A Theory and The Rule of Law*, 189.
416 MacCormick, *A Theory and The Rule of Law*, 190.
417 MacCormick, *A Theory and The Rule of Law*, 215.
418 MacCormick, *A Theory and The Rule of Law*, 228.
419 MacCormick, *A Theory and The Rule of Law*, 190.

From the point of view of their objectivity, the coherence theory has a very important influence on the status of facts. According to coherence theory, the category of correspondence is replaced by the category of coherence as the main way of making sense in law.[420] The category of correspondence is used to guarantee objectivity on the level of facts, even in very a strong sense. When the theory of coherence is applied, the status of legal facts changes its character from the point of view of their objectivity. To quote MacCormick about the procedure of reaching truth in the past, he claims that it is not the case that we cannot get at the truth about the past but only rarely can we be absolutely certain what the truth of the given matter is. Narrative coherence does not operate by self-applying an objective status, but always requires some subjective exercise of judgment.[421] Somebody always has to pass judgment.

How then can claims about the objectivity of legal facts hold up? One could claim that they are objective only in a weak sense because it is not possible to eliminate subjective elements. This has to be accepted as a part of the decision-taking process about legal facts and it does not preclude formulating statements about objective legal facts. But still one has to reveal what conception of objectivity one has in mind in order to uphold claims about the objectivity of legal facts.

At this stage it seems appropriate to reveal what kinds of elements comprise the process of formulating statements about the objectivity of legal facts.

Going step by step, the process of applying the theory of coherence to the legal facts means that first brute facts have to be grasped and then transformed into institutional facts. Secondly, the narrative-normative context forms the basis for the justification of this transformation.[422] The minimal condition for the transformation is that the fact it is coherent with its normative context and accepted by the community of legal professionals. All legal facts are contextualized entities and fit together in the same way as with narrative coherence.

Rational agents can transform brute facts into coherent legal narratives within a framework of common pragmatic rules.[423] That is why one could say that this perspective is not only a semantic narrative but also a semantic-pragmatic narrative.

---

420 Monica Den Boer, 'Two in one Trolley: Reflection on the Relation between MacCormick's Institutional and Narrative Theory of Law,' *International Journal of Semiotics of Law* IV/12 (1991) 263.

421 MacCormick, *A Theory and The Rule of Law*, 227–228.

422 Boer, 'Two in one Trolley,' 262–263.

423 Boer, 'Two in one Trolley,' 263.

5.4. The Relation between Brute and Institutional Facts

The classification of legal facts into brute and institutional facts begs the question about the relationship between these two types. To answer this, it is first necessary to explain the sources of origin of the facts.

Let us consider two examples of facts: tree and marriage. Trees existed before law and can exist without it, but marriage is the creation of a legal institution. Without the law in the 'ordinary world,' it is possible to say that we would not know about marriage, but we would still know what a tree is. That is why some authors claim that there are different kinds of facts in law. An institutional fact like 'marriage' consists of certain brute facts, like the signing of a register, but the institutional form of creating a marriage and its legal effects has its origin in law and this is what gives it its institutional character. Brute facts, like 'tree,' which have no institutional character, also exist in law. Firstly, because even such terms like tree are used in legal acts, though their notion is very often completely different from their definition in ordinary language. For example, the legal definition of natural area of water. If you have a natural area of water (in fields or woodland) of less than 1 hectare, it is understood as a water hole and is not subject to soil classification. As such, it does not have to registered with the Polish Land Registry. Larger areas of natural water class as lakes and have to be registered.[424]

The same applies to the definition of a human being. Cases of abortion generated the need for a precise description of when life as a human being starts in order to qualify whether or not abortions have a criminal character.

From the linguistic perspective, what constitutes the relation between these two kinds of facts are the semantic rules of how to set or interpret the meaning. This could be solved by the sources of the meanings of brute facts and legal facts. The first one should come from common language, the second from given institutional rules. When analysing court rulings or legal statutes, one can observe legal definitions in legal acts which represent the legislator's will in the understanding of certain listed legal facts. In this sense, they should be institutional facts, but one can find definitions of what would normally be regarded as brute facts in the 'dictionary given by legislator' in the legal statute. Through the legislator's definition, brute facts become legal facts; the meaning from common language has changed. Take, for example, the legislator's definition that a natural

424 Act of the 3 February 1995 on Protection of Agricultural and Forestry Land.

area of water In such cases, it is hard to distinguish which are brute facts and which are already legal facts.

As we can see, law has spread into human behaviour and the human world. Sometimes law is creating completely new concepts, for example, servitude; sometimes it just takes over concepts from external reality, such as computer terminology.

Authors who claim that there are both brute facts and institutional facts in law try to justify it as follows.[425] Institutional facts have their origins in legal norms; they come from legal institutions and they refer to brute facts. But what is important is that descriptions of brute facts are not equal in their institutional characterization. When a legal characterization of a fact is the same as the description of a brute fact, it means that it is still only a brute fact. Such an approach seems to assume that there are two worlds: the empirical world of experience and the legal world. However, when we take into account the normative legal order, it appears that a brute fact can have a different characterization in different cases, so the process of singling out brute facts that have the same characterization in law is not very helpful in explaining the relation between these two notions. This justification only provides an answer on the basis of an analytical assumption of what brute and institutional facts are and it is working within this network of notions.

A different explanation can be arrived at by putting in another line of argumentation. The legal world constitutes a completely different kind of reality because of its legal character. There are different kinds of habitants living there, namely subjects of law. Every subject can play many different roles at the same time. For example, one subject could simultaneously be a husband, employer, taxpayer, and a customer. Law also has its own time, narrative, and dynamism. When one looks through the glasses of law, one enters into the legal world and the condition to be there is to know the rules and the language. Imagine being a citizen of a certain country without knowing the language or the customs; it would be nearly impossible to participate in society and to understand it. The network of legal notions is imposed on everyone in a legal society.

In the legal world everything is legal, and it is not possible to find something that is not embraced by a legal category, otherwise it is would be outside legal world. The world is created through the language of the legislators. That is why, even brute facts which are not mentioned in legal statutes, are still considered in a legal context and will be involved in legal narration and through this can change their qualification into institutional facts.

425 See Studnicki, 'Przedmiot ustaleń,' 164.

That is why one could claim there are only institutional facts in law and there is no point in distinguishing between brute facts and institutional facts. Of course, the composition of institutional facts is based on empirical facts and institutional rules, but the process of institutionalization creates new entities that have a legal character. It is possible that in law, all facts are institutional.[426] At very least, one can say that the relation between both types of facts is questionable. As Weinberger stresses, social reality is penetrated with regulative and normative patterns and, because of them, the distinction between an everyday reality and an institutional reality is inconceivable.[427]

There are also approaches in the jurisprudential literature which say that, for lawyers, facts and law do not belong to two different worlds because otherwise there would be a chance that these worlds would never meet.[428] Lawyers do not refer to raw facts existing outside of any legal description. Life situations have to contain specific factors that can be designated only by legal concepts.[429] So, the answer to the question about determination of meaning or interpretation of legal facts could go as follows: it is not in the direction from the empirical world to legal world but the other way round; facts do not determine meaning, but rules determines what facts are. This point is coherent with Wittgenstein's proposition, which is why I will consider his theory of meaning and interpretation in relation to facts as the next step.

5.5. The Relation between Facts and the Paradigm of Interpretation

What is the relation of dependency between facts and their meaning; between their ontology and epistemology? Or, in other words, between ontology and semantics, because semantics plays the role of epistemology when dealing with facts on the level of language in determining how their meaning or interpretation is fixed.

426 See MacCormick, *An Institutional Theory of Law*.

427 Neil MacCormick and Ota Weinberger, *Grundlagen des institutionalistischen, Rechtspositivimus* (Berlin: Duncker&Humbolt, 1985) 28, As quoted by: Boer, 'Two in one Trolley,' 258.

428 See François Rigaux, 'The concept of fact in legal science,' in *Law, interpretation, and reality: essays in epistemology, hermeneutics and jurisprudence*, ed. Patrick Nerhot (Dordrecht, The Netherlands: Kluwer Academic Publishers, 1990) 48.

429 See Rigaux, 'The concept of fact,' 48.

It is possible to assume that, on the level of language, the role of epistemology is to discover and/or establish meaning. Wittgenstein said that there are no facts that determine meaning, so he breaks the relation between ontology and semantics, giving the priority to the process of setting meaning: the epistemology.

So, if facts have no influence on the way of setting or establishing meaning, there is no difference between brute, descriptive, and evaluative facts from Wittgenstein's point of view. Does this mean that all facts are created and that we could easily forget about objectivity? Taking the line of thinking offered by Wittgenstein, it could be as follows:

For Wittgenstein, meaning is treated as the core of the notion that could be objective; interpretation is the next level, which is dependent on individual elements and so the product of interpretation could be changeable in different cases. Meaning is a necessary introduction to interpretation and, only in this sense, could facts be objective in a stronger sense. Following this idea, meaning appears as something that has a firm core, which gives the possibility for interpretation, because without understanding there is no place for interpretation at all. The next important question is what makes certain interpretations objective? What kind of justification gives the right to claim that an interpretation is objective?

One answer proposed by the antirealists is that common acceptance of a certain community gives the justification for treating an interpretation as objectively valid.

Wittgenstein's thoughts represent the sceptical position, but it is not necessary to reject the possibility of objectivity in a stronger sense. Meanings of terms are not determined by facts, but this does not exclude the possibility of making claims about objectivity or make it necessary to consider it only in a minimal sense (a meaning that is applied and accepted by the majority of an interpreting community).

Considering the problem of dependency between facts and interpretation, one conclusion is that the meaning of facts is determined by a paradigm of interpretation and the conditions that are formulated by this paradigm. So the next problem that has to be considered is how this meaning is determined, and how the meaning of legal facts is settled in the context of normative legal reality, because the theory that determines meaning is also the part of the assumed paradigm.

5.6. Objectivity of Legal Facts: Semantic Reflections

As argued before, there is only one world that includes both facts and law. Setting legal facts could be a matter of grasping the meaning or the process of interpretation. It could be perceived as looking through the paradigm of interpretation or through the process of institutionalization, which makes legal facts what they are. So, further consideration about legal facts will be on the level of language, the semantic field. This enables us to reformulate the question about objectivity of legal facts into questions about the objectivity of meaning and objectivity of interpretation. Further consideration has to be directed on how the meaning is determined. If the meaning were to be fully determined, we would be able to talk about objectivity of legal facts in a strong sense; this is exactly how strong realists approach the theory of meaning. But this is only one of several possible controversial answers to this question. At the other extreme, the subjectivists challenge the determinacy of linguistic meaning, with the view that meaning is located in the individual subject. I would like to take a middle way and consider to what degree the meaning of words can be determined.

So, what kind of legal facts are determined and to what degree? If there are different kinds of legal facts, do they have different extents of determination in fixing or discovering their meaning? Or maybe, in the sphere of language, the type of legal fact is not important in this respect.

First, it is important to make a distinction between critical semantic theory and interpretative semantic theory. Generally speaking, semantic theories offer an explanation of what links a word with the object to which it applies. Critical semantic theories, as represented by Kripke and Putnam, claim that the basic link is an uncontroversial test of sharing by speakers. Interpretative semantic theories, as represented Roland Dworkin, claim that the necessary link is a theory or interpretation.[430] The next assumption that needs to be explained is what I mean by meaning.

5.6.1. Meaning

The key to further explanations is to make clear the difference between meaning and interpretation or application. It is not possible to discuss all the problems within this thesis, so, in what follows, I only aim to show what I understand by meaning and interpretation.

By meaning, I refer to the relation between empirical objects and the sense of words. It is important to stress that 'the meaning of words' and 'the meaning of words in their correct application' are not equal. The first is what speakers of a language generally share but correct application could be the matter of controversy.[431] This in turn raises the question of what are the sources of interpretative

430 See Endicott, 'Review book,' 508–512.
431 See Endicott, 'Review book,' 510.

authority[432] that says which interpretation is correct or incorrect? What are the instances that allow decisions to be taken about meanings?

If meaning is what speakers of a certain language generally share, what could be said about the objectivity of meaning of legal facts bearing in mind their diverse character? According to the analytical approach, legal facts have to be at least objective in the minimal sense because they are shared by the majority.

Let us consider this problem separately with regard to descriptive facts and evaluative facts. It seems to me that the same could not be said about evaluative facts and descriptive facts, because when evaluative ones are treated like an order to make an individual judgment or evaluation, it does not fulfil the test based on shared acceptance by all speakers. This is due to the complicated status of values.[433] In justifications by Polish judges, there are no references to acts of individual moral choice. Nevertheless, judges do make individual moral choices in order to achieve a suitable justification. There are fragments of justifications where judges were trying to base their choice of morality on the common acceptance test, like in the case of descriptive facts. Very often this process has just a robe of descriptive morality because it is one of the most successful ways of argumentation, but the real reason has its source in individual moral choice.[434] They cover an act of individual evaluation. But are evaluative facts really different from descriptive facts on the semantic level?

It seems to me that, from the point of view of Wittgenstein's position on the objectivity of meaning, facts are shaped in the same way, no matter whether they are descriptive or evaluative. Both are subjected to the test of common shared meaning.

5.6.2. Wittgenstein and Kripke

Now, I shall present the so-called antirealist approach to the theory of meaning, discussing mainly Kripke's interpretation of Wittgenstein's philosophy. Then I would like to consider the application of this theory to the legal discourse, especially to legal facts. Kripke's sceptical and non-sceptical analysis of Wittgenstein would give an answer to the question about the level of determination of meaning with regard to different types of legal facts. (Kripke's sceptical interpretation is

432 See Stanley Fish, 'Working In the Chain Gang, interpretation in the law and in literary criticisms,' *Critical Inquiry* 9 (1982–3).

433 Only objectivists could claim an objective status for evaluative statements about values.

434 See Nowacki, 'Domniemanie dobrej wiary,' 123.

commonly known as the sceptical approach[435]. A middle position is taken by Friderick Schauer,[436] who claims that formulated rules are not radically indeterminate, but unformulated rules are.[437])

5.6.3. Kripke's Sceptical Position

Kripke was criticized very strongly for his sceptical interpretation of Wittgenstein and it has been the topic of twenty-five years of controversy.[438] After all the many commentaries, today this position is called 'Kripkesteinism,' and is taken as new philosophical proposition in the theory of meaning, quite distinct from Wittgenstein's original position. His approach is quite controversial for many reasons but has been also defended as suitable for law.[439] Developing Kripke's position could bring us quite far from Wittgenstein to a very controversial point, namely the radical indeterminacy of meaning.

To enter into speculations on Wittgenstein's sceptical problem[440] one must go through the door of the thesis that there is no fact in the world that constitutes meaning.[441] This is the very basic assumption, which is incompatible with or even contradictory to the realist approach to the theory of meaning. Generally speaking, it means that a particular discourse is not primarily descriptive or fact stating. Such a discourse states no facts but instead gives expressions of certain attitudes. The meaning is derived from these expressions not from truth conditions.[442] Kripke offers the example of '57 + 65 = 5' to show that there is no fact determining meanings in this statement. He argues that the statement '57 + 65 = 122' is correct, not because there are facts which constitute it, but our community permits us to use certain signs like '+' in certain way; in this case, to mean addition.

---

435 See Charles M. Yablon, 'Law and Metaphysics,' in *Law and Legal Interpretation*, ed. Fernando Atria and Neil MacCormick (Dartmouth, ASHGATE: 2003) 371–384.

436 See Timothy A. O. Endicott, 'Linguistic Indeterminacy' in *Law and language*, ed. Thomas Morawetz, (Dartmouth: Ashgate, 2000) 689.

437 See Frederic Schauer, *Playing by the Rules. A Philosophical Examination of Rules-based Decisions-making in Law and in Life* (Oxford: Clarendon Press, 1991) 64–68.

438 See Martin Kusch, *A Skeptical Guide to Meaning and Rules. Defending Kripke's Wittgenstein* (Acumen: McGill-Queen's University Press, 2006).

439 See Yablon, 'Law and Metaphysics,' 371–384.

440 Saul A. Kripke, *Wittgenstein on Rules and Private Language. An elementary Exposition* (Oxford: Basil Blackwell, 1982) 145.

441 See Kripke, *Wittgenstein on Rules,* 15.

442 See Coleman and Leiter, 'Determinacy, Objectivity, and Authority, in Law,' 220.

Kripke's second argument is as follows: there is no such a thing as a fixed meaning of an expression because any use in the past does not determine its present or future use. This argument can be developed to say that conventional meaning is also not rigidly binding and could be subject to change. In addition, there is no such thing as a general rule, as Wittgenstein's infinitive regression argument demonstrates: 'But how can a rule show me what I have to do at this point? Whatever I do is, on some interpretation, in accord with this rule.' That is not what we ought to say, but rather: any interpretation still hangs in the air along with what it interprets, and cannot give any support. Interpretations by themselves do not determine meaning.[443]

The important point is that, if the understanding of an utterance or sign were a matter of advancing interpretation, then the interpretation would require its own interpretation, and so on, indefinitely.[444] So, as one can see, the problem is just moved one level higher – 'rules say how to interpret other rules.' It could lead to *regresus ad infinitum,* and be used as criterion for a meaning with no end.[445] The next important point in Wittgenstein's philosophy is that 'for him understanding, not interpretation is primary.'[446] He said also: 'there is a way of grasping a rule which is not an interpretation (. . .).'[447]

5.6.3.1. Kripke's Non-Sceptical Interpretation of Wittgenstein

Kripke was criticized for omitting the passage from Wittgenstein's Investigations saying that 'there is a way of grasping of rule which is not an interpretation but which is exhibited in what we call 'obeying the rule' and 'going against it' in actual cases.'[448] Kripke's so-called misunderstanding was that understanding consists in part of an interpretation, verbal or quasi-verbal, presenting itself to the mind.[449] In other words, Kripke treats interpretation as a part of meaning. It is not clear to me if interpretation was really misunderstood by Kripke or whether he was

---

443 See Ludwig Wittgenstein, *Philosophical Investigations* (Oxford: Wiley Blackwell, 2009) paragraph 198.

444 See Patterson, 'Objectivity and Normativity,' 339.

445 See Kripke, *Wittgenstein on Rules,* 43.

446 See Dennis Patterson, 'Wittgenstein on Understanding and Interpretation,' in *Philosophical Investigation* Vol. 29 No.2 (April 2006) 9.

447 See Wittgenstein, *Philosophical Investigations,* par. 201.

448 See Wittgenstein, *Philosophical Investigations,* par. 203.

449 See Jes Bjarup, 'Kripke's Case,' in *Law and Legal Interpretation,* ed. Fernando Atria and D. Neil MacCormick (Dartmouth: ASHGATE, 2003) 380.

fully aware of what he was omitting.[450] He said he didn't find it so important in analysing the main argument against private language.[451] (Anyway, I will treat Kripke's interpretation as a separate from Wittgenstein thoughts, although there is no possibility to analyse Kripke without Wittgenstein's 'Investigations' at the readers hands, of course.)

It has to be made clear that this not a problem of description; Kripke is fully aware of differences between justification and description. He is not asking if what he stated is the truth in the statement '57+65 = 122,' but how it is possible to justify that it is so. The point he is making is that we are not able to justify the use of rules on the basis of facts.

The main difference then between Wittgenstein and Kripke is that Kripke finds interpretation to be a part of meaning. This main difference between the two philosophers has great consequences in semantic theories. This distinction is the most problematic in thinking about meaning, mainly because of the 'mixing' of these two approaches. This is exemplified by radical authors, like Stanley Fish,[452] who once advocated interpretative semantic theory,[453] claiming that the meaning of the text is produced through the process of interpretation.

In opposition, Wittgenstein claims that we do not need any semantic theory to decipher reality. Language is a setting of games with loose relations, and meanings appear in the moment of acting. So, Wittgenstein breaks the realism-scepticism debate, arguing that rule following is not a mental phenomenon. He locates everything in action, especially in social action. Kripke's draws our attention to claims in Wittgenstein's Investigations that there is no difference between the philosophy of mathematics and the philosophy of mind. So, this is another argument for taking away meaning from individual minds, arguing that private language is not possible. Acceptance of community is what gives license in deciding about the rules that give meanings.

---

450 See Saul A. Kripke, *Wittgenstein o regułach i języku prywatnym* [*Wittgenstein about rules and private language*] (Warszawa: Aletheia, 2007) 6.

451 See Kripke, *Wittgenstein O regułach i języku prywatnym*, Preface to Polish edition.

452 This position was represented by S. Fish, until he adopted a less radical stand.

453 See Stanley Fish, *Is There a Text in this Class? The Authority of Interpretive Communities* (Cambridge, MA: Harvard University Press, 1980); He has changed his claims a few times, but the above claims are represented in this text.

5.7. Objectivity of Legal Facts

In order to find out in what sense legal facts should be objective, I sum up the most important points from the Wittgenstein's theory. I will then use them as assumptions to give an answer about the objectivity of legal facts.

(1) The meaning of words cannot be found by looking for their associations with particular objects. Instead, the meaning of words should be understood by the way in which they are used within their social context.
(2) The distinction between understanding and interpretation is as an elementary key to the conceptualization of meaning.

If the objectivity of legal facts can be regarded as objective on the basis of acceptance by the community, it reflects a way of legal facts becoming objective in a minimal sense, where the majority of the auditorium decides what a certain word means.

The main consequence of this is that the degree of objectivity is not dependent on the type of fact one is dealing with. When facts do not determine meaning, there is no difference between descriptive, evaluative, or any other type of facts. No matter what kind of facts are being settled, they are all constituted on the basis of common acceptance and the direction of determination goes from institutional rules, not from empirical constitution. This also means that all types of facts, including legal facts are objective to the same degree, but only with regard to their meanings, it also infers that there are no differences between them at the semantic level.

The differentiation of types of legal facts and its influence on the extent of their objective status has sense only on a metaphysic level. This obviously begs the question what sense legal facts could be objective on the metaphysical level, but this is outside the scope of my research. However, I would just like to mention briefly that even differentiation on the level of status of values has no meaning according to Wittgenstein's proposition. That is why there is no difference between cognitive and non-cognitive approaches and why this has no influence on the question of the objective status of facts on the semantic level.

On the basis of the above assumptions, I would like to analyse some specific problems with the objectivity of legal facts. First of all, if meaning is something that every speaker of a certain language shares, the implication is that the meaning of legal facts is objective, at least in a minimal sense. But what about interpretation and application, which are not commonly shared? This problem is especially seen in difficult cases, which are difficult exactly because of the lack of a single shared interpretation. In such cases, expressions like 'correct application,' 'correct meaning,' and 'objective legal fact' are viewed differently by opposing parties.

What follows from this is that the interpretation decides about the application and therefore has a major influence on it. So, what makes certain interpretations valid and what kind of justifications makes certain applications stronger than others? Is common acceptance a strong enough argument in the domain of law?

As indicated by legal practice, common acceptance is only one of several methods of argumentation. It is one of the most successful one, and can be very convincing in certain situations, especially in the context when one of the key values is common agreement. An example is a society based on democratic agreement.

However, common acceptance is only one of arguments used in the process of legal argumentation. In many of the Polish judge's justifications examined, especially the more difficult cases, arguments based on social acceptance are used, but amongst many other arguments.

To analyse the possibility of objectivity of interpretation, I would like to settle it in the context of the determination of the process of interpretation in law. My position can be summarized by the following quotation:

> If the interpretation is not determined, then there is no true answer to the question of how a certain situation is regulated by the law, therefore in such cases the law is not objective.[454]

The practical perspective could be delivered by analysing the judges' justifications. It could give an answer about the factual and postulated ways of following the doctrine of determinacy and objectivity. Very often the legislator takes the decision by means of legal definitions and it is also the task of judges in most cases.[455] But as I have shown, in a number of cases there is a problem with legal definitions. They also have to be interpreted as part of the judge's decision-making process. So, in this sense, judges contribute to determinacy and objectivity of law. In their justifications, lawyers and judges seem to speak about the law in terms that presupposed strongly objective standards, but after looking at what they actually do, the situation appears to be a little bit different. In practice, the sphere of subjectivity is extended, which is indeed necessary for lawyers and judges to do their jobs.

---

454 See Bulygin, 'Objectivity of Law in the View of Legal Positivism,' 225.
455 Bulygin, 'Objectivity of Law in the View of Legal Positivism,' 225.

In the next section, I would like to make a comparison between the above theories and practice of law. In particular, I would like to analyse the vagueness of language in legal definitions using examples from the Polish judicature.

5.7.1. Legal Definitions

Considering the problem of determination in the application of law, a good example could be delivered by the usage of legal definitions. They are perceived as the more determined part of law in the process of its application because the legislator gives both meaning and interpretation. The main aims of statutory definitions are to increase the certainty of law, improve the clarity of language, and to determine statutory meaning. However, one should check the hypothesis that legal definitions play that the role in the process of their application.

In the Polish legal system,[456] one of the main interpretive directives imposes a duty upon the judge to use statutory definitions (the 'legislator's meaning') as a first step in the process of interpretation. This is the first and the strongest of all the interpretive directives that have to be fulfilled in the process of the application of law.

Theory of interpretation questions to what extent the meaning is determined by the readers' understanding, the legislator's intent, or by other variables. So, even if the legislator defines some legal terms, it still does not guarantee the precision of legal expressions. When we analyse the process of application of legal definitions, we can realize how far they are from fulfilling their prescribed functions.

Statutory definitions in the process of application of law are still a source of doubts. Very often they are not ready-made or clear expressions. Legal definitions still need to be interpreted and problems in the process of application remain. I would like to make a short analysis of a working statutory definition in the process of application of Polish law. I will take into account three main spheres to show how complicated the application of legal definitions are:

456 It is important to stress that legal definitions in the Polish legal system are one of the most important principles in the interpretation process, and they have to be applied first. In other legal systems there is no such obligation. The person making interpretation can take into account the definition by the legislator but is not bound by it. For example, the Belgium legal system works according to such rules. See more, Mark Van Hoecke, *Law as Communication* (Oxford Portland Oregon: Hart Publishing, 2002) 131–134.

First and the most common is the problem with the interpretation of statutory definitions. Legal definitions are very often just starting point in the process of applying law. But as it is indicated in the jurisprudential literature 'a definition, as a legal rule, is interpreted the same as any other legal rule. Opinions that legal definitions should not be interpreted are limited to the situations when definitions are unequivocal from the point of view of linguistic rules. Their interpretation should be based on the references to other definitions or to dictionaries.'[457]

The second problem is the extent of applicability of legal definitions. Judges looking for legal definitions have to question whether it is only possible to apply a certain definition to one statute, many statutes, or whether it is limited to one branch of law or can be applied to others. There are also definitions that give references to other legal acts: for example, tax law has no definition of life annuity and as one may read in one of the court rulings 'it should be understood according to the definition given by civil law.'[458]

An attempt of answering this question could be done by showing Quine's and Kripke's positions. Quine names this problem the 'thesis of indetermination of translation,' in other words, there is no fixed meaning of statements no matter what language they are in. It means that its applicability could not be determined in a way that could be accepted as objective. Kripke goes one step further and attacks fixed meaning even within a single language. Law has exactly the kind of 'language' that can offer some proof in favour of Quine's and Kripke's theories and the problem of legal definitions illustrates this very clearly. Quine, on the basis of his theory allows us to apply a certain meaning no matter what the context is. Kripke allows for changing meaning in changing contexts. The extent of applicability of legal definitions illustrates the problem exactly.

The final problem is with recognizing or distinguishing legal definitions in legal texts[459]. Legal definition is such a definition, which we can find in legal texts and give a meaning to notions in a legal text. As we can learn from legal literature, there are many different types of definitions. They can be reconstructed from different parts of legal texts, from a few articles, from a whole statute, or even constructed using different statutes. Such definitions are described as

457 Maciej Zieliński, *Wykładnia prawa. Zasady. Reguły. Wskazówki* (Warszawa: Lexis Nexis, 2002) 205.

458 Agnieszka Bielska-Brodziak, 'Kłopoty z definicjami legalnymi,' [Trubles with a legal definitions] in *System prawny a porządek prawny* (Szczecin: Wydawnictwo Naukowe Uniwersytetu Szczecińskiego, 2008) 159–174.

459 Bielska-Brodziak, 'Kłopoty z definicjami legalnymi,' 159–174.

axiomatic[460]. Exaggerating, one could say that one could find or create a legal definition from almost anywhere in a statute given the many possible ways of constructing definitions.

Analysing these three problems can show the real role of a definition in the process of interpretation of legal texts. Of course, we can observe many easy cases where the 'legal dictionary' fulfils its prescribed function. But, there is a whole group of difficult cases that confirm that legal definitions do not help in more precise communication between legislator and courts. Contrary to a dominant opinion, there are even examples in difficult cases where legal definitions are used to justify interpretations that go in a different direction then the will of the legislator.

As one can see, there are some special conditions for setting meanings and it is almost impossible in the legal domain to make a generalization to embrace the practice of judging in one semantic theory. My observation leads rather in the direction of even more radical indeterminacy of meaning in law's domain. It is my view that judges and lawyers use many different strategies to make their argumentation more successful in order to justify their deep conviction for the position they want to argue for. That is why it is possible to find fragments in case law where the argumentation mixes different semantic interpretations, switching from realist to the antirealist positions to suit their needs.

5.7.2. The Semantic Theory of Kripke and Putnam

It is important to stress that there are two levels of consideration, the level of description of what judges are doing and the abstract level of the semantic theory of meaning. I do not question the possibility of application of Wittgenstein's approach to law or the coherence of semantic Kripke-Putnam, but only try to show its inconsistency with some examples from legal practice.

Semantic Kripke – Putnam is quite a controversial theory when applied to law. Authors in the jurisprudential literature write about many different aspects of controversy when applying the new semantic theory[461]. I will analyse only the aspect of common acceptance and common shared meaning in the process of applying law in Polish courts. The first argument says that there is no such thing as a fixed meaning of an expression based on justification by common acceptance. In consequence, there is possibility of changing meaning according to different usage in the past, present or in the future.

---

460 See Wróblewski, *The Judicial Application*, 234.

461 See Coleman and Leiter, 'Determinacy, Objectivity, and Authority, in Law,' 345.

The argument against making rule of usages of semantic Kripke – Putnam as a full theory in law is that the common acceptance is not always respectable in the law's domain, especially in hard cases. The practice of law shows many cases where meaning is set in very different ways. Meaning can be set without regard to or against common usage on the basis of the of law's authority. For example, take again the definition of tree, which according to Polish legislature must be 'above 1.20 meters,' or the attempt to formulate the definition of a human being in order to penalize abortion. There are also definitions that have no previous social practice of usage in common language (like a legal person) and are quite different from common understanding. There are a lot of examples that make legal language specific, for example: legal definition of 'night-time' which is understood as the 'time between 10.00 p.m. and 6.00 a.m..' From analysing Polish judicature, one can draw the conclusion than there is no single strategy in the process of interpretation. Judges very often quote the dictionary to find[462] the so-called linguistic meaning and, in spite of the primacy of using this kind of interpretative direction, they choose different meanings when, for example, considering non-linguistic elements, or interpreting the intention of the legislator.[463] They also justify their choice by arguing that a certain meaning is specific for law or belongs to the language of law and that is why the meaning is different.[464] There are a lot of situations where lawyers have to choose between meanings from common language and legal language and the choice is often done *ad usum*. For example: 'tax exemption' has a different meaning in common language and civil law and the courts use both meanings in their rulings. This specific feature of legal language, the creative power of legal language, makes common acceptance a secondary argument.

It is not very risky to claim that even semantic Kripke-Putnam is not suitable to apply fully in law. The theory does not cover all existing practices in law's

462 See more, Lawrence Solan, 'When Judges use the Dictionary,' *American Speech* Vol. 86 (1993) 50–57; Agnieszka Bielska-Brodziak, Zygmunt Tobor, Piotr Żmigrodzki, 'Co każdy prawnik o słownikach wiedzieć powinien,' [What every lawyer should know about the Dictionaries] *Przegląd Sądowy* No 7–8 (2008) 79–95.

463 See example, Resolution of the Supreme Court, 16 January 2004, III CZP 101/03, OSNC 2005/4/58.

464 See Judgment of the Supreme Administrative Court, 13 April 2005, FSK 1652/04, LEX no 166048. Judgment of the Supreme Administrative Court, 4 November 2005, FSK 2423/04, LEX no 187977; Resolution of the Supreme Administrative Court, 29 November 1999, FPK 4/99, Pr. Gosp. 2000/2/27.

domain. Maybe it works at the level of declaration of what judges are going to do, but on the level of action, it seems to be quite incoherent.

There are some legal philosophers who claim that interpretation is always indeterminate, and law is never objective. The main representative of this style of thinking is the Sceptical School of Genoa.[465] However, this approach is criticized on the grounds that 'all normative formulations can be ambiguous,'[466] and that it is an essential feature of language that at least some expressions have to be univocal. The sceptical approach about radical indeterminacy seems to be the consequence of identifying meaning with interpretation, as Kripke did.

Considerations about objectivity in terms of the determinacy and indeterminacy of law should also be done in the context of judicial discretion (decisions made on moral or political criteria), the normative gap, and inconsistencies in the legal system, and the problem of judicial activism versus formalism. It is not sufficient to consider them just under the penumbra of vagueness on the linguistic level. The problem of objectivity may go according to the schema of three pairs of notions:

- determination/indetermination,
- formalism/judicial activism,
- objectivity/subjectivity.

The above consideration may find its source in the problem of judicial activism and formalism. In the Polish judicature, the doctrine of formalism is very strongly represented, but theoretically almost impossible to defend.[467] Maybe this phenomenon explains some of the curiosities drawn from legal practice.

Summing up, the possible objective status of legal facts is a controversial thesis. Even when considered only at the semantic level, the justification for claiming that legal facts are objective is limited as to its meaning. The necessity

---

465 Sceptical School of Genoa: Giovani Tarello, *Dottrine giuridiche e ideologie sindacali* (Bologna: Il mulino, 1973); Riccardo Guastini, 'Rules, Validity and Statutory Construction,' in *Italian studies in law: a review of legal problems*, ed. Allessandro Pizzorusso (Dordrecht, The Netherlands: Kluwer Academic Publishers, 1992); Tecla Mazzarese, 'Grounds of Liability. An Introduction to the Philosophy of Law,' *Philosophia* Vol. 18 (1988); Pierluigi Chiassoni, 'Interpretive games: Statutory construction through Gricean eyes,' *Analisi e diritto* (1999): 79–99.

466 See Bulygin, 'Objectivity of Law in the View of Legal Positivism,' 228.

467 It is impossible to defend from the point of view of the character of judging. It is postulated by the division of power principle that judges should only apply law and not make it (through interpreting).

for interpretation and its application make the dream of objectivity unreal. Legal facts also need to be conceived in a broader context (as introduced in the section 4. on normative and narrative coherence of institutional facts). Physical facts from human reality are dependent on interpretation with reference to their normative and narrative frameworks[468]. So, institutional facts consist of brute facts and an institutional framework and they are perceived according to legal narrative rules. This kind of paradigm of interpretation, which is used to set or grasp the sense of legal facts, allows only a weak assumption of objectivity.

468 See Neil MacCormick, *Institutions of Law. An Essay in Legal Theory* (Oxford: Oxford University Press) 34.

Chapter VI Conclusions

Mapping objectivity with respect to its practical legal usage, in particular with respect to the way judges use it to justify legal decisions, allows me to formulate some critical remarks on the role of objectivity in the legal discourse, on the relationship between subjectivity and objectivity, in particular, the consequences for legal subjects. These remarks bring to the conclusions on the role of intersubjectivity as a suggested way out of the many difficulties described in the book.

This concluding chapter is organized as follows: Section 6.1. describes the ceremonial function of legal objectivity; Section 6.2. offers some reflections on the relationship between objectivity and subjectivity; finally, Section 6.3. analyses the key question of how intersubjectivity can fit the law.

6.1. The Ceremonial Function of Legal Objectivity

What judges perceive as right, correct, proper, rightful, legitimate, equitable, or reasonable, and what finally they agreed to accept, have all been called objective in the proposed analysis. One of the key questions, after mapping all the meanings is what is the function of decisions, evaluations, and legal facts which become objective by the power of naming them as 'objective' by the courts or judges? From the court rulings, there are many examples where certain criteria, judgements, evaluations, and decisions are treated as objective based on the authority given to them by law or judges. There are plenty of examples to illustrate this thesis, especially in the spheres of public law. Extracted from the court rulings, there is a whole separate group, which I classify as specific legal meanings of objectivity, where objectivity is given by the authority of law.

The overall impression from the research suggest that the use of objectivity in legal discourse does not go hand in hand with the simple linguistic intuition on how to use this term. Users of legal language use it according to their own aim which is strongly related to the very formal style of writing judicial decisions, and the special positioning of the judge in the legal system, profiting from the quality provided by strong concepts of objectivity in contexts which are not always justified.

One of the initial observations from practical usage is that objectivity seems to have a charm that lawyers are only too willingly taking advantage of. By far its most seductive feature is its great argumentative power. In legal discourse the use of the concept 'objectivity' could be perceived as an example of exercising power through words. There are many examples where 'objective' as an adjective is used to exclude other arguments from the discourse. It is a last resort argument in exercising discretion to legal subjects who are subordinate to law. Objectivity plays a role in deciding what is right or valid, but from a position of power rather than by any systematic presentation of arguments. The hierarchical character of legal discourse makes arguments introduced as objective automatically stronger than others just because of the position from which they are presented. When decisions, evaluations, etc., are introduced as 'objective' they become independent of the need for further convincing. Objectivity provides the easiest way to close the discourse and removes personal responsibility from the decisions taken.

This phenomenon is noted in the social and philosophical literature as a type of hidden power,[469] expressing its influences through language.[470] Many of the examples I have examined from the Polish case law confirm this. If lawyers really understand the ambiguous character of objectivity, the examples from the court justifications show that they are very unwilling to admit it. It would be very risky to suggest that judges do not realize the meaning of objectivity; rather they know what an idealistic and, at the same time, powerful construction it is, and still take advantage of '*le charme discret de l'objetivité.*'

'*Je sais bien, mais quand même*' sums up the cynical attitude described by Peter Sloterdijk[471] towards the actions of contemporary man. The same attitude could also describe judicial reality in what could be called the syllogistic method of applying law, which tries to pretend there is a scientific model of justification. Good examples of this can be found in the application of general clauses or discretionary clauses, where the style of interpreting statutes is based on methods that try to hide the impossibility of eliminating subjective evaluations (see Chapter 4). In light of the above, a statement of this 'false consciousness' ('*Je sais bien, mais quand même*') could be worded as follows: this is how it looks in my opinion, but I have to present my thesis in the body of possible argumentation for the easy acceptance by the community of judges; nevertheless it is based on independent objective criteria, it is commonly valid, and anybody in my position would argue in the same way. Very often, this is how judges see successful argumentation working in practice.

---

469 Zybertowicz, *Przemoc i poznanie*, 375.

470 Pierre Bourdieu, 'The force of law. Toward a Sociology of the Juridical Field,' *The Hasting Law Journal* 38 (1987), 805–53.

471 Peter Sloterdijk, *Krytyka cynicznego rozumu* [*Kritik der zynischen Vernunft,* 1983] (Wrocław: Wydawnictwo Naukowe Dolonośląskiej Szkoły Wyższej, 2008) 607.

I think that the application of objectivity by judges is a part of an unspoken code[472] (hidden elements behind the decision-making process) and through this they create a double understanding of objectivity. This can be observed in the division between what is said or declared by judges and what they actually do. It could be explained by the metaphor of double or false consciousness, which represents the state of mind when the subject is fully aware of what he is doing but chooses to apply double standards. Unwritten social knowledge and rules operating as an unspoken code have the function of contextualization and it determines the meaning of expressions.[473] When we consider the code of western lawyers, we have rules expressed in advance by the legislator, rules of logic that may be applied, and different types of legal reasoning based on the final decisions that have to be created. So, one can draw such a conclusion, that this unspoken code applied by lawyers is the last instance of deciding about the final interpretation, that, what a rule actually means, is decided when the final decision is taken. The final interpretation contains elements that are both revealed and hidden, and both 'objective' and subjective. The rule makers or legislators assess objectivity as one of the premises of law. Law has to be objective both at the level of abstract rules and their application in order to realize its main ideals, such as justice, equity, etc. From the institutional perspective, objectivity is necessary for all legal institutions in order to uphold the authority of law. How this is realized is through the unspoken code. When lawyers apply the law, they still have to uphold this vision, even though they realize that this is impossible in practice. This could be pictured as the magic transformation from the judge to the court, from person to institution, from subjectivity to objectivity, and from personal responsibility to the double standards of false consciousness. All lawyers are bound by this style of argumentation and this is reflected in the way lawyers present arguments and the way judges write their justifications.

The terminology of objectivity is representative of a scientific approach to law, which appears with the positivistic ambition of making statements valid for a certain discipline following argumentation based on the syllogistic model. As modern jurisprudence has shown, the scientific ambitions of law are not possible to realize. Law as a social science works in the context of society and, as such,

472 Bernard Jackson, 'Literal Meaning: Semantics and Narrative in Biblical Law and Modern Jurisprudence,' *International Journal for Semiotic of law* 13 (2000), 433–57.

473 Jackson, 'Literal Meaning' 447.

can never be objective and universal in the same way as the natural sciences.[474] However, the judicial style is strongly involved in the narration of objectivity.

6.1.1. The Analysis of the Style of Objectivity as Performing the Ceremonial Function

The style of writing legal justification, especially the construction of sentences, is also adapted to the narrative of objectivity, where the use of a passive voice dominates, indicating the passivity of the judge in the decisions making process. It also suggests that things happened by themselves and the facts themselves reach conclusions simply by occurring. This gives an impression of a kind of scientific statement, which is supposed to convincing about the truth of the argument. The construction of objectivity in this case, therefore, is a form of persuasion, widely accepted in the legal discourse. It should be emphasized that it is also used by other participants in the trial as rules of the game. The style of depersonalized writing is characterized not only by the frequent use of passive voice, but also by abstract verbs, but also citing theory, doctrine sentences, other rulings, or other authorities. The style of 'objectifying science' of judicial justifications should not only sound impersonal and true, but also wise. By using this style, judges indicate that they belong to a community of intellectuals who are selflessly making decisions about someone's case. Thanks to this, they can also be considered professionals because they are fluent in matters inaccessible to ordinary people. Creating complex constructions of legal categories such as: 'guilt in the objective and subjective meaning' or 'best interests of the child in an objective and subjective sense' etc. is a figure of speech used to create favourable impression.

Some relevant examples of these figures of speech are the following:

(a) it is objective, because it is not me who takes a decision. 'this is how it is, the reality speaks for itself.' In this case the judge has privileged access to this reality due to his position. In other words, this figure expresses a message of the judge: 'it is not me who decides here,'
(b) it is objective, because this is clear and obvious. this is the truth. In this case there appears a strong claim for authority. A decision is authoritative because arguments based on objectivity close the discourse, they are the last words followed by a period. The judge presents himself as

474 Andrzej Zybertowicz, 'The Success of the Natural Sciences Sociologically Explained,' *Studia Metodologiczne* 29 (1999), 11–34.

the one who knows more, as he has an access to secret knowledge of truth. Thanks to this, judges can keep their place in the hierarchy and apply a covert power. The hierarchy's principle is also meant to convince the parties that the judge, not them, are right,

(c) it is objective, because that is what the law says while the law is understood as a higher reality, which speaks the clearest truth and the judge is just the mouth to speak this truth,

(d) it is objective, because 'we all think that' – it is a figure which plays with authority of common reason and intersubjectivity by presupposing that this reasoning is what everybody shares. The question however remains who is 'everybody.'

The character of these expressions is ceremonial, not semantic. It serves to differentiate the judge from the so-called ordinary people, who only have their own individual subjective perspectives. This is undoubtedly a specialist discourse, it uses concepts and categories which are not known to ordinary people, but as it appeared from the analysis of the use of objectivity, they are also new to specialists, in the sense that the judges supplement the use of legal concepts with rhetoric elements aimed at persuading the audience, at the cost of a lack of transparency which, for the law, should be of paramount importance. Due to the high degree of complexity of the conceptual apparatus and the vastness of the legal matter, judges can use complicated, difficult-sounding or loosely related to science concepts, without a high risk of being exposed.

The way of writing justifications with the intention of depersonalizing the judge's decision, presenting it as impartial, true and transparent, paradoxically reveals a philosophical, cognitive, sociological and political orientation (in a broad sense). That is, it entails a specific vision of law and of its understanding, of the place of the judge in the legal system as someone applying the law in a scientific way, like revealed 'the only truth.' As a result, the style created by the judges to distinguish themselves from ordinary people, unwilling to speak as everyone else, results in creating a language that is hermetic, artificial, incomprehensible and sometimes inconsistent.

The popularity of the utilization of the 'narration of objectivity' indicates that this is an effective way to build a convincing justification, by maintaining the standards in force in the field: to speak the truth without revealing that it is my own, upholding the faith in one right way. Interestingly, the judges developed a writing method embodying a belief in the current 'right' style of writing, which is confirmed by the several cases of duplicated templates adopting this style, found in the analysis of judges' documents. Finally, as a consequence of adopting a depersonalized formal style, as sign of adaptability (Foucault), judges become convinced that they are the best professionals if they get rid of their own self.

Therefore, there appears a visible paradox related to the problem of particularism and universalism, or subjectivity and objectivity in the legal discourse, to which hermeneutics already draw attention: raising one point of view of the judge as universal decision, by the special positioning of the judge and at the same time by depersonalizing him. The paradox of this situation is that: to give validity to an individual decision, it should be presented as non-individual, and to give it universality it needs to be strengthened in the form of an institutional authority.

6.2. The Relationship Between Objectivity and Subjectivity

> 'There is a noticeable relationship between the idea of objectivity and the idea of the human individual, the idea of individuality as a value and the opposition of knowledge to the world'[475]

Objectivity and subjectivity in legal discourse are set as opposites that compete with each other, and the struggle is for the objectivity, where objectivity is supposed to win. Clumsy justifications of objectivity testify its weakness and need to defend it, while the paradigm of objectivity is breaking.

The key to determining the role of objectivity in legal discourse may be, as it seems, to determine the relationship between objectivity and subjectivity and how subjectivity is expressed and perceived in the legal discourse itself. In the Cartesian division between objectivity and subjectivity, duality is a category that organizes the world, giving priority and a claim to rightness to objectivity, and placing subjectivity on the opposite side, representing 'only an individual perspective. The domination of the enlightenment's order is the one in which what is rational is objective and what is emotional is subjective and, as such, excluded from the discourse.

Objectivity in law takes over the above traits and becomes the dominant category, with positive connotations, despite appearing in the context of cognitive judgments or justifying decisions. As it has a strong power of persuasion, not only the law, but the activities of the judge as its extension, are perceived as

475 Andrzej Zybertowicz, 'Przemoc i Poznanie, Studium z nie-klasycznej socjologii wiedzy' [Violence and Cognition, A study of Non-classical Sociology of Knowledge], (Toruń: Uniwersytet Mikołaja Kopernika, 1995), 84.

objective. As a consequence, what is 'subjective' in law is expelled from the discourse and marginalized.

By an identification with what is emotional and irrational, the 'subjective' is characterized as only individual perception contrasted with a rational objective assessment of legal standards. Subjective as individual does not deserve consideration, unless it is institutionally recognized as one of legal categories. An important, though not surprising, observation is the way in which opinions, judgements, and decisions perceived as subjective are treated. They are commonly eliminated from the discourse as arguments not deserving to be taken into account because of their insignificant character. In this way, arguments of opposing parties are eliminated. But if we look closer and deeper at the character of the arguments given by the two parties, we realize that almost all of their arguments have to be subjective in some sense. This point of view is the consequence of the contradictory character of the legal process: parties on trial deliver arguments and evidence to make their own positions stronger and more persuasive. On the other side, we have opinions, judgements, legal facts, etc.,[476] which have been recognized as objective and as such they serve to find the 'right place' in the process of justification. It is possible to observe certain trends and one of the most prevalent was the way the courts grasped objectivity in positive context and subjectivity in pejorative sense. This reductionist division of what is objective and subjective is highly controversial because, such a binary division is close to arbitrariness.

Such a perspective ignores the individual and historical experience in all its complexity and subjectivity is perceived as an unnecessary complication that hinders the mechanical process of undertaking decisions in a given matter. It follows that one can try to solve the problem with an argument from objectivity as an attempt to eliminate conflicting points of view. In a dispute where we have two or more points of view, the imperialist – objectivist way of thinking suggesting one possible truth is the easy solution.

The analysis of this research, while describing a crisis of the legal discourse pointing out the lack of developed tools to deal with this situation, exposes the tension between objectivity and subjectivity. There exists a tendency in the legal discourse with respect to the relationship between objectivity and subjectivity: the weaker the concept of the individual, i.e. the less subjectivity is taken

476 It is difficult to distinguish specific objects that are called objective. As objective are described very different types of referential subjects, even those that contradict common intuition, such as 'objective evaluation.'

into account, the greater the need for objectivity and *vice-versa*. It follows that the law does not create favourable conditions for taking into account subjectivity and individual differences, i.e. various forms of subjectivity, and shows a strong tendency to use ready-made, a priori constructed models as the narration of objectivity, going hand-by-hand with ontologizing legal institutions.

The key question for this problem is, if it then possible to establish a stronger position of intersubjectivity within the legal discourse? The main condition of intersubjectivity is communication, so by its very nature it is a more democratic solution that can be established when the parties agree. Clearly, this does not necessarily imply taking a common position, which is based on consent, because for intersubjectivity the most important aspects are transparency and the awareness of what we agree and what we disagree on. In other words, intersubjectivity is not so much a communication tool as it is a condition for it.

Perhaps, it is the lack of the aforementioned, developed relationship between objectivity and subjectivity that more clearly shows the inability to deal with subjectivity by eliminating it. The possible model should be based on intersubjectivity, however, with the inclusion of subjectivity and emotionality.

6.3. Does Intersubjectivity Fit the Law?

> 'A belief that once men are free from all the damaging myths of the past, they will have little difficulty understanding the proper shape of society.'[477]

The main conclusion appearing on the basis of the discourse analysis presented in this book is that in the legal discourse the most common occurrences of objectivity also include a relevant role for intersubjectivity. The description of various practices of using objectivity, in particular, indicates that along with objectivity identified with truth, there exists a whole scale of various practices of usages considered objective, which includes intersubjectivity, which refers to dialogue and takes into account the perspective of others. What should be emphasized about the relationship objectivity – intersubjectivity is, in fact, based on establishing some facts by means of dialogue or discursive practices interacting with others. That is why, as mentioned before, the legal discourse, due to its deliberative nature, creates more relevant conditions for the functioning of intersubjectivity than for objectivity.

---

477 Bruce Ackerman, 'Introduction,' in *Law and the Modern Mind*, 1974, As quoted by Brian Brix in his Introduction on new edition of: Jerome Frank, *Law and the Modern Mind* (Brentano: Transaction Publishers, 2009) XVI.

From a more general perspective, one can claim that where objectivity fails, there is a space for intersubjectivity. This issue is particularly visible considering the criticism of objectivity related to the relationship it implies between universalism and individualism. In particular, in legal context universal measures providing equal standards when applied to different type of subjects of law, result in inequality and low transparency.

Also, the socio-legal context of liberal democracies makes another problematic aspect of objectivity of law visible. In societies in which values were shared by the vast majority of citizens and plurality was not the rule, the idea of law as being objective in a strong sense was more in tune with the society itself. This was especially visible in the societies before the industrial revolution. Differently, in modern liberal societies in which there is no widespread agreement on many values, and many different points of view co-exist and differences are actually encouraged by the liberal political institutions, the idea of objectivity as imposed from a hierarchical superior entity is at odds with the society's values. On the other hand, the research presented in this book emphasized a flipside of the liberal framework as in the work of the judges, some aspects of the hierarchically imposed meaning of objectivity re-surfaces in the practical use they do of the concept. Let us look at these issues in more detail.

Objectivity with its universalism provides equal standards for everybody. However, by looking at this in more depth, it is possible to point out that objectivity and universalism cannot be required in every domain of law. For example, different spheres such as public and private law should be treated differently as private law demands to be more focused on the individual. That is why the legislator puts general clauses in legal acts to ensure that certain situations are evaluated individually. As demonstrated by the court rulings, judging such cases according to universal and objective criteria seems to lead to unjustified outcomes, as different cases need different systems of measures. This division between public and private law also presents certain intuitions about the different kinds of values involved. Public law represents the area of an objective, common space, whilst private law is bound with individual matters concerning particular subjects of law in their private space.

There is no denying that objectivity brings its positive consequences in the practical application of law. Objectivity fulfils a stabilizing function in societies and is the golden formula for the hierarchy that builds societies. In principle, it should also provide and protect the transparency of law. Together, these two aspects are excellent tools for imposing values on society that are valid for everyone and should be accepted by all rational human beings. Conversely, objectivity can play the role of masking power relations in societies and, in so doing, favour the interests of those in power, or the public authority over the rights of the individual. In other words, the legal discourse seems to be paying the price of a small contact with social life for being hermetic, for lack of dialogue with its subjects, for alliance with power and violence rather than with dialogue and recognition, for adhering to tradition rather than to an interaction with the present. This situation is certainly a sign of a deepening crisis, perhaps heralding a paradigm shift.

The German scholar, Karl Engisch describes an interesting example of the objectivity concept working in different types of societies. He defines 'subjective' as bound with the will of the author, and 'objective' as determined by the perception of contemporary society. The first represents a monarchy or dictatorship, where the focus is on the will of the legislator. The second represents a liberal democratic society, where the law is open for interpretation by liberal citizens.[478] Treating law as an interpretative or argumentative process allows us to support the assumption of objectivity in and its intersubjective dimension. If one wants an interpretation to be commonly accepted, then one must introduce the best possible argumentation to be discussed and finally accepted by the members of argumentative community. Here we meet a potential problem with applying intersubjectivity in legal discourse understood along these lines: to meet intersubjective standards requires that all the subjective elements taken into account are revealed.

Reliance on the majority's opinion or common acceptance can be considered the weakest form of objectivity, if any. Such a reasoning, however, would make little sense in the light of Richard Rorty's considerations on the topic. According to Rorty, solidarity and objectivity are opposites. By examining these two ideas, the main differences become more visible. Solidarity and objectivity embody two different types of rationality, the first one looks for consensus, the second one looks for truth. Solidarity has no need or care for metaphysics and objectivity. Validity is created on the basis of pragmatic justification. That is why this approach is still open to new propositions, new arguments, new hypotheses, and new vocabulary.[479] Objectivity traditionally embodies a rationality strongly rooted in metaphysics, looking for something that is true or grounded in empirical reality. The Age of Enlightenment, with its dominance of reason,

478 See Karl Engisch, Paul Bockelmann, and Arthur Kaufmann, *Ulrich Klug Beiträge zur Rechtstheorie* (Frankfurt Am Main: Vittorio Klostermann, 1926); Karl Engisch, *Vom Weltbild des Juristen* (Heidelberg: C. Winter, 1965).

479 See Richard Rorty, *Objectivity, Relativism, and Truth* 37.

strengthened objectivity, so these two traditions are completely different and they stand far apart. The idea of objectivity is strongly rooted in the consciousness of the European culture, based on the Cartesian dualistic rationality, making sense of discourse in relation to metaphysics. This is still visible in the ideology of application of law in its broader sense, where the discourse is presented in terms of what is true and what is false.

One could arrive at the point where it is a better claim that intersubjectivity suits better the continental legal culture than solidarity or objectivity in the minimal sense, in order to avoid the confusion with objectivity interpreted in its traditional sense. However, if one treats law as an argumentative process, using an argument about objectivity based on common acceptance with all its diversity and strong presuppositions, it still has very strong argumentative power. In societies based on democratic values, this operates quite successfully. This conflict embodies the domination of political philosophy over metaphysics or, as Rorty expresses it, priority of democracy over ontology. Antirealists actually call solidarity minimal objectivity, by reformulating the meaning of objectivity based on common acceptance and social practice. In the light of the above reasoning, intersubjectivity becomes a more transparent and adequate way to express thinking in plural, rather than a matter of individual judgements.

As modern and post-modern writers have constantly stressed, there are no great narrations that can fit the world into a single picture of how things should be. We have already seen their weaknesses. In the pluralistic, post-secular societies that we are living in, there is no agreement about shared common values. Looking closer at the justifications of judges reveals a certain type of schizophrenia, which is manifested in what I see as their split character between thinking and acting. This schizophrenia is caused by the emptiness and lack of new propositions to replace big ideologies, like the 19th century notion of objectivity, as they are crumbling down: we are still trying to act as nothing to act has happened. M. Zirk-Sadowski writes:

> uncertainty of law and weakness of justification of law is not a postmodern discovery, but only a description of what has been present in law from a very long time ago hidden behind great narrations of jurisprudence. What we see now is the demystification of a disenchanted law.[480]

---

480 Marek Zirk-Sadowski, 'Postmodernistyczna jurysprudencja?' [Postmodern Jurisprudence?] in Michał Błachut ed., *Z zagadnień teorii i filozofii prawa. Ponowoczesność* (Wrocław: Kolonia Limited, 2007) 22.

Some authors[481] have suggested that the problem of objectivity and subjectivity should be reformulated, but this debate has now gone out of fashion and is seen as leading nowhere. Maybe so, but I think the change of direction required is not the rejection of the notion of objectivity, but the adoption of the perspective offered by intersubjectivity.

481 See Rorty, *Objectivity, Relativism, and Truth*; Patterson, 'Objectivity and Normativity.'

Bibliography

Legal acts

- Act of 12 January 1991 on taxes and local fees (Journal of Laws 1991 No 9, Item 31 with amendments).
- Act of the 3 February 1995 on protection of agricultural and forestry land (Journal of Laws 2004 No 121 Item 1266; 2009 No 01 Item 22, amendment Journal of Laws 2009 No 1 Item 3).
- Principles of European Contract Law – Parts I and II revised 1998 (Parts I and II revised 1998, Part III 2002).
- Unidroit Principles of International Commercial Contracts (Rome, 1994, 2004, 2010, 2016).
- United Nations Conventions on Contracts for the International Sale of Goods signed in Vienna in 1980.

Literature

- Ackerman, Bruce. 'Introduction.' In *Law and the Modern Mind*, 1974.
- Aleinikoff, Thomas Alexander. 'Constitutional Law in the Age of Balancing.' *The Yale Law Journa.l* Vol. 96 No. 5 (April 1987).
- Alexy, Robert. 'Law, Normativity and Autonomy.' Paper presented during the workshop 'The Normative Dimension Of Law.' Organized by University Centre Saint-Ignatius Antwerp, Centre for Law & Cosmopolitan Values. 2009.
- Alexy, Robert. 'On the Structure of Legal Principles.' *Ratio Juris*. Vol. 13 No. 3 (September 2000).
- Alexy, Robert. *Teorie der Grundrechte*. Baden-Baden: Suhrkamp Verlag, 1985.
- Aristotle. *Nicomachean Ethics, book IV of the Eudemian Ethics*. Translated by Terence Irwin. Indianapolis: Hackett, 1985.
- Ascombe, Gertrude and Elizabeth Margaret. 'On Brute Facts.' In *Ethic, Religion and Politics. The collected Philosophical Papers of G. E. M. Ascombe*. Vol. 13. Oxford: Basil Blackwell, 1981.
- Barak, Aharon. *Judicial Discretion*. New Haven and London: Yale University Press, 1989.
- Barsalou, Lawrence W. 'Abstraction in perceptual symbol systems.' *Philosophical Transactions of the Royal Society of London: Biological Sciences*. Vol. 358 (2003) 1177–1187.

- Barsalou, Lawrence W. 'Perceptual Symbol System.' *Behavioral and Brain Science.* Vol. 22 Issue 4 (1999) 576–660.
- Bartlett, Katharine T. and Rosanne Kennedy. *Feminist legal theory: readings in law and gender.* Boulder: Westview Press, 1991.
- Bell, Derrick and Preta Bansal. 'The Republican Revival and Racial Politics.' *Yale Law Journal* 97 (1988): 1609–1621.
- Bell, Derrick. *And We Are Not Saved: The Elusive Quest for Racial Justice.* New York: Basic Books, 1987.
- Bielska-Brodziak, Agnieszka and Zygmunt Tobor, 'Słowniki a interpretacja tekstów prawnych' [Dictionaries and interpretation of legal texts]. *Państwo i Prawo.* Vol. 5 (2007) 20–33.
- Bielska-Brodziak, Agnieszka and Zygmunt Tobor, Piotr Żmigrodzki, 'Co każdy prawnik o słownikach wiedzieć powinien.' [What every lawyer should know about the Dictionaries] *Przegląd Sądowy.* No. 7–8 (2008).
- Bielska-Brodziak, Agnieszka and Zygmunt Tobor, Piotr Żmigrodzki. 'Opis semantyczny leksemów w słowniku ogólnym i jego doniosłość prawna' [The semantic description of lexemes in a general dictionary and its legal significance]. *Język Polski* 88/1 (2008) 3–13:
- Bielska–Brodziak, Agnieszka. 'Kłopoty z definicjami legalnymi' [Troubles with a legal definitions]. In *System prawny a porządek prawny.* Szczecin: Wydawnictwo Naukowe Uniwersytetu Szczecińskiego, 2008.
- Bjarup, Jes. 'Kripke's Case.' In *Law and Legal Interpretation.* Ed. Fernando Atria and D. Neil MacCormick. Dartmouth: ASHGATE, 2003.
- Blackburn, Simon. *Oksfordzki słownik filozoficzny.* [*Oxford Dictionary of Philosophy*] Translated by Cezary Cieśliński, Paweł Dziliński, Michał Szczubiałka, Jan Woleński. Warszawa: Książka i Wiedza, 2004.
- Blakeslee, Sandra. 'Cells That Read Minds.' *New York Times. Science* (January 10, 2006). Accessed 13 June 13 2016. http://www.nytimes.com/2006/01/10/science/cells-that-read-minds.html?_r=0.
- Bourdieu, Pierre. 'The force of law. Toward a Sociology of the Juridical Field.' *The Hasting Law Journal.* Vol. 38 (1987) 805–853.
- Brink, David O. 'Legal Interpretation, Objectivity, and Morality.' In *Objectivity in Law and Morals.* Edited by Brain Leiter. Cambridge: Cambridge University Press, 2000.
- Brink, David O. 'Legal Theory, Legal Interpretation, and Judicial Review.' *Philosophy and Public Affairs.* 17 (1988) 105–148.
- Brix, Brain H. 'Transaction Introduction.' In Jerome Frank. *Law and the Modern Mind.* New Brunswick: Transaction Publisher, 2009.

- Brodniewicz, Witold. *Postępowanie cywilne w zarysie.* [*Civil Procedure in an Outline*] Warszawa: Lexis Nexis, 1983.
- Bull, Hedley and Benedict Kingsbury, Adam Roberts. ed. *Hugo Grotius and International Relations*. Oxford: Oxford University Press. 1990.
- Bulygin, Eugenio. 'Objectivity of Law in the View of Legal Positivism.' *Analisi e diritto* (2004).
- Burns, Tony. 'Aquinas's Two Doctrines of Natural Law.' *Political Studies*. Vol. 48. Is. 5 (December 2000).
- Calmore, John O. 'Critical race Theory, Archie Shepp, and Fire Music: Securing an Authentic Intellectual Life in a Multicultural World.' *University of South California Law Review* (1992).
- Chamallas, Martha. *Application Feminist Legal Theory to Women's Lives. Sex, Violence, Work and Reproductions.* Temple University Press, 1996.
- Chiassoni, Pierluigi. 'Interpretive games: Statutory construction through Gricean eyes.' *Analisi e diritto* (1999): 79–99.
- Clark, Andy. *Being There: Putting Brain Body, and World Together Again*. Cambridge MA: MIT Press, 1997.
- Coleman, Jules and Brian Leiter. 'Determinacy, Objectivity, and Authority, in Law.' In *Law and Interpretation: Essays in Legal Philosophy*. Edited by Andrei Marmor. Oxford: Oxford University Press, 1995.
- Coleman, Jules. 'Truth and Objectivity in Law.' *Legal Theory*. 1 (1995).
- Cornell, Drucilla. *Imaginary Domain: Abortion, Pornography and Sexual Harassment*. New York & London: Routlege, 1995.
- Craig, Edward ed. *Concise Encyclopedia of Philosophy*. Vol. 8. London: Routlege 1998.
- Currie, Greg. 'Interpretation and Objectivity.' *Mind*. Vol. 102 (1993) 413–428.
- Dajczak, Wojciech. 'Problem "ponadczasowości" zasad prawa rzymskiego. Uwagi w dyskusji o "nowej europejskiej kulturze prawnej." ' [The problem of timelessness] *Zeszyty Prawnicze*. Vol. 5 Issue 2 (2005).
- Dajczak, Wojciech. *Dobra wiara jako symbol europejskiej tożsamości prawa* [Bona Fides as a Symbol]. Poznań: Księgarnia św. Wojciecha, 2006.
- Damasio, Antonio. *Descartes's error*. Random House. 2008.
- Daszkiewicz, Wiesław. *Prawo karne procesowe - zagadnienia ogólne.* [Criminal Procedur Law – general issues] Vol. I. Poznań: Branta, 1999.
- De Boeck, Annuck and Mark Van Hoecke. 'The Interpretation of Standards clauses in European Contract Law.' In *Standard Contract Terms in Europe: A Basis for and a Challenge to European Contract Law.* Edited by Hugh Collins. Wolters Kluwer, 2008.

- Delgado, Richard. 'The Inward Turn in Outsider Jurisprudence.' *William and Mary Law Review.* Vol. 34 (1993).
- Den Boer, Monica. 'Two in one Trolley: Reflection on the Relation between MacCormick's Institutional and Narrative Theory of Law.' *International Journal of Semiotics of Law.* IV/12 (1991).
- Derrida, Jacques. *Of grammatology*. Translated by G. Spivak. London: The Johns Hopkins University Press, 1976.
- Douzinas, Costas and Adam Gearey. *Critical Jurisprudence: The Political Philosophy of Justice.* Oxford and Portland, Oregon: Hart Publishing, 2005.
- Dworkin, Ronald. 'My Reply to Stanley Fish (and Walter Benn Michaels): Please Don't Talk About Objectivity Anymore.' In *The Politics of Interpretation.* Edited by W.J.T. Mitchell. Chicago and London: University of Chicago Press, 1983.
- Dworkin, Ronald. *Law's Empire.* Cambridge: Harvard University Press, 1986.
- Dworkin, Ronald. 'Objectivity and Truth: You'd Better Believe It.' *Philosophy and public affairs.* 25 (1996).
- Dworkin, Ronald. 'The Model of Rules.' In *An Anthology of law and legal theory.* Edited by Dennis Patterson. Oxford: Blackwell 2003.
- Dybel, Paweł. 'The problem with intersubjectivity.' In *Intersubjectivity*. Ed. Piotr Makowski. Kraków: Universitas, 2012. 17–28.
- Easterbrook, Frank H. 'The Role of Original Intent in Statutory Construction.' *Harvard Journal of Law and Public Policy*. Vol. 59 (1988).
- Ekelof, Olof. 'Free evaluation of evidence.' *Kallenberg, Svensk civilprocessratt.* Vol. II, Lund (1931).
- Endicott, Timothy A. O. 'Linguistic Indeterminacy.' In *Law and language.* Edited by Thomas Morawetz. Dartmouth: Ashgate, 2000.
- Endicott, Timothy A. O. 'Review book of Objectivity in Law by N. Stavropoulos.' *Law Quarterly Review* (1997).
- Engisch, Karl and Paul Bockelmann, Arthur Kaufmann. *Ulrich Klug Beiträge zur Rechtstheorie.* Frankfurt Am Main: Vittorio Klostermann, 1926.
- Engisch, Karl. *Vom Weltbild des Juristen.* Heidelberg: C. Winter, 1965.
- Fairclough, Norman. *Language and power. Second Edition.* Harlow: Pearson Education, 2001.
- Fay, Brian. *Contemporary Philosophy of Social Science. A Multicultural Approach.* Blackwell Publishing 1996.
- Feldman, Heidi Li. 'Objectivity in Legal Judgment.' *Michigan Law Review.* Vol. 92 (1994).

- Felman, Shoshana. *The Juridical Unconscious, Trials and Traumas in the Twentieth Century.* Cambridge and London: Harvard University Press, 2002.
- Finnis, John. *Natural Law and Natural Rights.* Oxford: Clarendon Press, 1980.
- Fish, Stanley. 'There is No Textual Position.' *San Diego Law Review.* Vol. 42 (2005).
- Fish, Stanley. *Is There a Text in this Class? The Authority of Interpretive Communities.* Cambridge, MA: Harvard University Press, 1980.
- Fish, Stanley. 'Working In the Chain Gang, interpretation in the law and in literary criticisms.' *Critical Inquiry.* 9 (1982–3).
- Fodor, Jerry A. *The Language of Thought.* Cambridge, MA: Harvard University Press, 1975.
- Foucault, Michel. *The Archeology of Knowledge and The Discourse on Language.* London and New York: Vintage Books, 2010.
- Frank, Jerome. *Courts on Trial: Myth and Reality in American Justice.* Princeton: Princeton University Press, 1973.
- Frankfurter, Felix. *Of Law and Life and Other Things That matter.* Edited by Philip B. Kurland. Harvard University Press, 1965.
- Gallese, Vittorio. 'The roots of empathy: the shared manifold hypothesis and the neural basis of intersubjectivity.' *Psychopathology.* Vol. 36 Issue 4 (2003) 171–180.
- Gilles-Gaston, Granger. *Le probable, le possible et le virtuel.* Odile Jacob, 1995.
- Gillespie, Alex and Flora Cornish. 'Intersubjectivity: Towards a Dialogical Analysis.' *Journal for the Theory of Social Behaviour.* 40 (2010) 19–46.
- Gizbert-Studnicki, Tomasz. 'Konflikt dóbr i kolizja norm ['Conflict of Goods and Collision of Norms']' *Ruch Prawniczy, Ekonomiczny i Socjologiczny.* No 1 (1989).
- Gizbert-Studnicki, Tomasz. 'Przedmiot ustaleń sądu w procesie cywilnym' [Object of court findings in civil procedure]. *Krakowskie Studia Prawnicze.* Vol. VII (1974).
- Gizbert-Studnicki, Tomasz. 'Podstawy argumentacji prawniczej' [Foundation of legal argumentation]. *Acta Universatis Wratislaviensis.* No. 1772 Prawo CCXLIV Wrocław (1995).
- Greenawalt, Kent. *Law and Objectivity.* New York, Oxford University Press, 1992.
- Grundmann, Stefan and Denis Mazeaud. ed. *General Clauses and Standards In European Contract Law: Comparative Law, EC Law, Contract Law and Codification.* The Hague: Kluwer Law International, 2006.

- Grzybowski, Stanisław. 'Struktura i treść przepisów prawa cywilnego odsyłających do zasad współżycia społecznego' [The Structure of the Civil Law Norms Reffering to Norms Regulating Social Relations]. *Studia Cywilistyczne.* No. 6 (1965).
- Guastini, Riccardo. 'Rules, Validity and Statutory Construction.' In *Italian studies in law: a review of legal problems.* Edited by Allessandro Pizzorusso. Dordrecht, The Netherlands: Kluwer Academic Publishers, 1992.
- Habermas, Jurgen. Notes on the post-secular society. Accessed November 22, 2015. http://www.signandsight.com/features/1714.html.
- Harris, Angela P. 'Foreword: The Jurisprudence of Reconstruction.' *California Law Review.* 82 (1994).
- Hart, Herbert. *The Concept of Law.* Oxford: Oxford University Press, 1994.
- Herbut, Józef ed. *Leksykon Filozofii Klasycznej* [*Lexicon of Classical Philosophy*]. Lublin: Towarzystwo Naukowe KUL, 1997.
- Hirschberg, Lothar. *Der Grundsatz der Verhältnismässigkeit.* Göttingen: Schwartz, 1981.
- Hoecke, Mark Van. 'Deep Level Comparative Law.' In *Epistemology and Methodology of Comparative Law.* Edited by Mark Van Hoecke. Oxford and Portland, Oregon: Hart Publishing, 2004.
- Hoecke, Mark Van. *Law as Communication.* Oxford Portland Oregon: Hart Publishing, 2002.
- Hutchison, William D. et al., 'Pain related neurons in the human cingulate cortex.' *Nature Neuroscience* 2 (1999).
- Hyslop, Alec. 'Other Minds.' In *The Stanford Encyclopedia of Philosophy* (Fall Edition). Ed. Edward N. Zalta. Accessed June 13, 2016. plato.stanford.edu/archives/fall2010/entries/other-minds/>. Section 1.
- Iacoboni, Marco. 'Grasping the Intentions of Others with One's Own Mirror Neuron System.' PLoS Biol. Vol. 3 Issue 3 (2005).
- Ingarden, Roman. 'Rozważania dotyczące zagadnienia obiektywności.' ['Considerations on the issue of objectivity']. In *U podstaw teorii poznania* [*At the Foundations of the Theory of Knowledge*]. Warszawa: PWN, 1971.
- Ingarden, Roman. *Spór o istnienie świata* [*Controversy over the Existence of the World*]. Warszawa 1987.
- Jackson, Bernard. 'Literal Meaning: Semantics and Narrative in Biblical Law and Modern Jurisprudence.' *International Journal for Semiotic of law.* Vol. 13 (2000) 433–457.
- Johnson, Micheal G. 'Language and Cognition in Products Liability.' *Language in the Judicial Process* (1990).

- Judycki, Stanisław. 'Tajemnica komunikacji pomiędzy osobami' [The mystery of interhuman communication]. In *Intersubjektywność* [*Intersubjectivity*]. Ed. Piotr Makowski. Kraków: Universitas, 2012: 87–114.
- Judycki, Stanisław. In *Powszechna Encyklopedia Filozofii*. Vol. 4. Lublin: Polskie Towarzystwo Tomasza z Akwinu, 2003.
- Kafka, Franz. *The Trial*. Translated by John Williams. Hertfordshire: Wordsworth Edition, 2008.
- Kant, Immanuel. *Critique of Pure Reason*. Translated by Norman Kemp Smith. London: St. Martins Press, 1965.
- Kant, Immanuel. *Krytyka czystego rozumu*. [*Critique of Pure Reason*] Translated by Roman Ingarden. Kęty, 2001.
- Kelly, Paul. 'Impartiality: a philosophical perspective.' In *Judicial integrity*. Edited by Andras Sajo and Lorri Rutt Bentch. Dordrecht, Netherlands: Brill, 2004.
- Kelman, Mark. *A Guide to Critical Legal Studies*. Cambridge and London: Harvard University Press, 1987.
- Kennedy, Duncan. *A Critique of Adjudication [fin de siecle]*. Harvard University Press, 1997.
- Kennedy, Duncan. 'Form and Substance in Private Law Adjudication.' *Harvard Law Review*. Vol. 89 (1976).
- Keysers, Christian. *The emphatic brain*. Kindle Edition, 2011.
- Klich-Rump, Jadwiga. *Podstawa faktyczna rozstrzygnięcia sądowego w procesie cywilnym* [*Factual Basis of Judicial Decision in Civil Trial*]. Warszawa: Wydawnictwo Prawnicze, 1977.
- Kokoszczyński, Marcin and Grzegorz Wierczyński. *System informacji prawnej w pracy sędziego*. LEX/el. 2011, chapter 5.
- Kołakowski, Leszek. *Obecność mitu* [*The Presence of Myth*]. Warszawa: Prószyński i S-ka, 1972.
- Kotz, Hein and Axel Flessner. *European Contract Law*. Oxford: Clarendon Press, 1997.
- Kramer, Matthew H. *Objectivity and the Rule of Law*. Cambridge: Cambridge University Press 2007.
- Kripke, Saul A. *Wittgenstein o regułach i języku prywatnym*. [*Wittgenstein about rules and private language*] Warszawa: Aletheia, 2007.
- Kripke, Saul A. *Wittgenstein on Rules and Private Language. An elementary Exposition*. Oxford: Basil Blackwell, 1982.
- Kripke, Saul. *Naming and Necessity*. Oxford: Basil Blackwell, 1980.

- Kripke, Saul. *Wittgenstein on Rules and Private Language*. Oxford: Harvard University Press, 1984.
- Kubal, Agnieszka. 'Why Semi Legal? Polish post 2004 EU Legal Migrants in the United Kingdom.' *Immigration, Asylum and Nationality Law*. Vol. 23 No. 2 (2009).
- Kurczewski, Jacek. 'Either Rightly or Like a Crook: Legal Culture of Polish Society after Communism.' *Sociolegal Studies*. Vol. 185 (2007) 33–60.
- Kusch, Martin. *A Skeptical Guide to Meaning and Rules. Defending Kripke's Wittgenstein*. Acumen: McGill-Queen's University Press, 2006.
- Laing, Ronald David and Herbert Phillipson, Lee A. Russell. *Interpersonal Perception: A Theory and Method of Research*. London: Tavistock Publications, 1966.
- Leiter, Brian. 'Law and Objectivity.' In *The Oxford Handbook of Jurisprudence and Philosophy of Law*. Edited by Jules Coleman, Scott Shapiro. Oxford: Oxford University Press, 2002.
- Leiter, Brian. 'Objectivity and the Problems of Jurisprudence.' *Texas Law Review*. Vol. 72 (1993).
- Leiter, Brian. *Objectivity, Morality and Adjudication*. The University of Texas School of Law, Public Law and Legal Theory Working Paper, No. 004, March 2000.
- Leiter, Brian. 'Objectivity, Morality, and Adjudication.' In *Objectivity in Law and orals*. Edited by Brian Leiter. New York: Cambridge University Press, 2001.
- Leiter, Brian. 'Rethinking Legal Realism: Towards a Naturalized Jurisprudence.' *Texas Law Review*. Vol. 76 (1997).
- Leszczyński, Leszek. *Tworzenie generalnych klauzul odsyłających* [*Setting up of General Referral Clauses*]. Lublin: UMCS, 2000.
- Łętowska, Ewa. *System Prawa Prywatnego* [Private Law System]. Vol. 5. Warszawa: C. H. Beck, 2006.
- Leyh, Gregory. *Legal Hermeneutics. History, Theory and Practice*. Berkeley, Los Angeles, Oxford: University of California Press, 1992.
- Litewski, Wiesław. *Jurysprudencja rzymska* [The Roman Jurisprudence]. Kraków: Wydawnictwo Uniwersytetu Jagiellońskiego, 2000.
- Locke, John. *Questions Concerning the Law of Nature*. Edited by Robert Horwitz and Jenny Strauss Clay, Diskin Clay. Ithaca: Cornell University Press, 1990.
- Łyda, Zbigniew. 'Bezstronność arbitra a zakaz zainteresowania w sprawie' [Impartiality of an Arbitrator and the Ban of Interest in the Case]. *Państwo i Prawo*. No. 2 (1996).

- Łyda, Zbigniew. 'Bezstronność arbitra a zakaz "zainteresowania w sprawie."' *Folia Philosophica*. No. 15 (1997).
- MacComick, Neil. *Rhetoric and The Rule of Law. A Theory of Legal Reasoning*. Oxford: Oxford University Press, 2005.
- MacCormick, Neil and Robert S. Summers. ed. *Interpreting Statute. A Comparative Study*. Dartmouth, 1991.
- MacCormick, Neil and Ota Weinberger. *An Institutional Theory of Law. New Approaches to Legal Positivism*. Dordrecht, The Netherlands: Kluwer Academic Publishers, 1986.
- MacCormick, Neil and Ota Weinberger. *Grundlagen des institutionalistischen, Rechtspositivimus*. Berlin: Duncker&Humbolt, 1985.
- MacCormick, Neil. *A Theory and The Rule of Law. A Theory of Legal Reasoning*. Oxford: Oxford University Press, 2005.
- MacCormick, Neil. *Institutions of Law. An Essay in Legal Theory*. Oxford: Oxford University Press, 2008.
- MacGowan, Miranda. 'Do as I do, not as I say: An Empirical Investigation of Justice Scalia's Ordinary Meaning Method of Statutory Interpretation.' *Mississippi Law Journal*. Vol. 78 (2008).
- Mackie, J. L. 'The Subjectivity of Values.' In *Moral Relativism*. Edited by Paul K. Moser, Thomas L. Carson. Oxford: Oxford University Press, 2001.
- MacKinnon, Catharine A. *Toward Feminist Theory of the State*. New York: Harvard University Press, 1989.
- Mańko, Rafał. 'Critical Legal Theory in the Central and Eastern Europe: in search of method.' *Acta Universitatis Lodziensis. Folia Iuridica*. Vol. 89 (2019) 5–14.
- Marmor, Andrei. *Positive Law and Objective Values*. Oxford, New York: Oxford Clarendon Press, 2001.
- Martyniak, Czesław. *Obiektywna podstawa prawa według Św. Tomasza* [*The Objective Foundation of Law according to Tomas Aquinas*]. Kraków: Towarzystwo Naukowe KUL, 2005.
- Marx, Karl and Friedrich Engels. *The German Ideology*. Edited by Christopher John Arthur. New York: International Publishers, 2004.
- Matczak, Marcin. 'Semantyka Kripkego-Putnama a język prawny.' Accessed November 18, 2015. http://pts.edu.pl/teksty/marmat.pdf.
- Matusov, Eugene. 'Intersubjectivity without agreement.' *Mind, Culture and Activity*. Vol. 3 Issue 1 (1993).
- Mazzarese, Tecla. 'Grounds of Liability. An Introduction to the Philosophy of Law.' *Philosophia*. Vol. 18 (1988).

- Moore, Michael. 'A Natural Law Theory and Interpretation.' *Southern California law Review.* Vol. 58 (1985).
- Moore, Michael. 'Moral Reality Revisited.' *Michigan Law Review.* Vol. 90 (1992).
- Mori, Junko and Makoto Hayashi. 'The Achievement of Intersubjectivity through Embodied Completions: A Study of Interactions between First and Second Language Speakers.' *Applied Linguistics.* Vol. 27. Issue 2 (2006) 195–219.
- Moser, Paul K. and Thomas L. Carson. ed. *Moral Relativism.* Oxford: Oxford University Press, 2001.
- Nagel, Thomas. *The View from Nowhere.* New York, Oxford: Oxford University Press, 1986.
- Nerhot, Patrick. 'Introduction.' In *Law, interpretation, and reality: essays in epistemology, hermeneutics and jurisprudence.* Edited by Patrick Nerhot. Dordrecht, The Netherlands: Kluwer Academic Publishers, 1990.
- Newell, Allen. 'Physical symbol systems.' *Cognitive science.* Vol. 4 Issue 2 (1980) 135–183.
- Nowacki, Józef and Zygmunt Tobor. *Wstęp do prawoznawstwa.* [Introduction to Jurisprudence] Warszawa: Oficyna a Wolters Kluwer, 2007.
- Nowacki, Józef. 'O przepisach zawierających klauzule generalne' [About Rules Contain General Referral Clauses]. In *Studia z Teorii Prawa.* Kraków: Zakamycze, 2003.
- Nowacki, Józef. 'Domniemanie dobrej wiary.' [Presumption of Good Faith] *Studia Iuridica Silesiana.* No. 5 (1979).
- Olivecrona, Karl. *Law as fact.* London: H. Milford, Oxford University Press, 1997.
- Ossowska, Maria. *Moral Norms. A Tentative systematization.* Amsterdam – New York – Oxford: North–Holland, PWN Warszawa, 1980.
- Ost, François and Michel van de Kerchove. *De la pyramide au réseau? Pour une théorie dialectique du droit.* Bruxelles: Publications des FUSL, 2002.
- Ost, François and Michel van de Kerchove. *De la pyramide au réseau? Pour une théorie dialectique du droit.* Bruxelles: Publications des FUSL, 2002.
- Patterson, Dennis. *Law and Truth.* Oxford, New York: Oxford University Press, 1996.
- Patterson, Dennis. 'Objectivity and Normativity.' *William & Mary Law Review.* Vol. 43 (2001–2002).
- Patterson, Dennis. 'Wittgenstein on Understanding and Interpretation.' In *Philosophical Investigation.* Vol. 29 No.2 (April 2006).

- Pavlakos, George. *Our Knowledge of Law. Objectivity and Practice in Legal Theory.* Oxford and Portland, Oregon: Hart Publishing, 2007.
- Perelman, Chaïm, *Logika prawnicza. Nowa retoryka* [Logique juridique]. Warszawa: Wydawnictwo Naukowe PWN, 1984.
- Perelman, Chaïm. *Imperium Retoryki* [*Empire of Rhetoric*]. Warszawa: Wydawnictwo Naukowe PWN, 2002.
- Perelman, Chaïm. *L'Empire rhétorique.* Paris: Vrin, 1977.
- Perelman, Chaïm. *O sprawiedliwości* [Justice at raison]. Warszawa: Wydawnictwo Naukowe PWN, 1959.
- Piętka, Henryk. *Słuszność w teorii i praktyce.* Warszawa: Instytut Wydawniczy Kasy Mianowskiego, 1929.
- Pietrzykowski, Krzysztof. 'Nadużycie prawa podmiotowego w prawie cywilnym' [Misuse of Right in Civil Law]. In *Nadużycie prawa.* Edited by Hubert Izdebski, Aleksander Stępkowski. Warszawa: Liber, 2003.
- Pintore, Anna. *Il diritto senza verità.* Torino: Giappichelli, 1966.
- Pintore, Anna. *Law without truth.* Edited by Bernard Jackson. Deborah Charles Publications, 2000.
- Płeszka, Krzysztof. *Uzasadnianie decyzji interpretacyjnych przez ich konsekwencje* [*Justification for Interpretative Decisions by its Consequences*]. Kraków: Tow. Aut. i Wydaw. Prac Nauk. Universitas, 1996.
- Podsiad, Antoni ed. *Słownik terminów i pojęć filozoficznych* [*Dictionary of philosophical terms*] Warszawa: PAX, 2000.
- Popper, Karl R. *Objective Knowledge. An Evolutionary approach.* Oxford: Oxford University Press, 1979.
- Postema, Gerald. 'Objectivity fit for Law.' In *Objectivity in Law and Morals.* Edited by Brian Leiter. Cambridge: Cambridge University Press, 2000.
- Prinz, Jesse J. *The Emotional Construction of Morals.* Oxford: Oxford University Press, 2007.
- Prinz, Jesse J. *Furnishing the Mind Concepts and their perceptual basis.* Cambridge MA: MIT press, 2002.
- Prosser, William L. *Handbook of the Law of Torts.* 4th ed. St. Paul: West Pub. Co, 1971.
- Pufendorf, Samuel von. *The Political Writings of Samuel Pufendorf.* Edited by Craig L. Carr. Oxford and New York: Oxford University Press, 1994.
- Putnam, Hilary. 'Are Moral and Legal Values Made or Discovered?' *Legal Theory.* Vol. 1 (1995) 5–19.

- Putnam, Hilary. 'Reply to Brian Leiter.' *Legal Theory.* Vol. 1 (1995) 69–80.
- Putnam, Hilary. 'The Meaning of 'Meaning.' In *Mind, Language and Reality: Philosophical Papers.* Cambridge: Cambridge University Press, 1975.
- Rawls, John. 'Kantian Constructivism in Moral Theory.' *Journal of Philosophy.* No. 77 (1980).
- Raz, Joseph. 'Notes on Values and Objectivity.' In *Objectivity in Law and Morals.* Edited by Brain Leiter. Cambridge: Cambridge University Press, 2000
- Rigaux, François. 'The concept of fact in legal science.' In *Law, interpretation, and reality: essays in epistemology, hermeneutics and jurisprudence.* Edited by Patrick Nerhot. Dordrecht, The Netherlands: Kluwer Academic Publishers, 1990.
- Ripstein, Arthur. 'Questionable Objectivity.' *Nous.* Vol. 27 (1993).
- Rorty, Richard. *Objectivity, Relativism, and Truth: Philosophical Papers.* Vol. I. Cambridge University Press: Cambridge, 1991.
- Rosati, Connie S. 'Some puzzles about objectivity of law.' Law and Philosophy. Vol. 23. No. 3 (May, 2004): 273–323.
- Rott-Pietrzyk, Ewa. 'Wzorzec rozsądnej osoby jako kryterium wykładni oświadczenia woli' [The pattern of reasonable person as an criterion of declaration of the interpretation of will]. In *Studia z wykładni prawa.* Edited by Czesław Martysz and Zygmunt Tobor. Katowice: Branta, 2008.
- Samuel, Geoffrey. 'Epistemology and Comparative law: Contribution from the Sciences and Social Sciences.' In *Epistemology and Method in Law.* Aldershot: Ashgate, 2003.
- Scales, Ann C. 'The Emergence of Feminist Jurisprudence: An Essay.' *Yale Law Journal.* Vol. 95 (1986).
- Schauer, Frederic. *Playing by the Rules. A Philosophical Examination of Rules-based Decisions-making in Law and in Life.* Oxford: Clarendon Press, 1991.
- Scheff, Thomas et al. *Goffman Unbound!: A New Paradigm for Social Science. (The Sociological Imagination).* CO: Paradigm Publishers, 2006.
- Schur, Richard. 'Critical Race Theory and The Limits of Autobiographical Reading; Patricia William's *The Alchemy of Race and Rights* Through Postcolonial Theory.' *Biography.* Vol. 25 No. 3 (2002).
- Seale, Clive. *Researching Society and Culture.* London, Thousand Oaks, New Delhi: Sage Publications, 2004.
- Searle, John R. 'How Performatives Work.' *Linguistics and Philosophy.* Vol. 12 No. 5 (1989).

- Searle, John R. *Speech acts: An essay in the Philosophy of Language.* Cambridge: Cambridge University Press, 1969.
- Searle, John R, *The Construction of Social Reality.* London, New York: The Free Press, 1995.
- Sen, Amartya. 'Objectivity and Position: Assessment of Health and Well-Being.' In *Health and Social Change in International Perspective. Health and Social Change in International Perspective.* Edited by Lincoln Chen, Arthur Kleinman and Norma Ware. Boston, Mass.: Harvard School of Public Health, 1994.
- Sen, Amartya. 'Positional Objectivity.' *Philosophy and Public Affairs.* Vol. 22 (1993).
- Sieckmann, Jan-Reinard. *Legal Reasoning: The Methods of Balancing: Proceedings of the Special Workshop held at the 24th World Congress of the International Association for Philosophy of Law and Social Philosophy (IVR), Beijing, 2009 Paperback - Dec 15 2010.* Franz Steiner, 2010.
- Sieckmann, Jan-Reinard. 'Legal System and Practical Reason. On the Structure of a Normative Theory of Law.' *Ratio Juris.* Vol. 5 Is. 3 (1992) 288–307.
- Siemek, Marek J. *Freedom, mind, intersubjectivity.* Warszawa: Oficyna Naukowa, 2002.
- Singer, Joseph. 'The Player and the Cards: Nihilism and legal Theory.' *Yale Law Journal.* Vol. 94 (1984).
- Sloterdijk, Peter. *Krytyka cynicznego rozumu.* [*Kritik der zynischen Vernunft,* 1983] Wrocław: Wydawnictwo Naukowe Dolonośląskiej Szkoły Wyższej, 2008.
- Smith, Patricia. ed., *Feminist jurisprudence.* New York: Oxford University Press, 1993.
- Solan, Lawrence. 'Learning Our Limits: The Decline of Textualism in Statutory Cases.' *Wisconsin Law Review* (1997).
- Solan, Lawrence. 'When Judges use the Dictionary.' *American Speech* Vol. 86 (1993) 50–57.
- Spruit, Leen. *Species intelligibilis. From Perception to knowledge. Classical roots and Medieval Discussions.* Leiden: E. J. Brill, 1994.
- Stavropoulos, Nicos. *Objectivity in Law.* Oxford: Oxford Clarendon Press, 1996.
- Stawecki, Tomasz. 'Instrumentalne traktowanie prawa – różne perspektywy.' [Instrumental approach to law- different perspective] In *Prawo I Ład Społeczny, Księga Jubileuszowa dedykowana Prof. Annie Turskiej.* Warszawa: PWN, 2000.

- Sulikowski, Adam. 'Perspektywy zastosowań metod Krytycznej Analizy Dyskursu w badaniach nad prawem: kilka uwag' [Some remarks on the prospects for applying the research approach of Critical Discourse Analysis to the study of Law]. *Wrocławskie Studia Erazmiańskie. Studia Erasmiana Wratislaviensia.* Vol. VIII (2014).
- Suwaj, Patrycja J. *Gwarancje bezstronności organów administracji publicznej w postępowaniu administracyjnym.* Wrocław: Kolonia Limited 2004.
- Szabo, I. 'Pojęcie słuszności w różnych systemach prawnych.' *Państwo i Prawo.* No. 5 (1971) 673–680.
- Szaniawski, Klemens. *O nauce, rozumowaniu i wartościach. Pisma Wybrane.* [*About Science, Reasoning and Values. Selected works*] Warszawa: PWN, 1994.
- Szubka, Tadeusz. *Antyrealizm semantyczny. Studium analityczne.* [*Semantic Antirealism. Analitical Study*] Lublin: Redakcja Wydawnictw KUL, 2001.
- Szymczak, Mieczysław. ed. *Słownik języka polskiego.* [*Polish Dictionary*] Warszawa, 1994.
- Tamanaha, Brian Z. *Law as a Means to an End.* Cambridge: Cambridge University Press, 2006.
- Tarello, Giovani. *Dottrine giuridiche e ideologie sindacali.* Bologna: Il mulino, 1973.
- Tobor, Zygmunt and Sławomir Tkacz. 'In dubio pro reo w prawie karnym.' [In dubio pro reo in Criminal Procedure] In *Studia z Wykładni Prawa.* Edited by Czesław Martysz. Bydgoszcz – Katowice: Branta, 2008.
- Tobor, Zygmunt. 'Iluzja wykładni literalnej.' In: Konstytucyjne uwarunkowania tworzenia i stosowania prawa finansowego i podatkowego. Białystok: Temida 2, 2010.
- Tobor, Zygmunt. 'Bezstronność sędziego.' ['Impartiality of a Judge'] *Przegląd sądowy.* No. 6 (2005).
- Tobor, Zygmunt. 'Iluzja Wykładni literalnej.' Post conference publication from Zjazd Katedr Prawa Finansowego i Podatkowego w Białowieży. In printing.
- Tuleja, Piotr. *Normatywna treść praw jednostki w ustawach konstytucyjnych RP.* [Normative Content of Rights of the Individual in Constitutional Acts of the RP] Warszawa: Wydawnictwo Sejmowe, 1997.
- Unger, Roberto M. *The Critical Legal Studies Movement.* Cambridge, London: Harvard University Press, 1983.
- Waligórski, Michał. 'Gwarancje wykrycia prawdy.' [Guarantees to detect the Truth] *Państwo i Prawo.* No. 8–9 (1953).

- Waltoś, Stanisław. *Proces karny. Zarys system.* [Criminal Procedure. An Outline of the system] Warszawa 2002.
- Weinberger, Ota. In *An Institutional Theory of Law*, Neil MacCormick and Ota Weinberger. Dordrecht: D. Reidel & Co, 1986.
- Weinberger, Ota. 'Objectivity and Rationality In Lawyer's Reasoning.' In *Theory of Legal Science*. Edited by Aleksander Peczenik. Dordrecht: D. Reidel Publishing Company, 1984.
- Weinberger, Ota. '*Prima Facie* Ought. A Logical and Methodological Enquiry.' *Ratio Juris*. Vol. 12 No. 3 (September 1999).
- Weismann, Friedrich. 'Verifiability.' *Proceedings of the Aristotelian Society*. Supplementary Volume 19 (1945): 119–150.
- William N. Eskridge Jr. and Philip J. Frickey. 'Statutory Interpretation as Practical Reasoning.' *Stanford Law Review* (1990).
- Willson, Margaret. 'Six views on Embodied Cognition.' *Psychonomic Bulletin and Review*. Vol. 9 Issue 4 (2003) 625–636.
- Winkielman, Piotr and Knutson, Brian and Paulus, Martin and Trujillo, Jennifer L. 'Affective influence on judgments and decisions: Moving towards core mechanisms.' *Review of General Psychology*. Vol. 11 Issue 2 (2007).
- Winkielman, Piotr and Niedenthal, Paula M. and Oberman, Lindsay. 'The embodied emotional mind.' *Embodied grounding: Social, cognitive, affective, and neuroscientific approaches* (2008).
- Winkielman, Piotr and Niedenthal, Paula M. Ucieleśniony, emocjonalny umysł społeczny [Embodied emotional social mind]. In: Psychologia poznania społecznego [Psychology of social cognition]. Wydawnictwo Naukowe PWN, 2009.
- Wittgenstein, Ludwig. *Philosophical Investigations*. Oxford: Blackwell Publishers, 1997.
- Wittgenstein, Ludwig. *Philosophical Investigations*. Oxford: Wiley Blackwell, 2009.
- Wittgenstein, Ludwig. *Philosophical investigations*. Trans. Bogusław Wolniewicz. Warszawa: PWN, 2000.
- Wittgenstein, Ludwig. *Philosophical investigations*. Trans. Gertrude E.M. Anscombe. Oxford: Blackwell, 1958.
- Wojciechowski, Bartosz. 'Dyskursywny model sądowego stosowania prawa – wybrane aspekty.' [Discursive model of judicial application of law. The chosen aspects] In *Filozofia prawa wobec globalizmu*. Edited by Jerzy Stelmach. Kraków: Wydawnictwo Uniwersytetu Jagiellońskiego, 2003.
- Woleński, Jan. *Epistemologia*. [*Epistemology*] Warszawa: PWN, 2005.
- Wolniewicz, Bogusław. Trans. *Dociekania Filozoficzne*. Warszawa: PWN, 2000.

- Wright, Crispin. *Realism, Meaning and Truth.* Oxford: Wiley-Blackwell, 1993.
- Wróblewski, Jerzy. *Sądowe stosowanie prawa.* [The Judicial Application of Law] Warszawa 1988.
- Wróblewski, Jerzy. *The Judicial Application of Law.* Edited by Zenon Bankowski and Neil MacCormick. Dordrecht, The Netherlands: Kluwer Academic Publishers, 1992.
- Wróblewski, Jerzy. *Wartości a decyzja sądowa.* [*Values and Judicial Decision*] Wrocław – Warszawa – Kraków – Gdańsk: Zakład Narodowy im. Ossolińskich, 1973.
- Yablon, Charles M. 'Law and Metaphysics.' In *Law and Legal Interpretation.* Edited by Fernando Atria and Neil MacCormick. Dartmouth, ASHGATE: 2003.
- Załuski, Wojciech. 'O trzech rodzajach empatii: pełnej, częściowej i skażonej' ['On Three Types of Empathy: the Complete, the Truncated, and the Contaminated']. *Logos i Ethos.* Vol. 46 Issue 2 (2017) 51–66.
- Zerubavel, Eviatar. *Social Mindscapes: An Invitation to Cognitive Sociology.* Cambridge, Massachusetts: Harvard University Press, 1997.
- Zieliński, Maciej. 'Obiektywność ustalenia faktów jako element praworządności stosowania prawa' [Objectivity of establishing facts as the element of rule of law application], Ruch prawniczy [Legal Movement]. Vol. 1 (1979).
- Zieliński, Maciej. *Wykładnia prawa. Zasady. Reguły. Wskazówki.* Warszawa: Lexis Nexis, 2002.
- Zirk-Sadowski, Marek. 'Postmodernistyczna jurysprudencja?' [Postmodern Jurisprudence?] In *Z zagadnień teorii i filozofii prawa. Ponowoczesność.* Edited by Michał Błachut. Wrocław: Kolonia Limited, 2007.
- Zirk-Sadowski, Marek. 'Wykładnia i rozumienie prawa w Polsce po akcesji do UE.' [The interpretations and understanding of law in Poland after the accession to EU] Paper presented on conference in Gniezno.
- Zirk-Sadowski, Marek. 'Instytucjonalny i kulturowy wymiar integracji prawnej.' [Institutional and cultural dimension of legal integration] In *Zmiany społeczne a zmiany w prawie. Aksjologia, konstytucja, integracja europejska.* Edited by Leszek Leszczyński. Lublin: Wydawnictwo UMCS, 1999.
- Zybertowicz, Andrzej. *Przemoc i poznanie: studium z nie-klasycznej socjologii wiedzy.* [*Violonce and Cognition. Non-classical Study of Sociology of Knowledge*] Toruń: Wydawnictwo Uniwersytetu Mikołaja Kopernika, 1995.
- Zybertowicz, Andrzej. 'The Success of the Natural Sciences Sociologically Explained.' *Studia Metodologiczne.* Vol. 29 (1999) 11–34.

Index of court rulings

1. Rulings of the Supreme Court of Poland

Resolutions:

- Resolution of the Supreme Court of 25 June 1953, C. Prez. 195/52, OSN 1953, OSNCK 1953/4/95.
- Resolution of the Supreme Court of 29 June 1995, III CZP 66/95, OSNC 1995/12/168.
- Resolution of the Supreme Court of 11 October 2001, I KZP 23/01, OSNKW 2001/11- 2/94.
- Resolution of the Supreme Court of 16 January 2004, III CZP 101/03, OSNC 2005/4/58.
- Resolution of the Supreme Court of 29 October 2004, I KZP 24/04.
- Resolution of the Supreme Court of 29 October 2004, I KZP 24/04, OSNKW 2004/10/92.
- Resolution of the Supreme Court of 3 August 2007, I PZP 7/07, OSNP 2008/5–6/55.
- Resolution of the Supreme Court of 15 October 2008, II PZP 10/08, OSNP 2009/9–10/112.

Judgements:

- Judgment of the Supreme Court of 18 Match 2009, IV KK 380/08, Biul.PK 2009/6/23.
- Judgment of the Supreme Court of 16 February 1978, IV KR 4/78.
- Judgment of the Supreme Court of 11 March 1997, III CKN 33/97, OSNC 1997/6–7/93.
- Judgment of the Supreme Court of 16 April 1997, II UKN 56/97, OSNP 1998/3/96.
- Judgment of the Supreme Court of 8 May 1998, I CKN 664/97, OSNC 1999/1/7.
- Judgment of the Supreme Court of 6 April 2000, III RN 150/99, OSNP 2001/1/4.
- Judgement of the Supreme Court, 23 of May 2000, II UKN 551/99.
- Judgment of the Supreme Court of 20 July 2000, I PKN 737/99, OSNP 2002/43.

- Judgment of the Supreme Court of 24 October 2000, WA 37/00, LEX No. 332949.
- Judgment of the Supreme Court of 4 October 2001, T I CKN 458/00, LEX no 52717.
- Judgment of the Supreme Court of 9 November 2001, III RN 145/00, OSNP 2002/19/450.
- Judgment of the Supreme Court of 9 November 2001, III RN 145/00, OSNP 2002/19/450.
- Judgment of the Supreme Court of 22 November 2001, I PKN 680/00, OSNP 2003/20/488.
- Judgment of the Supreme Court of 11 February 2002, II KKN 475/99, LEX No. 53038.
- Judgment of the Supreme Court of 12 September 2002, IV CKN 1266/00, not publicated.
- Judgment of the Supreme Court of 26 September 2002, III CKN 213/01, OSNC 2003/12/169.
- Judgment of the Supreme Court of 28 November 2002, II CKN 1047/00, LEX No. 75344.
- Judgment of the Supreme Court of 9 December 2002, IV KKN 508/99, LEX No. 75496.
- Judgment of the Supreme Court of 11 February 2003, IV KKN 312/99, LEX No. 77436.
- Judgment of the Supreme Court of 23 October 2003, VCK 311/02, LEX No. 82272.
- Judgment of the Supreme Court of 23 October 2003, V CK 311/02.
- Judgment of the Supreme Court of 11 December 2003, II CK 315/02, OSNC 2005/1/13.
- Judgment of the Supreme Court of 1 April 2004, II CK 130/03, OSNC 2005/4/68.
- Judgment of the Supreme Court of 30 September 2004, IV CK 713/03, OSNC 2005/9/160.
- Judgment of the Supreme Court of 13 April 2005, II PK 258/04, OSNP 2005/22/356.
- Judgment of the Supreme Court of 15 June 2005, II PK 276/04, OSNP 2006/3–4/42.
- Judgment of the Supreme Court of 15 June 2005, II PK 276/04.
- Judgment of the Supreme Court of 12 January 2006, II KK 29/05, OSNKW 2006/4/41.

- Judgment of the Supreme Court of 15 November 2006, I BP 12/06, OSNP 2008/1–2/3.
- Judgment of the Supreme Court of 1 October 2007, IV KK 232/07, OSNwSK 2007/1/2147.
- Judgment of the Supreme Court of 8 January 2008, I UK 172/07, OSNP 2009/3–4/51.
- Judgment of the Supreme Court of 21 January 2008, III KK 403/07, OSNKW 2008/6/45.
- Judgment of the Supreme Court of 22 April 2008, II UK 215/07, LEX No. 448853.
- Judgment of the Supreme Court of 14 November 2008, II PK 88/08, LEX No. 490339.
- Judgment of the Supreme Court of 4 December 2008, II PK 134/08, LEX No. 483282.

Orders:

- Decision of the Supreme Court of 4 December 1969, I CZ 124/69, LEX No. 6629.
- Decision of the Supreme Court of 7 November 1984, No. II CZ 117/84, LEX No. 8643.
- Decision of the Supreme Court of 7 June 2001, V KKN 75/01, LEX No. 51843.
- Decision of the Supreme Court of 10 July 2001, II KKN 538/98, OSNKW 2001/9–10/80.
- Decision of the Supreme Court of 23 November 2001, III KKN 109/99, LEX No. 51578.
- Decision of the Supreme Court of 23 November 2001, III KKN 109/99.
- Decision of the Supreme Court of 21 January 2003, III KO 59/02, LEX No. 77010.
- Decision of the Supreme Court of 13 January 2004, V KK 170/03, LEX No. 109496.
- Decision of the Supreme Court of 13 January 2004, V KK 170/03.
- Decision of the Supreme Court of 29 September 2004, I KZP 18/04, OSNKW 2004/9/89
- Decision of the Supreme Court of 20 October 2005, II KK 184/05, OSNKW 2005/12/120.
- Decision of the Supreme Court of 15 December 2006, III CZP 112/06, LEX No. 260365.

- Decision of the Supreme Court of 30 July 2008, II KK 68/08.
- Decision of the Supreme Court of 5 May 2009, I UO 3/08, LEX No. 509056.

2. Ruling of Polish Constitutional Tribunal

Judgments:

- Judgment of the Constitutional Tribunal of 14 March 1995, K 13/94.
- Judgment of the Constitutional Tribunal of 18 January 2000, K 17/99, OTK 2000/1/4.
- Judgment of the Constitutional Tribunal of 23 January 2003, K 2/02.
- Judgment of the Constitutional Tribunal of 7 January 2004, K14/03, votum separatum.
- Judgment of the Constitutional Tribunal of 7 January 2004, K 14/03, OTK-A 2004/1/1.
- Judgment of the Constitutional Tribunal of 13 July 2004, P 20/03, OTK-A 2004/7/64.
- Judgment of the Constitutional Tribunal of 7 February 2005, SK 49/03, OTK-A 2005/2/13.
- Judgment of the Constitutional Tribunal of 7 February 2005, SK 49/03.
- Judgment of the Constitutional Tribunal of 12 September 2005, TK SK 13/05, OTK-A 2005/8/9.
- Judgment of the Constitutional Tribunal of 13 December 2005, SK 53/04, OTK-A 2005/11/134.
- Judgment of the Constitutional Tribunal of 16 January 2006, SK 30/05, OTK-A 2006/1/2.
- Judgment of the Constitutional Tribunal of 16 January 2006, SK 30/05, OTK-A 2006/1/2.
- Judgment of the Constitutional Tribunal of 21 March 2006, K 13/05, OTK-A 2006/3/31.
- Judgment of the Constitutional Tribunal of 19 April 2006 of the Constitutional Tribunal, K 6/06, OTK-A 2006/4/45.
- Judgment of the Constitutional Tribunal of 29 November 2007, SK 43/06, OTK-A 2007/10/130.
- Judgment of the Constitutional Tribunal of 8 July 2008, P 36/07, OTK-A 2008/6/103.

Orders:

- Decision of the Constitutional Tribunal of 6 May 2005, Ts 42/05, OTK-B 2005/3/150.
- Decision of the Constitutional Tribunal of 25 May 2005, SK 1/04, OTK-A 2005/5/59.
- Decision of the Constitutional Tribunal of 22 February 2006, K 48/04, OTK-A 2006/2/25..
- Decision of the Constitutional Tribunal of 6 February 2007, P 33/06.
- Decision of the Constitutional Tribunal of 22 November 2011, K 10/10.

3. Rulings of the Supreme Administrative Court

Resolutions:

- Resolution of the Supreme Administrative Court of 20 March 2000, FPS 14/99, ONSA 2000/3/92.
- Resolution of the Supreme Administrative Court of 29 November 1999, FPK 4/99, Pr. Gosp. 2000/2/27.

Judgments:

- Judgment of the Supreme Administrative Court of 1 June 1998, II SA 534/98, LEX No. 41763.
- Judgment of the Supreme Administrative Court of 13 December 1999 (until 2003.12.31) in Warsaw, IV SA 1671/99, ONSA 2001/1/29.
- Judgment of the Supreme Administrative Court of 22 March 2000 (until 31 December 2003) in Warsaw, II SA 2169/99, LEX No. 61953.
- Judgment of the Supreme Administrative Court of 6 March 2003 (until 31 December 2003) in Warsaw, V SA 1923/02, ONSA 2004/2/62.
- Judgment of the Supreme Administrative Court of 13 April 2005, FSK 1652/04, LEX No. 166048.
- Judgment of the Supreme Administrative Court of 4 November 2005, FSK 2423/04, LEX No. 187977.
- Judgment of the Supreme Administrative Court of 31 January 2006, II OSK 475/05, LEX No. 245659.
- Judgment of the Supreme Administrative Court of 14 December 2006, II OSK 75/06, LEX No. 319183.

- Judgment of the Supreme Administrative Court of 10 July 2007, II OSK 1032/06, LEX No. 368207.
- Judgment of the Supreme Administrative Court of 20 September 2007, II GSK 255/07, LEX No. 374829.
- Judgment of the Supreme Administrative Court of 4 June 2008, II OSK 268/08, LEX No. 465053, OwSS 2008/4/93.

4. Rulings of Polish Voivodeship Courts

- Decision of the Voivodeship Administrative Court in Poznań of 21 October 2008, II SA/Po 656/08.
- Judgment of the Voivodeship Administrative Court in Łódź of 14 January 2009, I SA/Łd 899/08.
- Judgment of the Voivodeship Administrative Court in Łódź of 18 March 2008, II SA/Łd 57/08.
- Judgment of the Voivodeship Administrative Court in Poznań of 1 December 2011, IV SA/Po 1044/11.
- Judgment of the Voivodeship Administrative Court in Szczecin of 23 April 2009, I SA/Sz 104/09.
- Judgment of the Voivodeship Administrative Court in Warsaw of 27 April 2007, VI SA/Wa 319/07.
- Judgment of the Voivodeship Administrative Court in Warsaw of 4 March 2008 r., IV SA/Wa 1149/07.
- Judgment of the Voivodeship Administrative Court in Wrocław of 16 November 2011, I SA/Wr 717/11.
- Judgment of the Voivodeship Administrative Court in Wrocław of 24 January 2008 r., IV SA/Wr 630/07.
- Judgment of the Voivodeship Administrative Court in Wrocław of 8 November 2011, II SA/Wr 587/11.

5. Rulings of the Polish Appealed Courts

- Judgment of the Court of Appeal in Katowice of 21 January 2005, I ACa 1313/04, LEX No. 147135.
- Judgment of the Court of Appeal in Poznań of 11 January 2007, I ACa 833/06, LEX No. 298413.
- Judgment of the Court of Appeal in Warsaw of 4 May 2007, I ACa 668/06.
- Judgment of the Court of Appeal in Warsaw of 14 May 2007, I ACa 668//06, OSA 2008/12/39.

- Judgment of the Court of Appeal in Katowice of 15 May 2008, II AKa 13/08, LEX No. 447031.
- Judgment of the Court of Appeal in Wrocław of 30 May 2008, I ACa 371/08, OSAW 2008/4/113.
- Judgment of the Court of Appeal in Warsaw of 20 November 2008, VI ACa 704/08, Dz.U. [Journal of Laws] UOKiK 2009/2/16.
- Judgment of the Court of Appeal in Katowice of 5 March 2009, V ACa 484/08, LEX No. 508538.
- Judgment of the Court of Appeal in Wrocław of 27 October 2011, II AKa 261/11.

6. Rulings of the Polish District Courts

- Judgment of the District Court in Ostrołęka of 22 May 2014, II Ka 109/14.
- Judgement of the District Court in Kraków of 11 December 2014, IV Ka 60/14.

Name Index

DIA-LOGOS
Schriften zu Philosophie und Sozialwissenschaften
Studies in Philosophy and Social Sciences

Edited by
Tadeusz Buksiński & Piotr W. Juchacz

"*Dia-Logos. Studies in Philosophy and Social Sciences* is a peer-reviewed book series publishing valuable monographs and edited volumes on various aspects of philosophy and social sciences. The series is intended to be an interdisciplinary forum of deliberation according to our firm belief that challenges of the contemporary world require common and multilevel research. The *Dia-Logos* series does not represent a single ideology or school of thought, but it is open to different trends and various styles of reflection, trying to understand better the contemporary world. We invite the submission of manuscripts of monographs and edited volumes from academic philosophers and social scientists."

Bd. / Vol. 1 Piotr W. Juchacz / Roman Kozłowski (Hrsg.): Freiheit und Verantwortung. Moral, Recht und Politik. 2002.

Bd. / Vol. 2 Norbert Leśniewski / Ewa Nowak-Juchacz (Hrsg.): Die Zeit Heideggers. 2002.

Bd. / Vol. 3 Marek Kwiek (ed.): The University, Globalization, Central Europe. 2003.

Bd. / Vol. 4 Ewa Czerwińska-Schupp (Hrsg.): Philosophie an der Schwelle des 21. Jahrhunderts. Geschichte der Philosophie, Philosophische Anthropologie, Ethik, Wissenschaftstheorie, Politische Philosophie. 2003.

Bd. / Vol. 5 Danuta Sobczyńska / Pawel Zeidler / Ewa Zielonacka-Lis (eds.): Chemistry in the Philosophical Melting Pot. 2004.

Bd. / Vol. 6 Marek Kwiek: Intellectuals, Power, and Knowledge. Studies in the Philosophy of Culture and Education. 2004.

Bd. / Vol. 7 Marek Kwiek: The University and the State. A Study into Global Transformations. 2006.

Bd. / Vol. 8 Andrzej Przylebski (Hrsg.): Das Erbe Gadamers. 2006.

Bd. / Vol. 9 Ewa Czerwińska-Schupp (ed.): Values and Norms in the Age of Globalization. 2007.

Bd. / Vol. 10 Tadeusz Buksiński (ed.): Democracy in Western and Post-Communist Countries. Twenty Years after the Fall of Communism. 2009.

Bd. / Vol. 11 Marek Zirk-Sadowski / Mariusz Golecki / Bartosz Wojciechowski (eds.): Multicentrism as an Emerging Paradigm in Legal Theory. 2009.

Bd. / Vol. 12 Bartosz Wojciechowski: Philosophical Approach to the Interculturality of Criminal Law. 2010.

Bd. / Vol. 13 Marek Nowak / Michał Nowosielski (eds.): (Post)transformational Migration. Inequalities, Welfare State, and Horizontal Mobility. 2011.

Bd. / Vol. 14 Tadeusz Buksiński (ed.): Religions in the Public Spheres. 2011.

Bd. / Vol. 15 Bartosz Wojciechowski / Piotr W. Juchacz / Karolina M. Cern (eds.): Legal Rules, Moral Norms and Democratic Principles. 2013.

Bd. / Vol. 16 Ewa Nowak / Dawn E. Schrader / Boris Zizek (eds.): Educating Competencies for Democracy. 2013.

Bd. / Vol. 17 Tadeusz Buksiński (ed.): Identities and Modernizations. 2013.

Bd. / Vol. 18 Karolina M. Cern: The Counterfactual Yardstick. Normativity, Self-Constitutionalisation and the Public Sphere. 2014.

Bd. / Vol. 19 Vito Breda / Lidia Rodak (eds.). Diverse Narratives of Legal Objectivity. An Interdisciplinary Perspective. 2016.

Bd. / Vol. 20 Marek Woszczek: Platonic Wholes and Quantum Ontology. Translated by Katarzyna Kretkowska. 2015.

Bd./Vol. 21 Roman Hauser / Marek Zirk-Sadowski / Bartosz Wojciechowski (eds.): The Common European Constitutional Culture. Its Sources, Limits and Identity. 2016.

Bd./Vol. 22 Aigerim Raimzhanova: Hard, Soft, and Smart Power – Education as a Power Resource. 2017.

Bd./Vol. 23 Roberto Franzini Tibaldeo / Graziano Lingua (eds.): Philosophy and Community Practices. 2018.

Bd./Vol. 24 Marta Soniewicka: After God – The Normative Power of the Will from the Nietzschean Perspective. 2017.

Bd./Vol. 25 Tomasz Jarmużek: On the Sea Battle Tomorrow That May Not Happen. A Logical and Philosophical Analysis of the Master Argument. 2018.

Bd./Vol. 26 Krzysztof Brzechczyn (ed.): New Perspectives in Transnational History of Communism in East Central Europe. 2019.

Bd./Vol. 27 Ewa Nowak: Advancing the Human Self. Do Technologies Make Us "Posthuman"?. 2020.

Bd./Vol. 28 Lidia Rodak: Judicial Objectivity. Limits, Merits and Beyond. 2020.

www.peterlang.com

www.ingramcontent.com/pod-product-compliance
Ingram Content Group UK Ltd.
Pitfield, Milton Keynes, MK11 3LW, UK
UKHW021344130926
8556IPUK00047B/290

9 783631 652145